P9-CFS-281

CLASSIC PATCHWORK & QUILTING

❖

By Margit Echols

SEDGEWOOD® PRESS
New York, N.Y.

Dedication
To Dave, side by side

Acknowledgements
Special thanks to Verdalee Tomberlaine and Terrence Lindall for my one-woman show this year at the Greenwood Museum in Smyrna, New York, where many of the new pieces in this book were shown. Verdalee's constant faith, support and encouragement have made all the difference.

I also wish to thank the following people and suppliers for generously providing many of the products used in *Classic Patchwork & Quilting:* Jean Tofani; Norman Jernigan, Norman's Handmade Reproductions; Monta Lea Kramer, Q-Snap Frames; Larry Bilotti, Laura Ashley; Robin Steele and Nancy Walsh, V.I.P.; Priscilla Miller, Concord Home Sewing Fabrics; Roseann Carter, Country Rose Workshop; Helyn's Hoops; Doug Boyd, The Maine Bucket Co., Inc.; David Johnson, Norwood Looms; Calico Cupboard; Debra Hostetler, Stencils and Stuff; and Fairfield Processing for all the batting and pillow foams.

Credits:
Cover and endpapers: Concord Home Sewing Fabrics

Pg. 9 Thread cabinet: Country Rose Workshop; "D" Hoop: Helyn's Hoops; Quilting Stencils: Stencils and Stuff; Raised Edge Thimble: Come Quilt With Me

Pg. 16 Quilting Frame: Norwood Looms; Quilting Stencils: Stencils and Stuff

Pg. 25 Fabrics: Laura Ashley; V.I.P.

Pg. 31 Fabrics: Laura Ashley; Collection of the author

Pg. 34 Fabrics: Collection of the author

Pg. 41, 42 Fabrics, wallpaper, sheets, lace panels: Laura Ashley; Pencil post bed, Shaker night stand, Step stool: Norman's Handmade Reproductions; Pillow forms: Fairfield Processing Corp.

Pg. 58, 59 Fabrics: Collection the author

Pg. 60 Fabrics: Stratford Hall collection, V.I.P.

Pg. 73, 77 Fabrics: Concord Home Sewing Fabrics; quilting frame: Q-Snap Frames; pillow form: Fairfield Processing

Pg. 81, 84 Fabric: American Wildflower collection, V.I.P.; display chest: Norwood Looms

Pg. 93, 98 Fabrics: V.I.P., Laura Ashley; Food Stuffs: Rowhouse Press; Pine Buckets: The Maine Bucket Co., Inc.; Colonial Apple Cone: Country Manor Gift Shop

Pg. 109, 113 Fabrics: V.I.P.; Pillows: Fairfield Processing; Calico Christmas Ornaments: Rowhouse Press

Pg. 129, 135 Fabrics: Rose Fever Collection, V.I.P.; Round Band Boxes: Calico Cupboard; (octagonal band box made by the author)

Sources

Laura Ashley, Inc.
714 Madison Avenue
New York, NY 10021

V.I.P., Div. of Cranston Print Works, Co.
1412 Broadway
New York, NY 10018

Concord Home Sewing Fabrics
1359 Broadway
New York, NY 10018

Fairfield Processing Corp.
P.O. Box 1130
88 Rose Hill Ave.
Danbury, CT 06813

Norman's Handmade Reproductions
Route 6, Box 695
Dunn, NC 28334

Q-Snap Frames
P.O. Box 38
Parsons, TN 38363

Norwood Looms
505 S. Division St. Box 167
Fremont, MI 49412

Rowhouse Press, Dept. CP&Q
P.O. Box 20531
New York, NY 10025

Country Manor Gift Shop
Rt. 211, Box 234
Sperryville, VA 22740

The Maine Bucket Co., Inc.
32 Manning Avenue
Lewiston, ME 04240

Calico Cupboard
24 N. State St.
Westerville, OH 43081

Country Rose Workshop
P.O. Box 0298
Cave Springs, AR 72718
(800) 776-1699

Stencils and Stuff
312 Daniel Lane
Strasburg, OH 44680

Helyn's Hoops
911 City Park
Columbus, OH 43206

Come Quilt With Me, Inc.
P.O. Box 021063
Brooklyn, NY 11202-0023

For Sedgewood® Press:
Director: Elizabeth P. Rice
Project Editor: Viviene Faurbach
Editorial Assistant: Valerie Martone
Production Manager: Bill Rose
Design: Remo Cosentino/Bookgraphics
Photography: Schecter Lee
Illustrations: Margit Echols

Distributed by Meredith Corporation, Des Moines, Iowa.
ISBN: 0–696–02336–9

Library of Congress Catalog Card Number: 90–89–061424

Printed in the United States of America

10 9 8 7 6 5 4 3 2 1

CONTENTS

Dear Quilter:

The unique quilt designs in *Classic Patchwork & Quilting* were developed by fabric artist and quilter Margit Echols especially for this book.

We are delighted to bring you Margit's lyric designs, which combine fabric and color as only an artist can, to produce works of enduring beauty. Whether you are a beginning quilter or have been quilting for years, we are sure you will be inspired by several of these unusual yet classic projects.

For almost a decade Sedgewood has published full-color, hardcover craft books written by accomplished artists and writers who share their designs and provide clear, accurate instructions. We hope you will enjoy *Classic Patchwork & Quilting*, and that the projects you select and make will give you great satisfaction.

Sincerely,

Connie Schrader

Connie Schrader
Editorial Project Manager

INTRODUCTION

Enthusiasm for quilts in this country today is unparalleled since the first half of the twentieth century. Today's quilters are demanding more and more of themselves. We are becoming more determined, even aggressive, about how far we push both our technique, which now rivals that of our sisters of the past, and our design, which we draw from past and present worlds of quiltmaking as well as from the other visual arts. We are shedding our diffidence and claiming recognition as artists. Because we are beginning to recognize the value of our work, we consider it an investment in ourselves and our future. Even if we make something simply to beautify our homes, we now know that it can have impact not only on our own lives but on future generations as well.

When I was finishing up my last book, *A Patchwork Christmas,* I was looking forward to taking some time off and getting back to all the unfinished business I'd left behind. In spite of my decision to give quiltmaking a rest for a while, other ideas began to surface, and I found myself planning new designs for our bedroom, the Christmas tree, the dining table, or for no particular purpose other than seeing how certain prints and colors would work together. I think what started me off again was the new fabrics.

Another season had come around at the mills, and I visited the showrooms to see the new lines. I'm always surprised at how many more new fabrics there are to choose from, just when I think that, by now, all possibilities must be exhausted. Depression-era prints were coming back, in larger patterns and bright pastels. There were new chintzes with printed medallions, borders, and other details that could be cut up and pieced in imaginative combinations. In addition to the standard lighter-weight prints, certain companies were introducing heavier home decorating fabrics with glazed finishes suitable for upholstery, curtains, dust ruffles, and pillows, as well as quilts. And I discovered silks again, unequaled in richness of color and texture.

When I'm planning a new quilt, I sometimes start with a design, then hunt around for the right fabric. But usually it's the fabric I react to first—one of the reasons I'm a quiltmaker and not a painter. Then I play around with the design that I think will make best use of the fabric.

When I found so many new fabrics, I was like a kid in a candy store. I piled myself up with yards of new designs and couldn't wait to get home and begin playing with them.

At about this time, I was asked to do another book. Even though I wasn't looking forward to getting involved in a new book so soon after the last one, many of the designs I was thinking about would be appropriate, so I was delighted for the excuse to get to work. Otherwise, I would have felt obliged to put off all new work until the other demands in my professional life were met.

I used to view my quiltmaking as secondary to other, more important obligations. I stopped one day and examined my uneasiness at putting long hours into a quilt when I could, or should, be working. It suddenly occurred to me that this *is* my work, and it has been for some time. Everything else, my books, shows, teaching—my business, in other words—is a direct outgrowth of the quilts I make. Today, even if I weren't a professional, I would sanction the time I spend making quilts as essential to the legacy I will leave behind. I hope you feel the same way about your quiltmaking, whether or not it's the way you make your living.

Quilts are beginning to receive the recognition they deserve as a vital part of our nation's history, so keep that in mind when you're working on your own quilts, and remember that they will also become an important part of *your* history.

With that, I invite you to sample this new collection I've had such fun putting together. There's something here for everyone: for those who don't have much time or experience, and for those who wish to stretch a bit and tackle something challenging. Some projects are quick and easy; others will provide you with hours of enjoyment. Feel free to make any changes you like to suit your own ideas or specifications.

If you've never made a Log Cabin before (every quilter should try at least one), consider starting with the Double Zigzag Log Cabin (page 32). This unusually dramatic design, inspired by an antique quilt made of brown and purple printed cottons that I saw in the window of an antiques store, is easy to make.

There are also two other Log Cabin quilts to try. One, also easy to make, was designed as part of a room setting complete with matching pillows and accessories. The last one, much more challenging because it's double-sided, is for all you veterans who've made Log Cabins before and would enjoy trying one with a new twist.

Flying Boxes is a great introduction to Baby Blocks, a simple enough quilt, or so it seems, except that it takes great skill to assemble well. By adding two triangles to the basic block, it's suddenly much easier to make and just as dramatic.

The Flower Basket Medallion demonstrates an interesting

approach to designing a quilt by surrounding a central motif with a series of borders.

The Harvest Appliqué is my tribute to the Baltimore quilt. Inspired by my own "Food Stuffs," a witty crop of stuffed fruits and vegetables, I've sewn a garden full of table linens, kitchen accessories, and a quilt using an easy-to-handle freezer-paper technique.

Designing a new group of Christmas tree ornaments each year is becoming a tradition with me. This year it's Santa, Mrs. Santa, and an elf—Santa's Helper. There's also a group of tiny red-and-white quilt blocks that I made as tree ornaments. They could also be made into miniature quilts by repeating one of the designs or by combining all of them in a mini-sampler quilt. Their larger counterparts are pillows made with the same patterns I used on page 48. These patterns could be used for quilts as well.

Finally, I've included a group of accessories—a bag for your quilts, a sewing or make-up case, a tote bag, and a shoulder bag.

There's a section on basic quiltmaking techniques, with general instructions to use as a reference when you need one. If this is your first try at making quilts, I suggest reading through Quilting Basics before getting started, so that you can become familiar with how things are done.

The sewing instructions have been carefully planned to guide you step by step through each project. Because I've seen so many unreadable instructions and poorly drawn patterns, I was determined, when I began to write books of my own, to make clarity and accuracy my trademarks. Nothing is more frustrating than getting stuck in the middle of a quilt with instructions that aren't clear and patterns that don't fit.

My intention is to offer you new designs with a taste of the past, to make these designs accessible through accurate patterns and instructions, and most of all, to fire the enthusiasm I know we share for making quilts.

Margit Echols

QUILTING BASICS

PATTERNS

All patterns in this book are drawn full size, with ¼-inch seam allowances. Cutting and sewing lines are clearly marked on all patterns (Diagram 1).

Arrows appear on some of the pattern pieces to indicate which side, or sides, of the pattern should line up with the horizontal or vertical grain of the fabric (Diagram 1). Patterns with straight edges that do not have arrows, such as squares or rectangles, should be positioned in the same way.

Some pattern pieces have notches (Diagram 1) which should be clipped into the fabric as indicated—up to, but not through, the stitching line. Use notches to match up edges when sewing pieces together.

Corners on triangular, diamond, and odd-shaped pieces are squared off to eliminate excess fabric (Diagram 1).

To trace the patterns by hand, use a pencil, tracing paper, and a straight edge. Be sure to trace carefully, because inaccurate patterns can create problems. Note the name of the design, the number of the pattern piece, and any other important markings, such as notches and arrows on each piece.

The tracing-paper pattern pieces can either be used as is, by cutting them out and pinning them to the fabric, or they can be mounted with spray glue on lightweight cardboard. First, apply the glue to a piece of cardboard the same size or slightly larger than the sheet on which the patterns have been traced. Lay the tracing paper on top of the cardboard and smooth it down with your hand. Allow the glue to dry, then cut out all the pieces with a pair of scissors or an X-acto knife with a steel straight edge.

A convenient way to make sturdy, long-lasting templates is by using non-slip plastic available in sewing and quilt supply stores. Trace the patterns on the plastic with a pencil, as you would on tracing paper, and cut them out. Some template plastic is marked with a ¼-inch grid, which can be helpful in tracing most square or rectangular pattern pieces.

Cardboard and plastic templates are not meant to be pinned to the fabric. Lay them on the fabric one at a time, hold them in place with your hand, and trace around their edges with a pencil or fabric marker. Make sure that no extra seam allowance is added and the markings remain exactly the same size as the pattern.

Be sure the pieces are properly marked with their piece numbers and name of the design so you can sort them out should they get mixed up with templates belonging to other designs. Store the templates in an envelope marked with the name of the design.

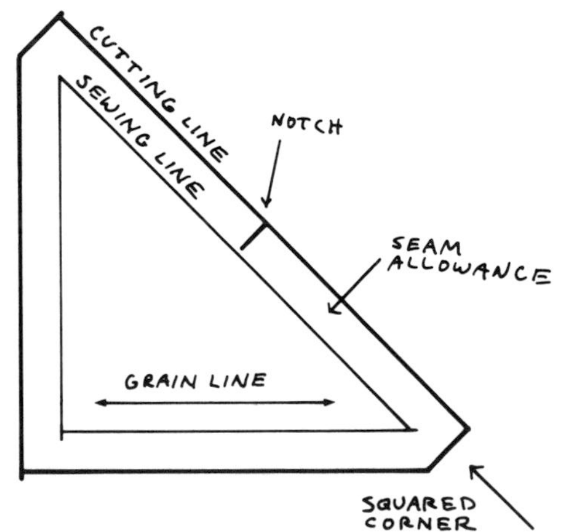

Diagram 1. Sample pattern piece.

FABRIC

The best fabrics for quilts are cotton and cotton blends. Most quilters prefer 100 percent cotton, but if it isn't available, cotton blends can be used. With quilters in mind, many fabric companies today are producing extensive home sewing lines of coordinating prints and solids. To pre-shrink and test color fastness, machine wash and dry all cottons or cotton blends at least once before cutting. If any fabrics show a tendency to run, wash them as many times as necessary to remove all residual dye.

Silk, satin, velvet, and wool also make wonderful quilts, but can be more difficult to handle than cotton. Beginners should use cotton until they feel ready to take on more exotic materials. Such fabrics, of course, should not be washed, but handled according to the nature of their fiber content. Because of their stretchiness and texture, knits do not work well in quilts and are thought to detract from the look of even the best-made pieces.

Although fabrics of different weights and textures can be mixed in a patchwork project, bear in mind that thicker fabrics require larger seam allowances. Some may be smooth and slippery, so extra care should be taken in combining heavier fabrics since they may resist being stitched together evenly. Before cutting out all the pieces for a project, it's always wise to assemble at least one quilt block as a test to see how the fabrics will behave.

It is impossible to give exact yardages for most of the designs in this book, since your own color choices will establish the required amounts. However, to help you establish fabric requirements, a list preceding the instructions for each design states how many of each pattern piece will be needed. In addition, approximate yardage requirements are given. To avoid running short of fabric, it's always better to buy a little more than you think you might need. Should you run short, though, don't panic. Some of the most interesting quilts are those that vary somewhat from block to block, having been made with fabrics available at the time rather than with purchased yardage.

CUTTING

Always use a pair of good, sharp scissors to cut fabric. You can work more quickly if you cut through four layers of fabric at a time instead of two.

Cutting wheels are very useful for cutting out pieces with straight sides—for example, strips for strip piecing. Hold the circular blade against a steel or thick plastic straight edge, apply pressure, and roll the blade along the side of the straight edge.

Position the patterns on the fabric so that arrows point in the same direction as the grain. Be sure the sides of square or rectangular pattern pieces also align with the grain of the fabric. Examine printed fabrics to determine whether or not the print is a one-way design. Most prints look fine going in any direction, but the placement of a print with a one-way pattern—such as a stripe—should be considered carefully with the overall design of the quilt in mind.

Unless you've mounted them on cardboard, pin the pattern pieces in place on the fabric and carefully cut out each shape. Accurate cutting will substantially affect a design and how it looks when it's finished. No amount of pressing will correct uneven seams that pucker. If using plastic or cardboard pattern templates, trace around them with a pencil or marker with the point held right up against the edge of the pattern. The addition of extra seam allowance resulting from marking cutting lines that are even slightly larger than the pattern will cause a piece to "grow," and for a design with many pieces this can become a real problem.

MARKING

Various kinds of marking pens and pencils are available. Any hard lead pencil, of course, can be used, but there are also gray pencils, which leave a lighter mark, and yellow and white pencils that are good for marking dark fabrics.

Water-soluble marking pens are useful, too, since the ink can be removed with a damp cloth. Before marking a whole project, test the pen on a sample piece of fabric to be sure the ink is really removable. Be careful not to hold the pen point down in one place too long because the ink will continue to flow, making it difficult to remove with only a damp cloth. If there's too much ink in the fabric, washing will probably be the only way to get it all out. So, keep a light touch and mark quickly.

Chalk markers that dispense a thin line of powdered chalk are probably the safest, since the residue can be easily brushed off. They are available in a variety of colors for marking light and dark fabrics. They are easy to use and quite accurate, but here again, it is advisable to use a light touch. I discovered this when marking white fabric with blue chalk. The fabric was lightweight, and even though I marked the wrong side, the blue lines showed through on the right side of the quilt top. It wasn't very obvious, but you could see it if you looked closely. Although most markings will wash out, I'd rather not have to wash a quilt just after finishing it.

Mark fabrics with pile or a nap on the wrong side, and use a pencil or marker that makes marks that won't have to be removed with water.

Until sewing a ¼-inch seam becomes automatic, beginners may feel the need to mark stitching lines as well as cutting lines. If this is the case, mark stitching lines on the wrong side of the fabric with a "quilter's quarter," a ¼-inch-wide metal or plastic sewing aid. Line up the edges of the quilter's quarter with the edge of the fabric and mark along the inside edge. Since most patchwork projects have a lot of pieces, marking the stitching lines on each piece may soon become tiresome. It usually doesn't take long to get used to sewing seams of a constant, even width, so it probably won't be necessary to mark stitching lines for very long.

There are other sewing guides that will help you sew a consistent ¼-inch seam allowance. The zipper foot on my machine is just about ¼ inch in width, so I use it as a guide. My machine also has a seam-allowance gauge on the metal plate next to the zipper foot. If your sewing machine doesn't have a gauge, you can use a piece of masking tape as a guide. Place it so that the edge of the tape is ¼ inch away from the needle and parallel to the side of the zipper foot. If you keep the edge of your fabric even with the edge of the tape, you will maintain a ¼-inch seam allowance.

PIECING

One of the benefits of living in the twentieth century is that a quilter can choose to piece by hand or machine. You should feel free to sew whichever way is most comfortable for you. It is true, however, that many quilts look best when the finishing—the final quilting when all layers are stitched together—is done by hand. Hand quilting produces a lovely, soft texture that is generally thought to be more appealing than machine quilting. Even so, wonderful quilts have also been quilted by machine, so no single rule seems to apply to every project.

ASSEMBLY-LINE PIECING

When instructions call for the assembly of many of the same types of pieces, it will save time to run each set of pieces through the machine one right after the other without stopping. After stitching the first set together, leave the presser foot down and continue stitching beyond the edges of the fabric about ½ inch to 1 inch, then feed the next piece beneath the presser foot and continue stitching (see Diagram 2). Repeat until all pieces in the step have been assembled. Clip the threads between the pieces when finished. These threads will stay twisted and keep the seams secure enough so that you can press them open and move on to the next step.

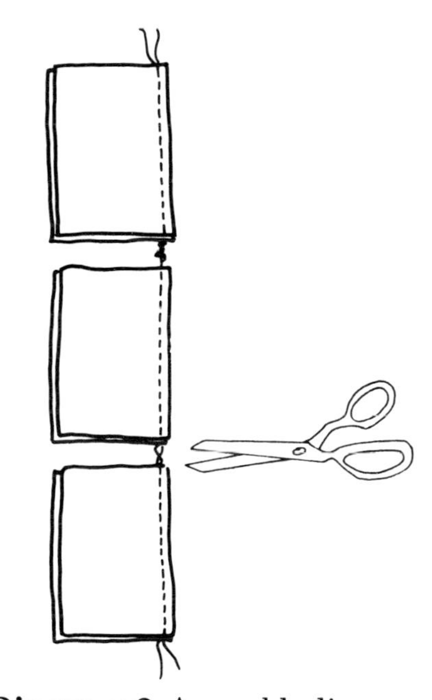

Diagram 2. Assembly-line piecing.

PRESSING

The sewing instructions for each project include frequent references to pressing seams open or, on occasion, to one side. Seams will usually lie flatter when pressed open, and a completed piece always looks better when seams have been pressed after every step.

Many quilters believe a quilt will be stronger if the seams are pressed to one side, and this is certainly true for hand piecing. When machine piecing, I would opt for beauty rather than strength since I don't intend to subject my quilts to heavy everyday use and repeated washings. Too much work and time go into each quilt for it not to be treated as a treasured object. Whether you prefer to press seams open or to one side, be careful not to stretch any of the pieces out of shape.

ENLARGING THE QUILT TOP

Most quilt tops can be enlarged by adding quilt blocks. If the instructions call for twelve blocks, for example, you can increase the overall dimensions by adding four more blocks to one side.

To increase the size of the quilt without adding more blocks, separate the blocks you have with sashes—strips of fabric sewn between blocks. These sashes can be almost any width, preferably not much wider than one-fourth the size of the blocks. They can repeat one of the colors used in the block or can introduce a contrasting color.

For additional width, add borders around the outside of the quilt top.

ASSEMBLING THE QUILT TOP

After the quilt top is completed, it is ready to be assembled into a sandwich with the batting and back. The best and easiest kinds of batting to work with are those available in most sewing or quilt supply stores. Most brands are polyester, although commercial cotton batting is also available. Cotton batting may not be quite as easy to closely quilt by hand as polyester batting. Cotton and wool batts, of course, were used in the past. They were hand-carded and carefully distributed on the backings before the quilt tops were placed on top and basted. Originally, the three layers were quilted together in order to hold the batting in place. The closer the lines of quilting were to each other, the less likely it was that the batting, which was loose, would bunch up and move around. With today's commercial battings, there's little danger of this happening.

Commercial battings come in several weights: regular, low-loft, and high-loft. The thinner the batting, the easier it will be to produce small stitches. Each weight is available in several sizes—from small sizes for small projects, such as baby quilts, to large sizes for king-size quilts.

Some quilts are backed with fabric in one of the colors in the pieced top. Others are backed with contrasting fabric. This is a matter of personal preference, but keep in mind that it's not a good idea to use a dark fabric for the back if the quilt top is light in color, especially if the batting is thin. The backing can show through and make the quilt top look shadowy or dark.

If the color of the quilting thread contrasts strongly with the top or the backing, extra care should be taken to keep the stitches regular in size. Uneven stitches will be much more obvious on a contrasting color.

Most cotton and cotton blend fabrics are 45 to 48 inches wide. Some are 36 inches wide. When buying yardage for a backing, it will be necessary to calculate how much fabric the project will require if its dimensions exceed the width of the fabric. It may take two or more lengths pieced together to accommodate the size of the project. For example, if a quilt measures 90 × 90 inches, it will require two 2-yard lengths of 48-inch fabric, or a total of 4 yards for the backing.

To assemble the quilt top, batting, and back, spread the back wrong side up on the floor, on a low-pile carpet if possible. The nap on the carpet will keep the fabric from slipping, making it easier to work with. If a carpet isn't available, tape the edges of the fabric to the floor with masking tape to prevent it from slipping underneath the batting and quilt top.

Place the batting on top of the back and smooth it out. Stretch the batting slightly, but not too much, to remove any slack. Place the quilt top right side up on top of the batting and carefully smooth it out until it looks square and free of any bubbles.

Working from the center of the quilt out toward the edges, pin all three layers together (without catching pins in the carpet) at least every foot or so along the edges. Pick up the quilt, turn it over, and straighten it out face down on the floor. Check to see that the back hasn't moved during pinning. If necessary, turn the quilt over and re-pin as needed until all layers are smooth and straight.

Baste all three layers together by hand, starting from the center and basting horizontally out toward the sides. Baste horizontal rows, working down toward the bottom, then up to the top. Then baste vertical rows from top to bottom. A sunburst pattern also works well.

THE FRAME

Quilting can be done without a frame, but quilts that have been frame-quilted have an especially smooth, flat appearance. It might be difficult at first to get used to quilting with a frame, because the sewing surface is taut and seems to resist flexing as the needle is pushed up and down at an angle through the quilt. With a little practice, however, most quilters eventually come to prefer using a frame, since the results are so pleasing.

Although different frames will have different instructions for attaching the quilts, a cloth tape is usually stapled to each of the cross bars, and the top and bottom edges of the quilt are pinned or basted to these bars (Diagram 3). Stretch the edge of the quilt a bit when attaching it to the tape. Make sure the top and bottom edges of the quilt are directly in line with each other so there's no diagonal pulling when they're rolled up.

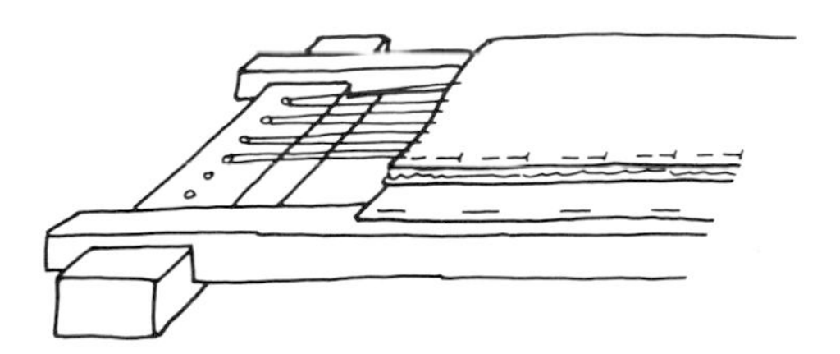

Diagram 3. Baste quilt to tape. Roll up and stretch tightly. Lash sides to side pieces.

When the top and bottom edges are fixed in place, roll the quilt up tightly from both ends until the center is exposed between the cross bars and tightly stretched. Lace the sides of the quilt to the sides of the frame with needle and thread, or use a length of cloth tape pinned to the sides, depending on your preference and how the frame is constructed. Stretch the quilt firmly and evenly throughout, because once the quilt is removed it will retain the shape it has acquired during this step. I pull the quilt very taut, so that there is no sagging in the middle and so that the fabric bounces back up if pressed down.

For a long time, I used a simple frame made for me by our neighbor, though I thought a frame that would tilt would be a good improvement and might make quilting a little easier by allowing me to work with my head up instead of bent forward. After carefully studying the ads for frames in quilting magazines, I finally took a big step and ordered the one pictured here. To me it is the Steinway of quilt frames; working with one as substantial and beautifully constructed as this is a joy. If you're a serious quiltmaker, treat yourself well. Don't skimp on good tools, especially one that's as important as a frame. Invest in one that will make long working hours a pleasure instead of a chore.

Another type of frame I recently discovered made with PVC pipe, designed and produced by Monta Lea Kramer, a fellow quilter (see page 73), is available in many sizes for lap quilting, and there is also a

wonderful standing model, the best portable frame I've ever seen. It's lightweight, can be put together and taken apart easily, does not require pinning or basting into the frame, and holds the tension perfectly. The design is so simple and elegant. I took the standing model with me on vacation and was delighted with how easy it was to transport and set up.

There are also hoops—lap hoops, standing hoops, and standing hoops with universal ball joints, which allow the work to be turned at any angle. The quilt is first spread out on top of the inner ring. Then the outer ring is placed on top of the quilt and forced down over the inner ring, tightly stretching the quilt. The set screw on the outer ring is then tightened to hold the quilt rigidly in place. Hoops work very well and are especially useful to people who don't have space for a floor frame.

QUILTING

Once it is stretched, the quilt is ready to mark. Mark the quilting designs on the right side of the fabric as lightly as possible, though still sufficiently visible to prevent straining your eyes. Make your selection of a marking tool according to whether you intend to remove your marks from the finished quilt by washing. Some quilters avoid this step by marking with a pencil so lightly that the lines virtually disappear during the quilting process.

The quilt designs can be drawn on the fabric with the aid of a ruler or by using commercial or homemade stencils. You can make your own stencils by drawing on lightweight cardboard and cutting the designs out with an X-acto knife. Stencil-cutting kits containing electric hot pens and a roll of plastic are advertised in quilt magazines and may be available in sewing and quilt supply stores. Because so many wonderful designs are available, I prefer to buy most of my stencils and hand-cut the few I can't find.

The simplest and most common way to mark a quilt is with "outline" quilting. Whatever the motif is, you can quilt around it ¼ inch away from its edge, using as a guide a quilter's quarter or a transparent ruler marked in ¼-inch increments.

Quilting is done with one hand holding the needle over the surface of the quilt. The other hand is positioned underneath to guide the needle as it comes through the fabric and direct it back up to the top. It is advisable to protect your fingers on both hands. I use a thimble with a ridge around the top for my quilting finger, which keeps the needle from slipping off the tip. I still haven't found anything I'm happy with for my fingers underneath. Some quilters use thimbles on these fingers also. Quilting without any thimbles at all means the needle will dig into the skin slightly, and over time a callus will build up.

Quilting is easiest with a fairly short needle. The thinner the needle,

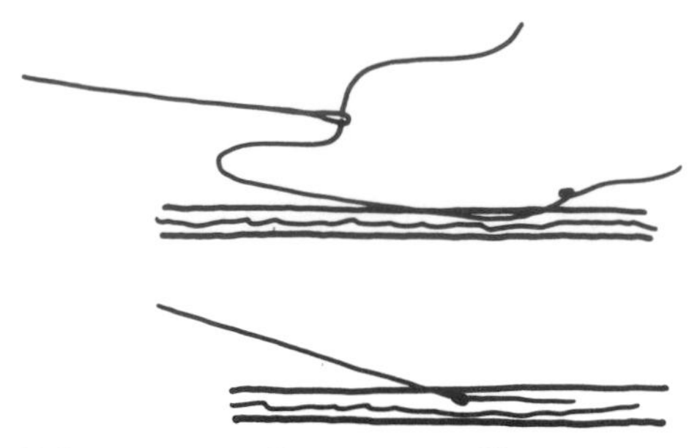

Diagram 4. Insert needle between layers. Pull knot through to inside.

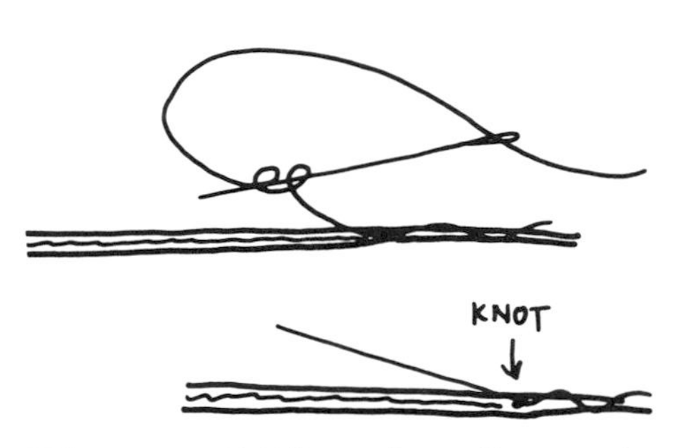

Diagram 5. Wrap thread around needle to make knot. Pull knot through to inside. Push needle up and clip thread.

the more easily it will pass through the fabric. Try not to choose a needle so thin that the eye is too small to thread easily.

To keep the thread from twisting, pull it through a piece of beeswax, a procedure that also seems to make the thread stronger. Tie a knot at the end of the thread, and insert the needle through the top layer of the quilt about an inch away from where you want to start quilting. Pull the needle up through the fabric at the starting point—right up to the knot. Tug gently until the knot pops through the top layer. The knot will now be concealed between the quilt top and back (see Diagram 4). Knots should never show on the front or back of the quilt.

To finish a line of quilting, wind the thread around the needle two or three times where it comes up at the surface of the quilt. Pull the needle through to make a knot at this point. Insert the needle just one stitch-length beyond this point between the top and back. Bring the needle up about 1 inch away and pop the knot through so it lies between the two layers (Diagram 5). Pull the thread slightly, and clip it at the point where it comes up through the fabric. The end of the thread will disappear between the layers.

How the actual quilting is done is a matter of preference. You will have to experiment to discover the quilting technique that is most comfortable for you. It is generally agreed that a series of running stitches—at least two to four stitches at a time—is better than quilting one stitch at a time. A series of running stitches usually produces a straighter line than the single stitch method. Make the stitches even and as small as you comfortably can. It is thought by many, and I think wrongly, that there should be as many as 11, even up to 13, stitches per inch, but I've seen many lovely quilts in which the stitches weren't small at all. My stitches are usually 10 to the inch, depending on how thick the fabric and batting are. If they're too small, they become hard to see and not as pretty, in my opinion, as a clearly visible line of even stitches. If you plan to enter your quilts in shows and contests, you will find that small stitch size is very important to judges. Observe the work of other quilters to learn how your own stitching technique and speed can be improved.

Quilting can also be done by machine. The only disadvantage is that larger quilts can be cumbersome and hard to handle when guided through the machine, especially if there are a lot of curves. I have found that basting wherever I intend to sew produces the best results.

When planning a large piece, it might be wiser to think about quilting the blocks one at a time and assembling them after they're finished. Great care must be taken to make sure that the quilt top and back feed through the machine at the same rate so that they don't pull away from each other and pucker. It might help to stretch the quilt firmly while sewing (gently when sewing on the bias): your right hand in front of the presser foot and your left hand behind it. Very pleasing results are possible with machine piecing as long as all layers remain smooth and flat and don't pull away from each other. To make knots at each end of a line of quilting, simply backstitch over the first and last stitches.

BINDING THE QUILT

Once all the quilting is finished, the quilt can be removed from the frame. The edges then need to be finished with a binding, which can be of any size. Self-binding, the same color as the overall color of the quilt, or a contrasting color can be used. The following instructions are for making a ½-inch-wide binding for a low-loft quilt.

A binding with a ½-inch finished width on a low-loft quilt requires 2-inch-wide strips of fabric cut on the bias or on the straight of the grain. The advantage of a bias binding is that it is more flexible and can be shaped around corners and curved edges. To prepare strips for a bias binding, fold over on a diagonal one end of a rectangle of fabric so that it is even with the selvage edge (Diagram 6).

Press a crease along this fold, which is the true bias of the fabric. Unfold and mark off the fabric in 2-inch-wide diagonal strips, using the crease as the first line (Diagram 7).

Cut as many bias strips as needed to go around the entire perimeter of the quilt, and stitch the ends together as shown in Diagram 8. Press seams open.

An even faster way to cut large quantities of bias trim is to begin with a rectangle of fabric twice as long as it is wide. Mark diagonal cutting lines as described above. Then cut off the triangles left over at each end and set them aside. With right sides facing, pin the edges of the fabric together, staggering the strips so that the bottom ends move over one place (Diagram 9). Machine-stitch the edges together in this position to make a tube. Starting at one end of the tube and following the marked lines, cut out one continuous bias strip.

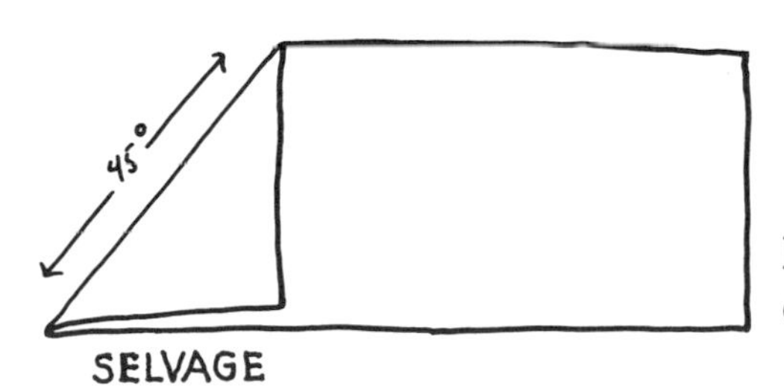

Diagram 6. Fold fabric on the diagonal.

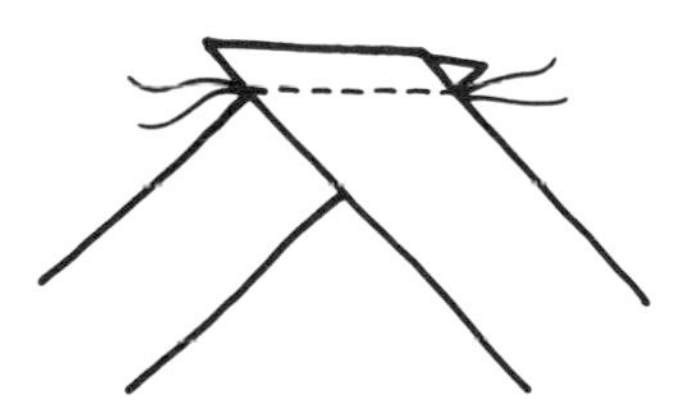

Diagram 8. Stitch strips together, end to end.

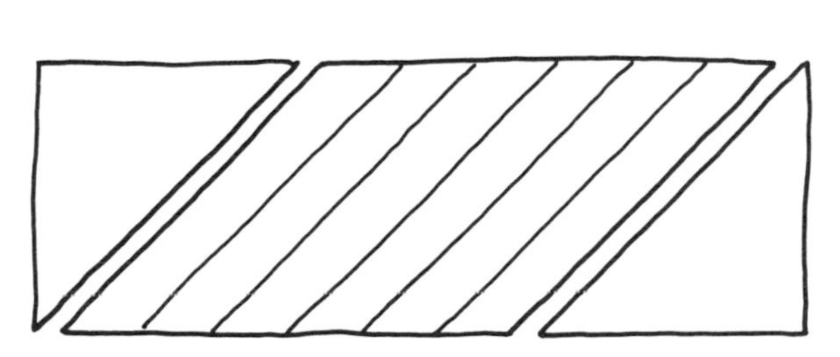

Diagram 7. Cut 2-inch-wide diagonal strips.

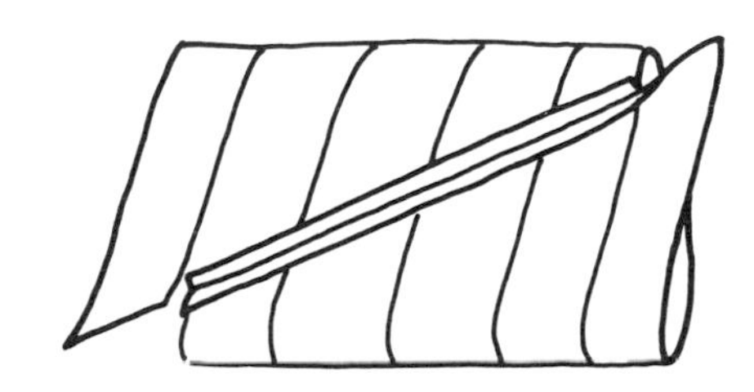

Diagram 9. Cut tube of fabric into one continuous bias strip.

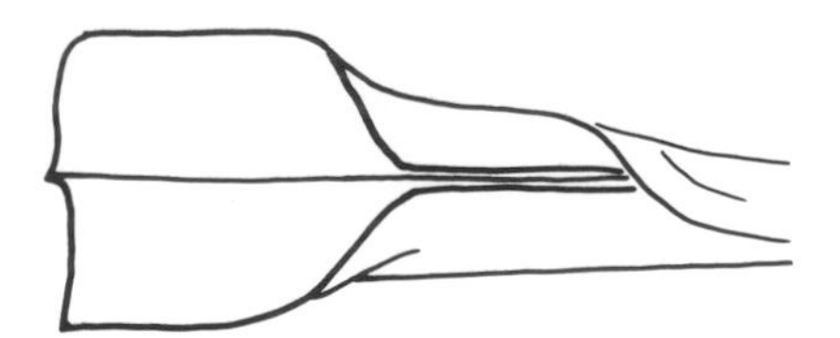

Diagram 10. Preshape bias binding.

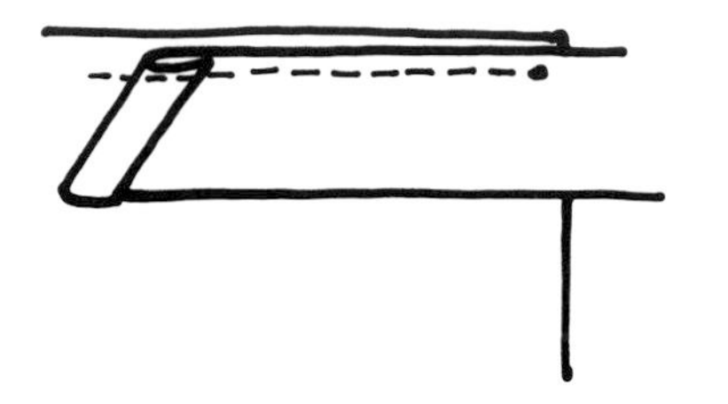

Diagram 11. Fold end over and stitch binding to quilt.

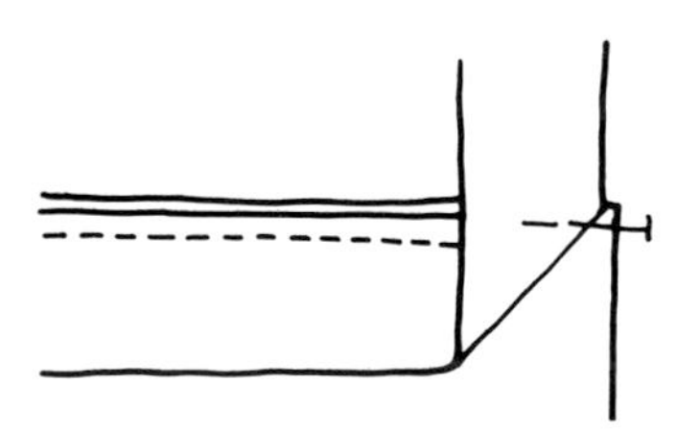

Diagram 12. Fold binding up and pin.

If you like, you can preshape the completed binding strip before attaching it to the quilt by folding and pressing it in half first, and then folding the sides in toward the middle and pressing again (Diagram 10). This can be accomplished even more easily with a tape pressing aid, a simple gadget available in most quilt and fabric shops.

Start the binding in the middle of one side, not at a corner. Fold over one end of the binding and, using a ½-inch seam allowance, sew the binding along one edge on the top of the quilt, matching the edge of the binding to the edge of the quilt. Stitch to within ½ inch of the corner and then backstitch (Diagram 11). Lift the presser foot, remove the quilt, and clip the threads.

Fold binding up so that it is perpendicular to the seam, crease the fold, and pin (see Diagram 12).

Fold the binding down to form a ½-inch tuck, insert the needle exactly at the point where the first stitch line ended, lower the presser foot, and continue sewing (Diagram 13). Sew a few inches and check to see that the corner will miter neatly with just the right amount of binding, and correct if necessary before continuing on to the other corners.

To finish, fold the binding over to the back of the quilt, fold the edge under ½ inch, and slipstitch the binding to the quilt by hand. Fold the corners carefully into neat miters. Continue sewing about 1 inch beyond the starting point and trim. Slipstitch the binding by hand (Diagram 14).

A nice finishing touch for any hand-made project would be your signature embroidered on the lower right-hand border, or anywhere else it can be seen. If you plan to show your quilt in public, it's always wise to add the year it was made and a copyright notice, a C inside a circle to protect your design. I usually embroider my name, the date, and copyright notice in thread of the same color as the fabric on which it is stitched. This makes the information visible, but not intrusive. At other times, if it's right for the overall design, I use a contrasting color. Other information, such as the name of the town or city in which you live, the person or purpose you made it for, which could later be of personal or historic interest, can also be embroidered on the back.

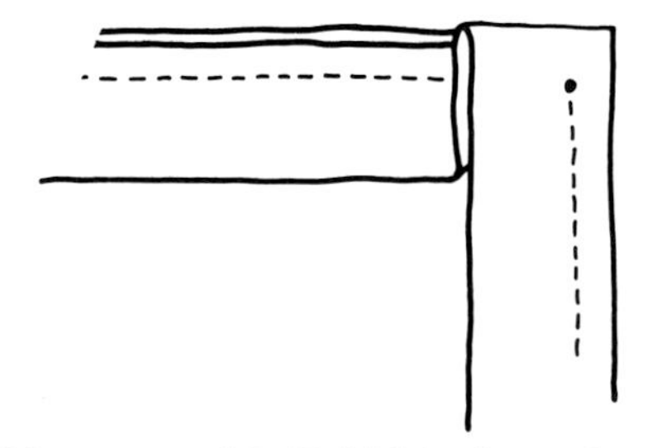

Diagram 13. Fold binding down at corner.

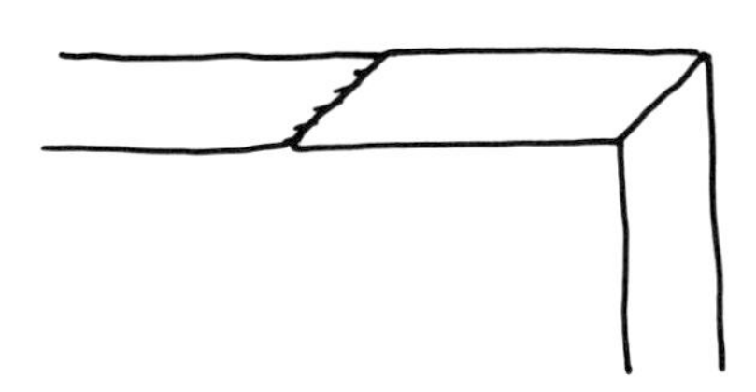

Diagram 14. Slipstitch overlap to binding.

HANGING AND DISPLAYING QUILTS

When displaying quilts on beds or on the wall, a few things should be kept in mind. Quilts should be kept out of direct sunlight to prevent fading. Drawing the curtains or blinds when the room in which a quilt is displayed is not in use will be helpful in reducing exposure to light. Quilts also should be protected from extreme changes in temperature and humidity.

Quilts should never be suspended with nails, staples, tacks, or push pins. They can be hung from a pole inserted through a muslin sleeve which is attached across the top of the wrong side of the quilt. The sleeve should be wide enough so the pole can be inserted easily. In the seam that joins the binding to the top of the quilt, baste the top of the sleeve through all three thicknesses. Baste the bottom of the sleeve to the back of the quilt without going through to the front. Insert the pole through either end of the sleeve and hang it on the wall.

You could also use a strip of Velcro about two inches wide and as long as the top width of the quilt. Baste the soft side of the Velcro strip across the top. Staple the other side of the strip to a flat board attached to the wall. To hang, stretch the top of the quilt slightly when attaching the two strips of Velcro to each other. Quilts can be easily removed and rotated with this method.

The safest way to hang a quilt is to baste it to a sheet, which is then stretched tightly over a wood frame. To relieve the quilt from the stress of its weight as much as possible, baste it to the sheet around all four sides and throughout the entire surface in vertical and horizontal rows. Then hang the frame on the wall like a large picture frame.

Quilts should not be displayed for indefinite periods of time. They'll need a rest from vertical hanging and from the wear and tear of being used on beds. If you have more than one quilt and can rotate your collection, you will also welcome the visual change. If artwork of any kind remains in the same place too long, we get so used to it that eventually we fail to noticc it.

CARE OF QUILTS

Because modern commercial batting is so well made, it can be washed easily without bunching up or shifting between the rows of quilting. As long as the fabrics are preshrunk and colorfast, there's no reason why a cotton quilt can't be washed by hand using a mild detergent. It's not a good idea, however, to wash quilts by machine because the agitating action causes too much stress. Hand washing is probably easiest in a bathtub or large sink. Never scrub or rub layers together. Gently press the water through the quilt. Drain the water, refill the tub, and repeat the process until the water remains clear. Then drain the water off for the last time, press out as much of it as possible, and gently blot the quilt with towels, laying it flat to dry. If it is put outside to dry, to prevent fading, be sure it is kept out of direct sunlight. Do not hang a wet quilt on a clothesline. The excess weight will put too much strain on the fibers and stitching. Quilts can be dry-cleaned, but after a while they don't look or smell quite as bright and clean as they do when they're hand-washed.

Antique quilts, of course, must be handled with special care. It is best to discuss the cleaning they require, and can survive, with an antiques dealer or an expert in textile conservation.

All quilts, new or old, should be folded in acid-free tissue paper and stored in acid-free cardboard boxes. See that they are clean and free from dirt which might invite pests. Never store quilts in plastic bags, especially for long periods of time. They will be deprived of air circulation and exposed to chemicals which may be harmful to the fibers. There is also a danger that mildew-causing moisture might be trapped inside. If they are to be stored on wood shelves or in drawers or trunks (even cedar), protect them from the acids in the wood with clean muslin or acid-free tissue. Some quilters make cotton sleeves that resemble pillowcases for each quilt. Refold your quilts every six months so the folds fall in different places, and insert crumpled tissue paper in each fold to prevent permanent creasing.

To avoid creasing altogether, wrap your quilts, several at a time, around a tube that's at least as long as the width of your quilts. Be sure to cover the tube with acid-free paper, or use a cotton sheet as protection against any harmful chemicals the paper tube may contain. Wrap the outside of the quilts with another sheet, and store them upright in a closet.

Quilts are meant to be used—if not on beds, then displayed where they can been seen and appreciated. Any quilt will age over time, but if properly cared for, it can be enjoyed for generations.

GLOSSARY

Appliqué. Two basic techniques, patchwork and appliqué, are generally used for quilt tops. Appliqué is the process by which individual shapes are cut from one fabric and sewn by hand or machine to a background of contrasting fabric.

Backing. The back, or underside, of a quilt, which can be made from an old, soft sheet or pieced with several lengths of fabric.

Basting. Long hand stitching, or machine stitching sewn with the longest possible stitches, used to hold in place two or more layers of fabric before final stitching.

Batting. The soft filling between the quilt top and the backing. Commercially produced polyester or cotton, or hand-carded cotton or wool, can be used, as well as flannel sheets or thin, soft blankets.

Bias. Fabric is woven with horizontal and vertical threads. The diagonal direction of this weave is called the *bias*.

Binding. Edge finishing for quilts, pillows, or other objects, usually made with bias strips of fabric long enough to bind the entire outside edge.

Block. Most quilt tops consist of a series of blocks, or squares, which are pieced or appliquéd. These can be repeats of the same design or a collection of many different designs. It is easiest to work on small sections, or blocks, and assemble them later into a larger piece.

Finger pressing. Instead of pressing seams open or to the side with an iron, you may prefer at times simply to run across the seams with your fingers or thumbnail. This will very nearly accomplish the same purpose and prevent certain fabrics, such as velvet or wool, from losing their naps.

French knot. An ornamental knot made with embroidery thread. The thread is wrapped several times around the needle, which is held on the surface of the fabric where the thread comes through from the back of the fabric. After the needle is pulled through the loops, it is then pushed through the fabric at the same place.

Miter. The diagonal fold at the corner on a border or hem where two pieces of fabric are cut at an angle and joined together.

Nap. The pile—that is, the short fuzzy ends of threads—on the surface of fabrics such as corduroy and velvet.

Patchwork. Unlike appliqué, in which any shape may be shown on top of a background, patchwork is the technique of joining adjacent pieces, which must be sewn together to fit together perfectly.

Piecing. The sewing together of geometric shapes to create a design.

Quilt. A quilt consists of three layers: a top, a soft or fluffy filler, and a back. To quilt is to sew through these three layers by hand or machine to produce lines of stitching in some sort of ornamental design or pattern. In the past, quilting was used primarily to keep the batting, which may have been loose and unstable, from shifting around during use or washing. Today, with many types of stable batting available, this stitching is often more ornamental than practical.

Quilting. The ornamental stitching that holds in place a quilt top, back, and batting.

Sashes. Strips or borders used between blocks to create a grid.

Setting. After all the blocks for a quilt have been made, they are assembled into an overall pattern called a *setting*. The quilt block designs can be arranged in more than one setting.

Stencil. A paper, cardboard, plastic, or metal template used to trace or paint designs onto fabric.

Tack. Several short stitches made by hand or machine to hold two or more pieces in place.

Template. A pattern mounted on stiff paper or cut from plastic or metal for use in tracing or cutting.

Top-stitching. Ornamental or functional hand or machine stitching that shows on the right side of the fabric.

PILLOWS

If you're like most quilters, you probably experiment with various color and fabric combinations before cutting everything you need for a quilt. Then you're stuck with leftover test blocks with no place to go. These blocks never need go to waste: simply make them into pillows.

Patchwork and appliqué pillows make great gifts, and they're a lot less demanding than a quilt. Starting with pillow-size projects is a good way for a beginner to become acquainted with traditional designs and quiltmaking techniques without feeling overwhelmed by a big project. Before making the Log Cabin with Cornerstones quilt on page 38, for example, make a pillow with four blocks such as the red and white one shown on page 110. If you like the results and feel comfortable with the technique, go ahead and make the quilt.

In this section there are instructions for making pillows with several edge finishes and three types of closures.

ASSEMBLING THE PILLOW

In addition to a pieced top, you will need a piece of matching or contrasting fabric of the same size for the pillow back, plus a piece of fabric (preferably white) to line the patchwork top and a piece of batting (optional) to give the top extra body.

Spread out the lining, smooth the batting on top of the lining, and lay the pillow top right side up on top of the batting. Pin all three layers together and machine baste ⅛ inch all around the outside edge. The layer of batting adds a soft, plump appearance to the pillow top, but it is not essential and can be omitted if you don't plan to quilt the pillow top. If you wish to quilt the top, however, a layer of batting will give dimension to your stitches. All quilting—whether by hand or machine—should be done at this point.

EDGE FINISHING

Double Ruffle

This ruffle, made with a strip of fabric folded in half lengthwise before gathering, provides a finished edge without hemming and permits the right side of the fabric to show on both sides. To make a 2-inch-wide double ruffle, cut four 5-inch-wide strips that, depending on how full you want the gathered ruffle to be, are 1½ to 2 times the length of one side of the finished pillow top. For example, if the pillow is a 10-inch square, cut four 5 × 15-inch or four 5 × 20-inch fabric strips. Or simply cut and piece a 5-inch-wide strip that measures 1½ to 2 times the perimeter of the pillow top. One-third yard of 44-inch-wide fabric will yield enough 5-inch-wide strips to make a generous double ruffle for a 10-, 12-, or even a 14-inch square pillow.

Sew the strips together end to end to make one continuous loop. Press the seams open. Fold the ruffle in half lengthwise, right side out, and press the fold into the ruffle. With the largest stitch on your machine, stitch through both thicknesses ⅛ inch from raw edges around the entire edge of the ruffle. Add a second row of stitching ⅛ inch away from the first, starting and stopping at the same place. To gather the ruffle, pull the threads at one end of both rows of stitching at the same time (Diagram 1).

Pin the ruffle to the outside edge of the pillow top with the folded edge of the ruffle toward the center (Diagram 2). If using a ruffle composed of four equal pieces, the seam lines can be positioned at each corner or at the center sides of the pillow top. This will help you judge how much ruffle should be distributed along each side of the pillow. If using a ruffle made of one continuous strip, fold it in quarters, clip a notch at each fold and use the notches as placement guides. Distribute the gathers with more fullness at the corners. Sew the ruffle to the pillow top just inside the stitch lines.

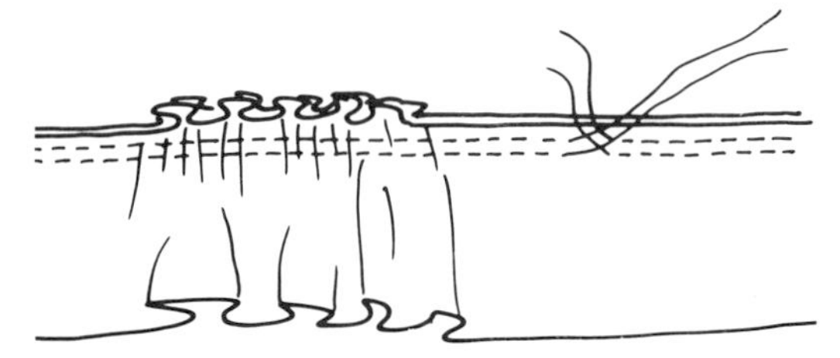

Diagram 1. Pull threads to gather ruffle.

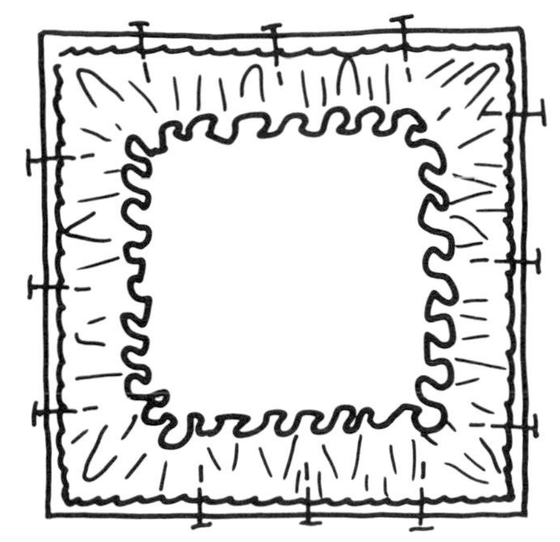

Diagram 2. Pin ruffle to pillow top.

Single Ruffle

A ruffle of a single thickness can be made in the same way as the Double Ruffle (page 26), except that the outer edge must be finished with a hem or some sort of trim, such as lace.

For a 2-inch-wide single ruffle, cut 3-inch-wide strips in the lengths described for the Double Ruffle. Sew the strips into one continuous loop. Press the seams open.

To make a hem, fold one of the sides over twice and stitch a ¼-inch hem along the entire edge. Add two lines of machine basting along the other edge for gathering, and proceed as for the Double Ruffle.

A row of lace edging can be added. Some laces are finished on both edges and can be attached to the ruffle with one row of stitching. Others will have one raw edge which will have to be sewn into the edge of the ruffle as it is hemmed (Diagram 3).

Diagram 3. Add lace edging to single ruffle.

Cord Edge

Cut and assemble approximately 1½ yards (for a 10- to 12-inch square pillow) of 1-inch bias binding according to instructions for binding the quilt, page 19. Replace the presser foot with a zipper foot. With the right side out, fold the bias strip over a 1½-yard length of cord and stitch close to the cord. Pin and stitch the cord to the outside edge of the right side of the pillow top, with the ends overlapping in the middle of one side. Before turning the corners, clip the seam allowance of the binding at corners up to, but not through, the stitch line (Diagram 4). To finish, follow instructions for assembling the pillow, page 26.

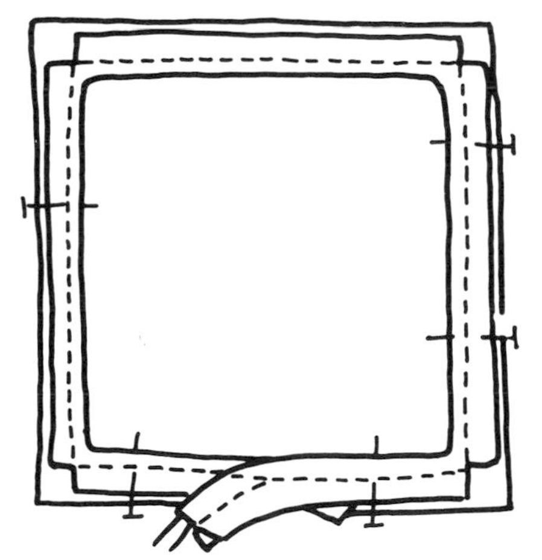

Diagram 4. Overlap ends of cord.

Diagram 5. Fold end of binding over ½ inch and sew to top.

Edge with Half-Inch Binding

One of the simplest and nicest ways to finish a pillow is to bind it as you would the edge of a quilt.

Prepare 1½ yards of 2-inch bias binding according to instructions for binding the quilt, page 19. With right sides facing and the starting end of the binding folded over ½ inch, sew the binding around the pillow top ½ inch from the edge (Diagram 5). Miter the corner and extend the binding ½ inch beyond the starting point and trim. For instructions on mitering corners, see page 23.

Leaving one side open, sew the pillow top to the pillow back, *wrong* sides facing inside. Insert the pillow form or batting and close the opening by hand or machine. Fold the binding over to the back of the pillow, tuck the edge under ½ inch, and slipstitch the binding to the pillow by hand.

To wash the pillow top, you will have to take out the stitching on one side and remove the pillow form. The pillow can be finished with a zipper.

CLOSURES

The following instructions are for three types of pillow closures: simple closure by hand, overlapped fabric back, and a lapped zipper.

Closure by Hand

With right sides facing, pin the pillow back to the pillow top. Keep the ruffle, if used, tucked inside toward the center. Starting about 1 inch before the corner on one side, sew the top to the back around three sides, ending about 1 inch past the corner on the fourth side. Stitching around both corners on the fourth side makes it easier to close the opening after the pillow is turned right side out and stuffed.

Clip the corners and turn the pillow right side out. Insert the pillow form or batting, turn the edges of the opening inside ½ inch, and whipstitch closed by hand. To wash, clip hand stitching and remove the pillow form.

Overlapped Fabric Back

This is another simple closure which consists of two pieces of fabric that overlap each other on the back of the pillow. The pillow is inserted into the opening between them.

You will need to cut two pieces instead of one for the pillow back. Cut both pieces the same width as the top, but 2 inches longer than half the length. An 11-inch top, for example, requires two 11 × 7½-inch pieces. For both pieces, fold one long side over twice and stitch a ¼-inch hem. Lay one piece over the other so that together they measure

11 × 11 inches with the hemmed edges overlapping in the center (Diagram 6). Machine baste the pieces together at the sides where edges overlap. With right sides facing, lay pillow back on pillow top and pin in place (keep ruffle, if used, tucked in toward the center of the pillow). Stitch around all four sides. Clip corners and turn. Insert the pillow form through the opening where the two back pieces overlap.

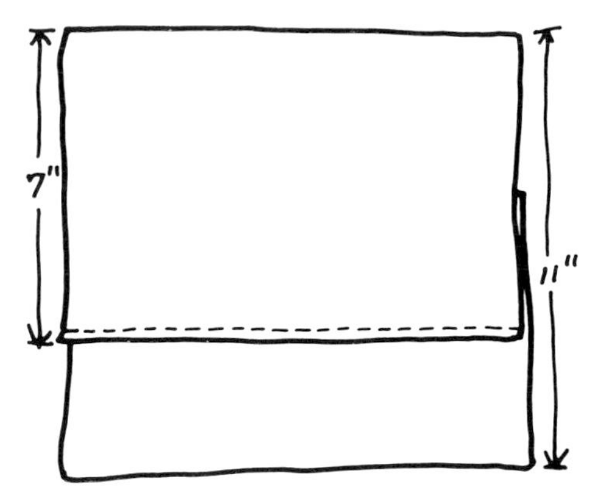

Diagram 6. Overlap two back pieces.

Lapped Zipper

Select a zipper that is 2 inches shorter than the size of the finished pillow. For example, if finished pillow measures 12 inches, buy a 10-inch zipper.

With the right sides of the pillow front and back facing, stitch them together on one side 1 inch from each end; backstitch for strength (Diagram 7). Press the seam open along the entire length of side.

Replace the presser foot with a zipper foot. With wrong side of back facing up, fold out the seam allowance of the pillow top. Place the unzipped zipper face down with the teeth on center seam line (zipper tab and stop should be at points where stitching ends). Stitch down the length of the zipper, ¼ inch from teeth, sewing through pillow front seam allowance (Diagram 8).

Close the zipper, turn it face up, and smooth the seam allowance away from zipper. Top-stitch down length of zipper through seam allowance about ⅛ inch from seam near zipper teeth (Diagram 9).

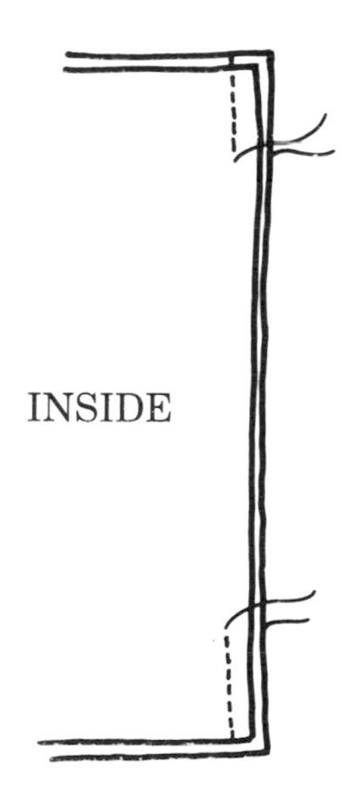

Diagram 7. Stitch one inch in from seam line on each end of one side.

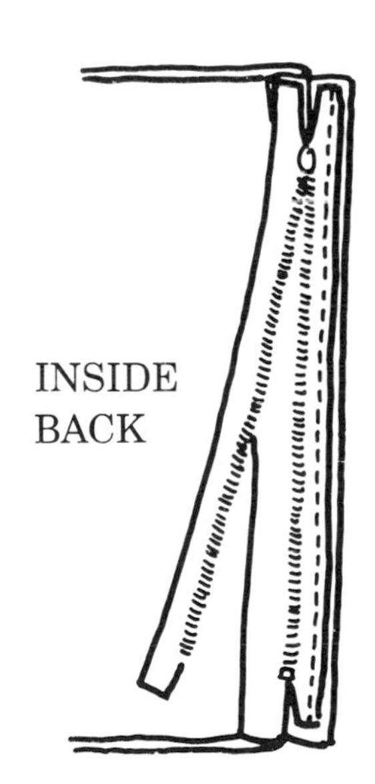

Diagram 8. Stitch one side of zipper to pillow front seam allowance.

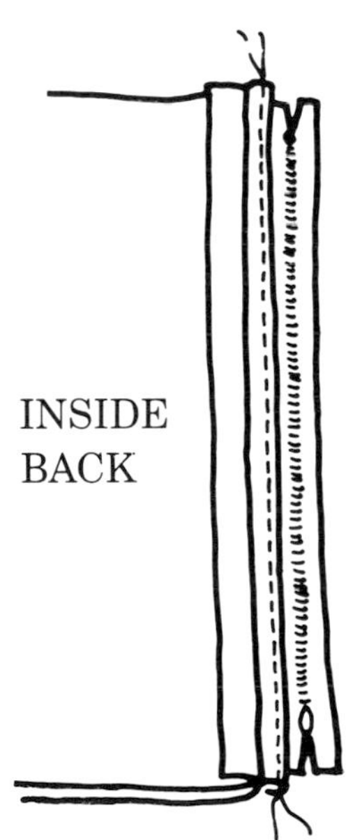

Diagram 9. Flip zipper and top-stitch seam allowance to zipper tape.

Spread open the front and back of the pillow, and turn zipper face down on the seam. Starting at the top of the zipper, stitch across the seam from pillow front to pillow back, turn corner and stitch zipper tape to pillow back down the length of the zipper. Turn corner at the other end and stitch across from back to front (Diagram 10).

With right sides facing, pin pillow front and back together around three remaining sides (Diagram 11). Be sure to open the zipper a few inches after pinning sides so that the pillow isn't sewn shut with the zipper closed. Sew the front to the back around three sides, starting and stopping just above the tab, and stop at head and foot of zipper. Clip corners, trim seams, and turn the pillow right side out. Insert pillow form and zip closed.

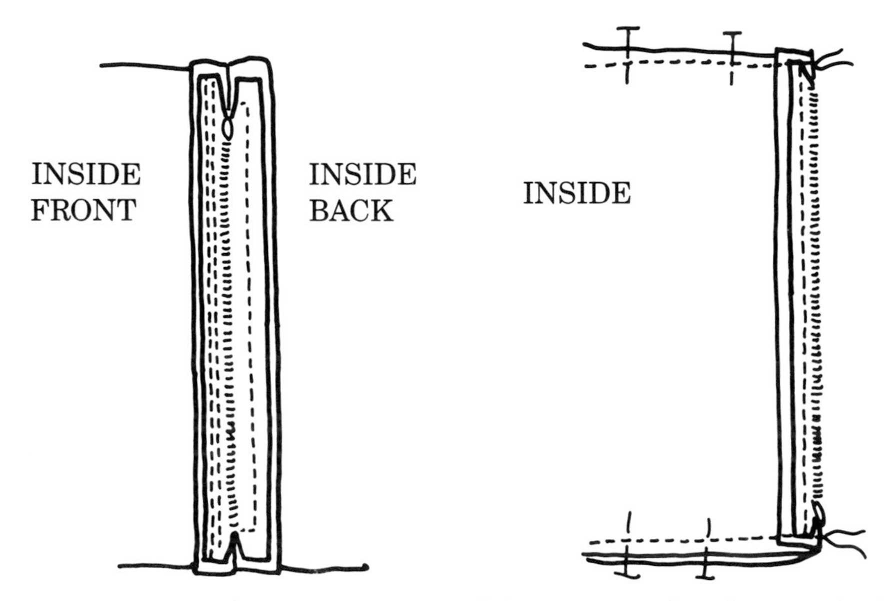

Diagram 10. Stitch other side of zipper in place.

Diagram 11. Stitch around other three sides of pillow.

LOG CABIN FEVER

DOUBLE ZIGZAG LOG CABIN

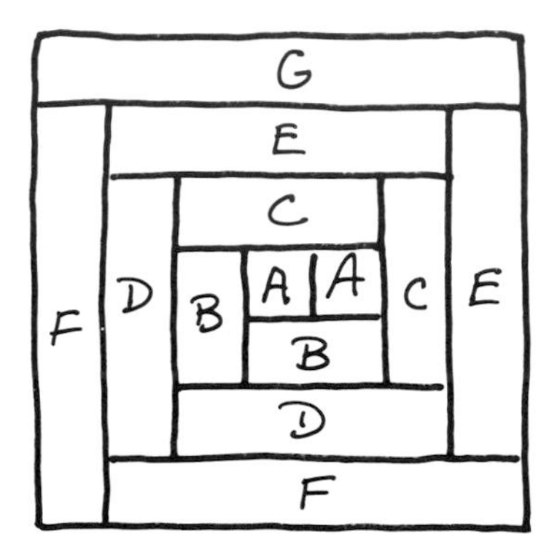

Piecing Diagram

Block **A**

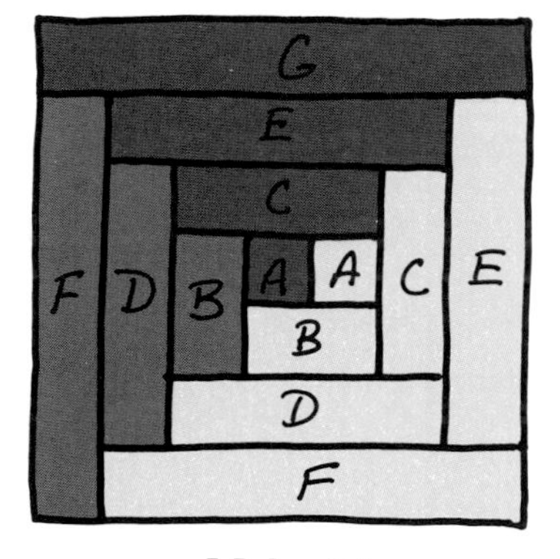

Make 24

Block **B**

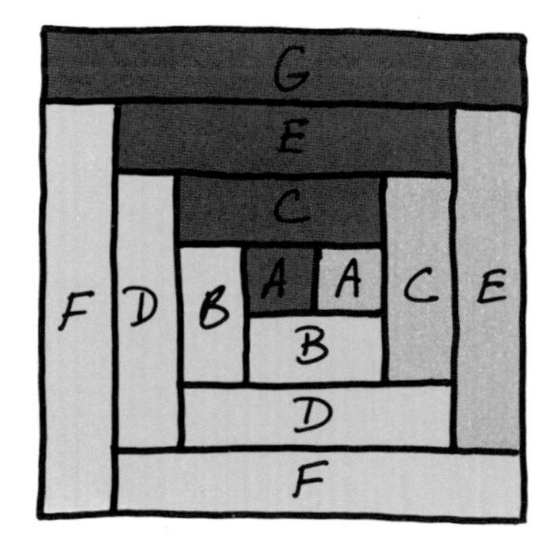

Make 24

Every quiltmaker makes at least one Log Cabin, a symbol of our nation's past. There are good reasons for its popularity. Log Cabin designs are among the most graphic and visually exciting, yet the basic block is simple and easy to make: you start with a square and add a strip, one at a time, to each side, spiraling out from the center until you reach the size you want.

Because each block is divided diagonally into light and dark colors, the log cabin is one of the most versatile of all quilt designs. Try it. Before deciding on which setting to use, make all the blocks you'll need. Then lay them out on the floor. By changing the position of the blocks—that is, the direction of light and dark—you can create an endless number of designs to choose from. Some of the possibilities are shown on page 44.

There are many types of Log Cabin blocks and just as many ways to make them. In this section there are instructions for three designs: a Double Zigzag, which is easy to make and very striking; a Log Cabin with Cornerstones, more detailed, but still easy to make; and a Reversible Log Cabin, a fascinating and challenging construction that produces different patterns on the front and back.

In making all of these designs, remember that it is a great timesaver to cut your fabric into strips and use the patterns provided to cut the strips into the appropriate lengths. Don't worry about leftover strips. These can be used in smaller projects, such as the pillows shown on page 48.

DOUBLE ZIGZAG LOG CABIN

The simple construction of this Log Cabin makes it quick and easy to assemble. I made mine out of silks, which require more careful handling than cottons because they're slippery and tend to get away from you. If you're a beginner, consider making one in cotton first. Solid cottons and sateens would be just as lovely, and the finished piece would have an Amish look.

Even though this pattern uses a common structure for a Log Cabin block, I used colors in a rather unusual way to create a double zigzag pattern that looks almost three dimensional: This effect requires the same block colored two ways, as ***Block A*** and ***Block B***. I used a basic plan of black with two shades of blue (light and dark) and two shades of red (light and dark). Feel free to use any colors you like; there's no telling how many other designs are possible if you change the placement of light and dark colors.

The finished size of each block is 3½ × 3½ inches and there are forty-eight blocks, twenty-four of ***Block A*** and twenty-four of ***Block B***. ***Block A*** requires ¼ yard of maroon fabric; ***Block B***, ¼ yard of magenta; ***Blocks A*** and ***B***, ½ yard each of light and dark blue; and ***Blocks A*** and ***B*** ⅔ yard each of black. The finished size of the quilt is 35 × 42 inches.

MATERIALS

Fabric

Block A

Pattern piece	Number of pieces
A	1 black, 1 light blue
B	1 light blue, 1 maroon
C	1 black, 1 light blue
D	1 light blue, 1 maroon
E	1 black, 1 light blue
F	1 light blue, 1 maroon
G	1 black

Block B

Pattern piece	Number of pieces
A	1 black, 1 magenta
B	2 dark blue
C	1 black, 1 magenta
D	2 dark blue
E	1 black, 1 magenta
F	2 dark blue
G	1 black

Two 7½ × 35½-inch black borders

Two 7½ × 42½-inch black borders

4½ yards 3-inch black bias binding

One 36½ × 42½-inch piece of black cotton sateen for the back

Forty-eight 4½-inch medium-weight muslin squares to back each block

Approximately 1½ yards of fabric will accommodate the borders and binding. Borders can be cut across the width of 44-inch-wide fabric. The leftover fabric can be used for the binding.

Other Materials

One 36 × 43-inch piece of polyester batting

SEWING INSTRUCTIONS

Cutting

To shorten cutting time, cut your fabrics into 1-inch strips using a rotary cutter, a thick clear plastic (or steel) ruler, and a cutting mat. Then cut the strips into the proper lengths using the patterns pro-

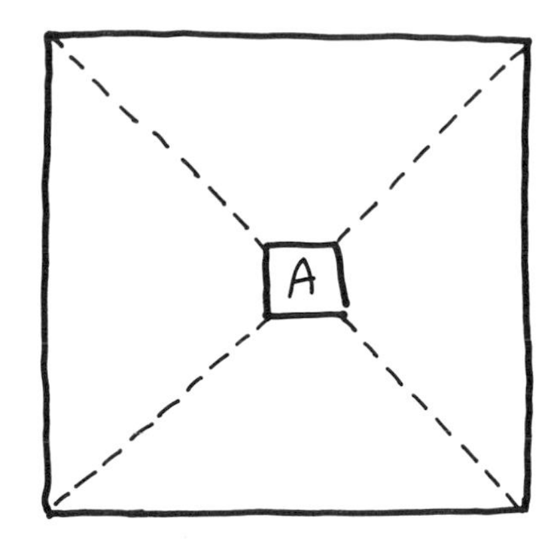

Diagram 1. Sew first **A** in center of muslin square.

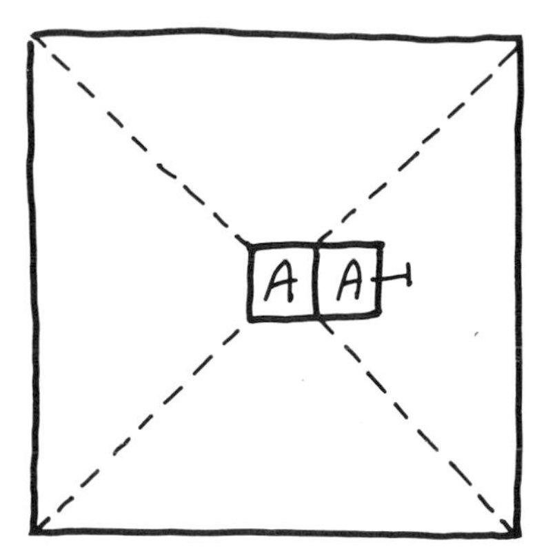

Diagram 2. Sew second **A** to first **A**.

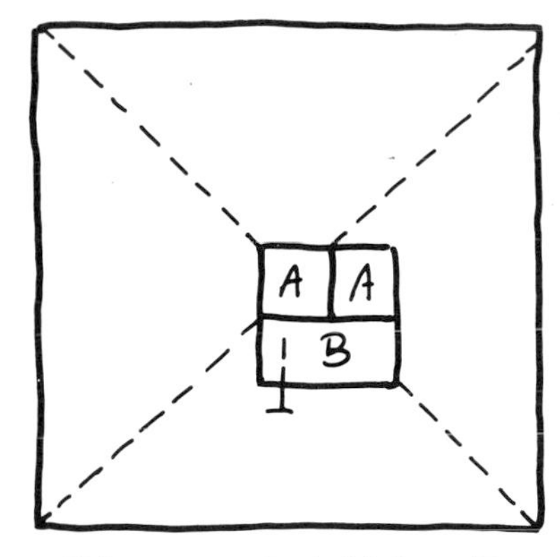

Diagram 3. Add first **B**.

vided. I like to mount the pattern pieces on cardboard before cutting them out. It makes them firm and easy to use, and I don't have to pin them in place before I cut the strips.

Piecing

Note: The following instructions apply to both Blocks **A** and **B**. Refer to the diagrams for placement of light and dark. I like to make eight blocks of one type at a time. If you'd like to also, just repeat each step eight times as you go. If you decide to use silks, do *not* use an iron; finger press only.

1. Fold a muslin square in half diagonally and crease the fold with your thumb. Fold it in half diagonally in the other direction and crease it in the same way to make an "X" across the square.

2. Place one **A** (black) in the center of the X and stitch all the way around, ⅛ inch from the outside edge (Diagram 1).

3. With right sides together, place the second **A** (color) on top of the first **A** and sew them together along the right side. Finger press the second **A** to the right, away from the center of the square (Diagram 2). Pin the outer side in place before adding the first **B**. Pinning in this way helps square up the edges of the pieces with each other and prepares the work for the addition of the next piece.

4. With right sides together, sew the first **B** along the bottom side of the two **A** pieces. Finger press open, away from the center, and pin (Diagram 3).

5. With right sides facing, sew the second **B** along the next side where **A** and **B** are joined. Finger press open, away from the center, and pin.

6. Add the first **C** to the next side in exactly the same way (Diagram 5). Continue adding the remaining **C, D, E, F,** and **G** pieces in the same way, spiraling out in a clockwise direction from the center to the outside edge. Keep checking the diagrams of the **A** and **B** blocks respectively for the correct position of light and dark colors.

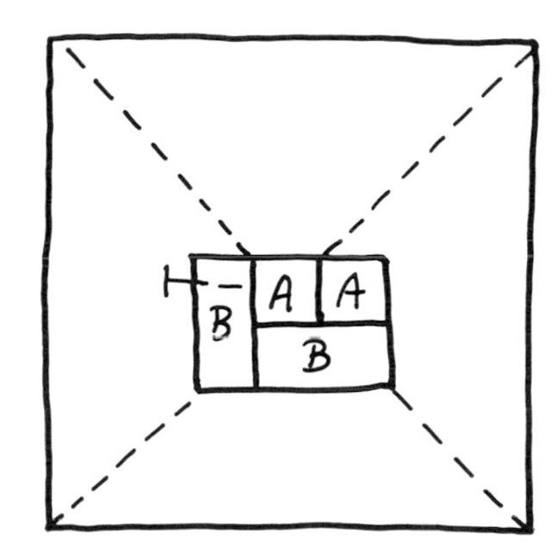

Diagram 4. Add second **B**.

Make 12

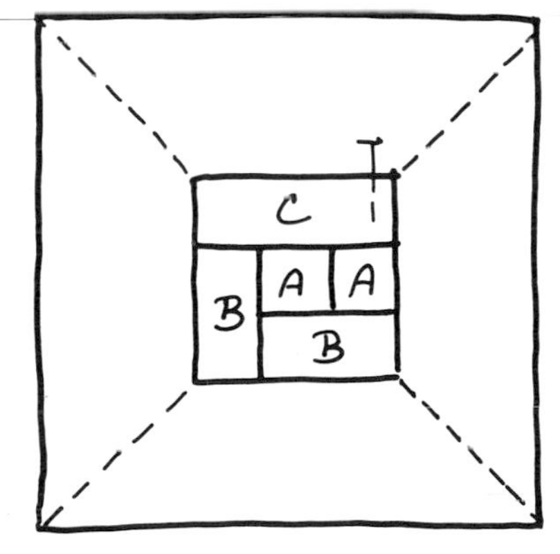

Diagram 5. Add first **C**.

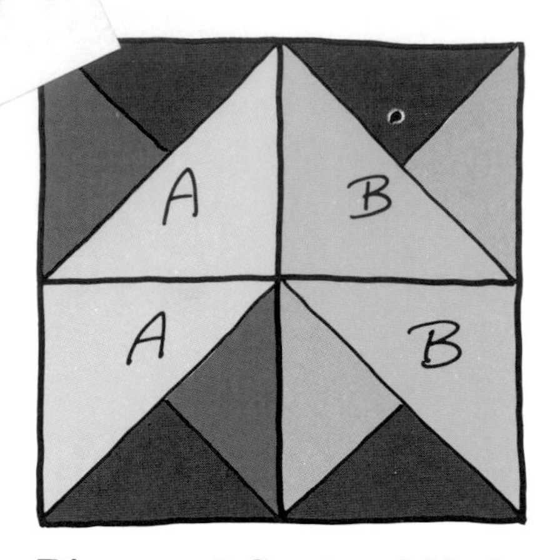

Diagram 6. Sew two **A** blocks together and two **B** blocks together to make one unit.

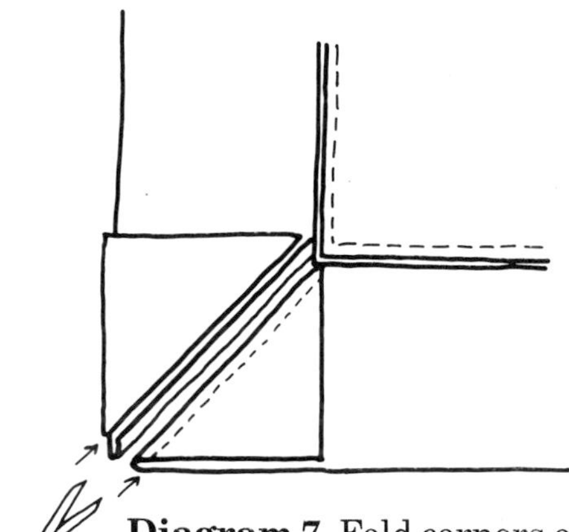

Diagram 7. Fold corners of borders and trim.

Assembly

7. The muslin squares are slightly bigger than the size of the finished block and should be trimmed to size when the blocks are finished.

8. Sew two **A** blocks together according to Diagram 6. Sew two **B** blocks together. Finger press the seams open, or lightly steam without pressure. Sew the **A** and **B** blocks together according to Diagram 6. Finger press seams open. Repeat for a total of twelve four-block units.

9. Sew three units together in a row. Finger press seams open. Repeat for four rows. Sew the four rows together to complete the quilt top.

10. Sew one 7½ × 35½-inch border to the top and bottom of the quilt top, stopping ¼ inch from each corner. Sew one 7½ × 42½-inch border to each side of the quilt top, stopping ¼ inch from each corner.

11. To miter the corners, fold over both ends of the borders to create a diagonal line from the inner edge at the corner of the quilt top to the outer edge of the borders. Leaving enough fabric for a ¼-inch seam allowance, make a diagonal cut of 45 degrees, following the fold line (Diagram 7). Sew the diagonal ends together at each corner. Finger press seams open.

12. With the wrong side up, lay out the 36½ × 42½-inch piece of fabric for the back. Place the batting on top, and the Log Cabin top on top of the batting, making sure there are no wrinkles in any of the three layers. Pin the layers together throughout and baste them together by hand. Machine baste around the outside edge. Add the 3-inch bias binding for a 1-inch border. (For detailed instructions on quilt assembly, see page 14).

13. Hand tack the three layers together at the corners of the blocks. You may also wish to hand stitch, in the ditch, in the seamlines between the blocks, and the seams between the blocks and borders.

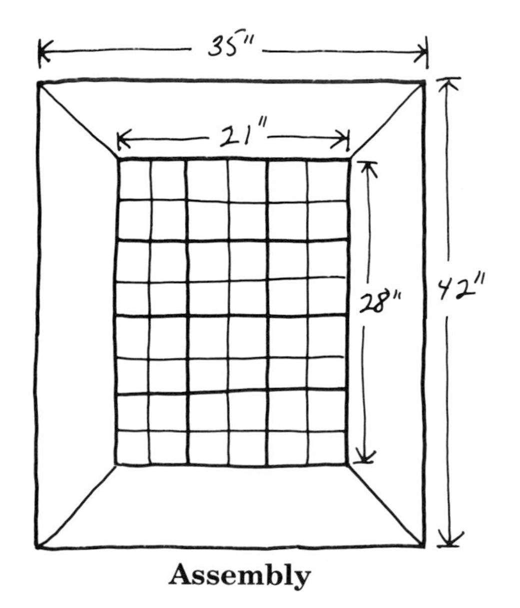

Assembly

DOUBLE ZIGZAG LOG CABIN

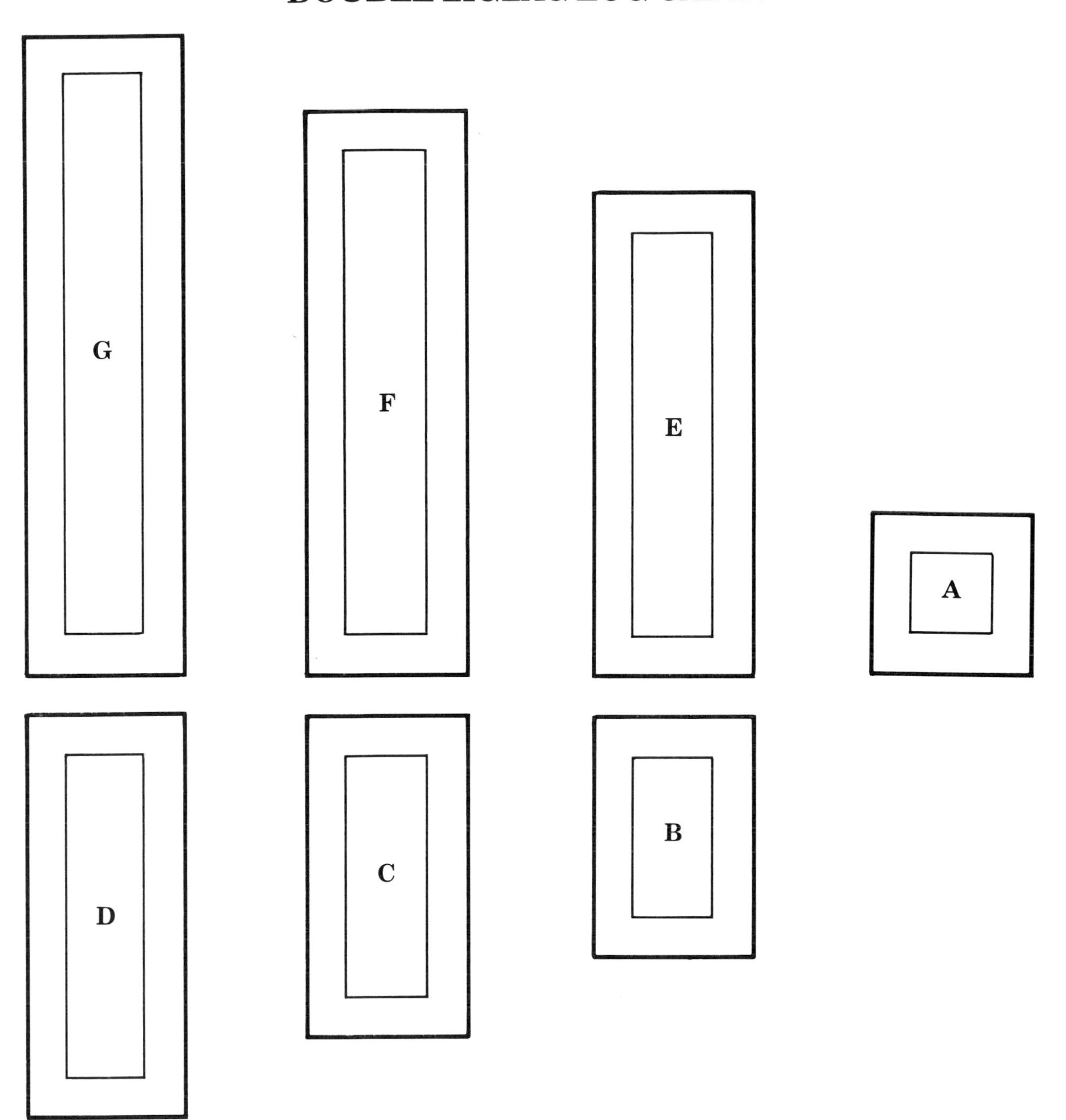

LOG CABIN WITH CORNERSTONES

Certain textile companies have very distinctive fabric collections, and one I've been a fan of for some time is Laura Ashley. I haven't used their fabrics much in my quilts, because they're too good in the way fine sheets with 200 stitches to the inch are too good. The weight and the thread count make them harder to hand quilt than lighter, softer fabrics with looser weaves. It's hard to push a needle through all the layers, especially when two of them are heavier and more closely woven than what you're accustomed to. I suspect that most quilters feel this way and, on the whole, tend to shy away from these and other home decorating fabrics, even though the Laura Ashley stores carry pre-cut pieces for quilting.

In spite of these considerations, my attraction to Laura Ashley fabrics remains as strong as ever, and I've begun to design quilts I can make with home decorating fabrics that require no hand quilting. The first of these is the Log Cabin with Cornerstones.

It can be a pleasure when designing a room to have the option of working with an extensive and versatile line of coordinating fabrics and products. One of the advantages of this approach is that a quilt can become the focus of a larger decorating scheme. The room you see on page 41—including curtains, wallpaper, sheets, lamp shades, and a quilt as centerpiece—is an example of one such environment.

If you decide to plan a room around your quilt, instructions for making curtains and other accessories are available in books such as *Vogue Sewing for the Home*, Harper & Row, 1986.

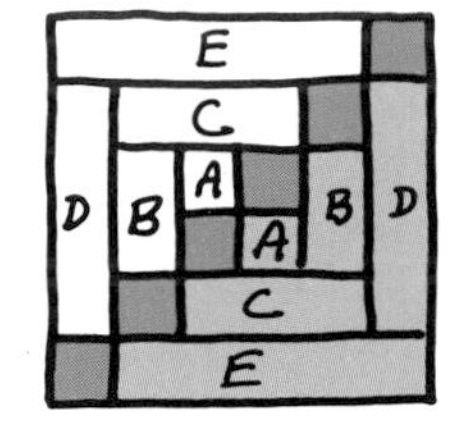

40 blocks: Color A

The exciting thing about the Log Cabin is the number of overall designs you can make by changing the position of the blocks. To illustrate: The blocks were set out and photographed in several ways (page 44) before I settled on one shown on page 42. Many other arrangements are possible.

This Log Cabin is made with cornerstones, little squares sewn to the ends of the strips before they're sewn to the blocks, a simple procedure which adds interest without adding a lot of time and effort. Although all the blocks are the same in construction, the cornerstones are done in two colors listed as Color A and Color B.

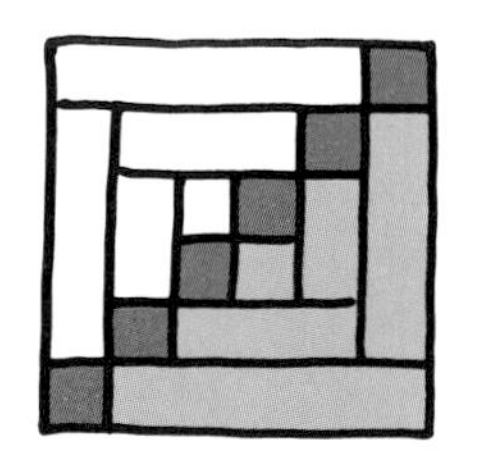
40 blocks: Color B

The following instructions are for a 78 × 96-inch quilt that requires eighty 9½ × 9½-inch blocks (9 × 9-inch finished) and a 3½-inch border. The overall size of the quilt can be changed by adding or subtracting the number of blocks, or more strips can be added to each block.

Note: I like to cut and sew up to ten blocks at a time—just enough to make things go quickly, but not too many to tire me out. For those of you who would like to do the same, I've included a cutting chart and instructions for ten blocks.

MATERIALS

Fabric (for 80 blocks)

Pattern piece	Number of pieces	Yardage
A	480 for cornerstones (240: color A, 240: color B)	⅔ yard of each color
	160 (80 light, 80 dark)	¼ yard of each color
B	160 (80 light, 80 dark)	½ yard of each color
C	160 (80 light, 80 dark)	⅔ yard of each color
D	160 (80 light, 80 dark)	¾ yard of each color
E	160 (80 light, 80 dark)	1 yard of each color

Fabric (for 10 blocks)

Pattern piece	Number of pieces
A	60 for cornerstones (color A or B)
	20 (10 light, 10 dark)
B	20 (10 light, 10 dark)
C	20 (10 light, 10 dark)
D	20 (10 light, 10 dark)
E	20 (10 light, 10 dark)

6 yards of 44-inch (or wider) fabric for the back

Eighty 10½-inch cotton squares (can be cut or torn from an old white sheet)

Other Materials

Queen size (90 × 108) batt, cotton or polyester

8½ × 8½-inch cardboard square (pattern for batting)

9½ × 9½-inch cardboard square with 3½ × 3½-inch square cut from center (pattern for marking blocks)

Note: Because the iron will touch the batting during pressing, I recommend using a cotton batt. If using a polyester batt, finger pressing may be advisable to prevent the iron from sticking to the batt.

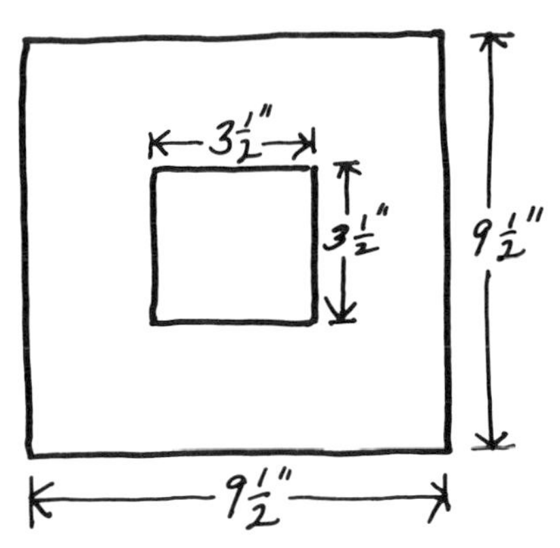

Pattern for Marking Blocks

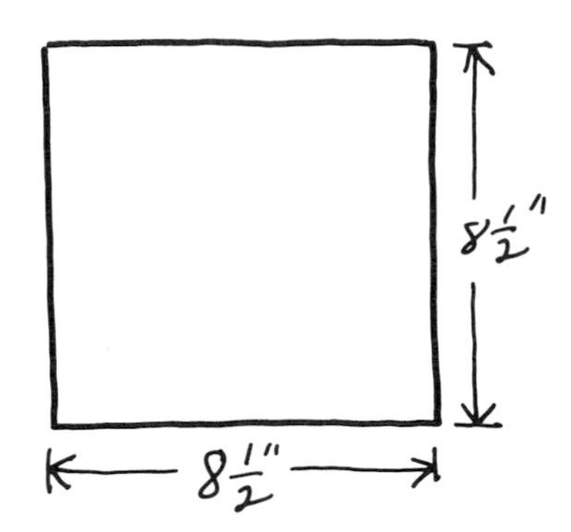

Pattern for Batting

SEWING INSTRUCTIONS

1. Press a 10-inch cotton square. Center the cardboard pattern for marking blocks (9½-inch square with a 3½ × 3½-inch cutout) on top of it. Trace around both the outside and inside edges. If you're using cotton batting, omit the inside square until later.

2. Place an 8½ × 8½-inch piece of batting inside the larger penciled square and pin at each of the four corners (Diagram 1). If you're using polyester batting, the smaller, penciled square will show through. This is a guide for positioning the center unit for the Log Cabin. The pencil line won't be visible through cotton batting, so if you're using cotton, mark the smaller inside square on the batting at this point. Repeat for ten blocks.

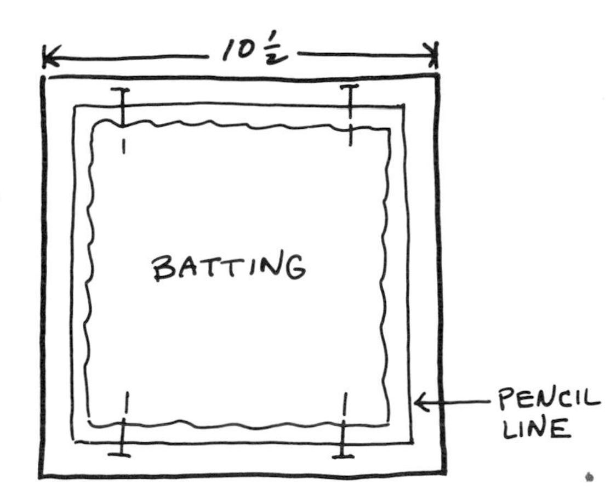

Diagram 1. Pin batting inside penciled square.

Diagram 2. Sew each **A** to a cornerstone (**A**).

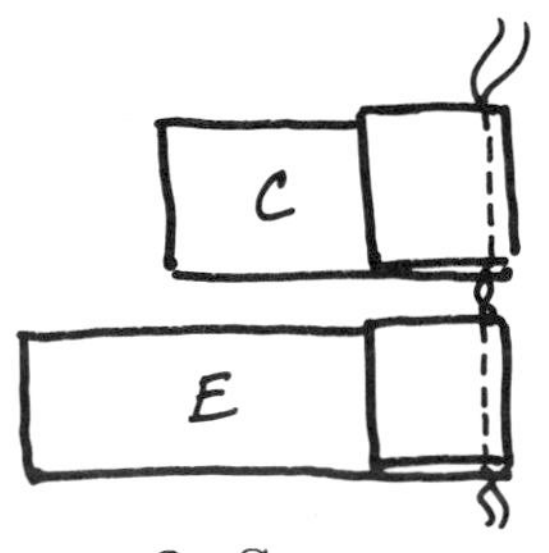

Diagram 3. Sew one cornerstone to each **C** and **E**.

3. Sew each light and dark **A** to a cornerstone (that is, an **A** piece in Color A or B) for a total of twenty units (Diagram 2). Clip threads between each unit and press seams open. Sew the remaining cornerstones to one end of each **C** and **E** (Diagram 3). Press seams open.

4. Matching seams at intersections, sew an **A-A** unit with a light square to another **A-A** section with a dark square, alternating their position so the light and dark squares end up at opposite corners (Diagram 4). Repeat for a total of the ten units. Press seams open.

5. Place one of the completed units in the center of one of the batting squares just inside the smaller square marked in pencil. With a large stitch, machine baste ⅛ inch around entire edge of the center unit (Diagram 5). Repeat for all ten blocks.

6. Sew a light **B** to the side of the center unit that has the light **B**. Sew a dark **B** to the opposite side (Diagram 6). Repeat for each block. Press or finger press each **B** toward outer edge of the block.

7. Matching seams at intersections, pin and sew a light **C** with cornerstone to the top of the center unit and a dark **C** with cornerstone to the bottom (Diagram 7). Repeat for each block. Press or finger press toward outer edge of the block.

8. Sew a light **D** to the side of the center unit that has the light **A** and **B**. Sew a dark **D** to the opposite side (Diagram 8). Repeat for each block. Remove pins holding the batting in place; by now they'll be getting in the way. Press or finger press each **D** toward outer edge of the block.

9. Matching seams at intersections, pin and sew a light **E** with cornerstone to the top of the center unit and a dark **E** with cornerstone to the bottom (Diagram 9). Repeat for each block. Press or finger press each **E** toward the outer edge of the block.

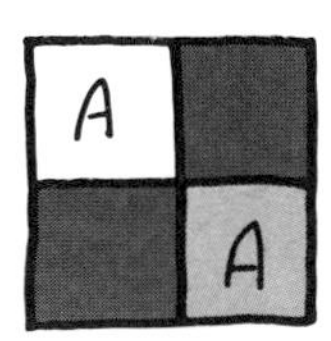

Diagram 4. Sew **A-A** units together to form square.

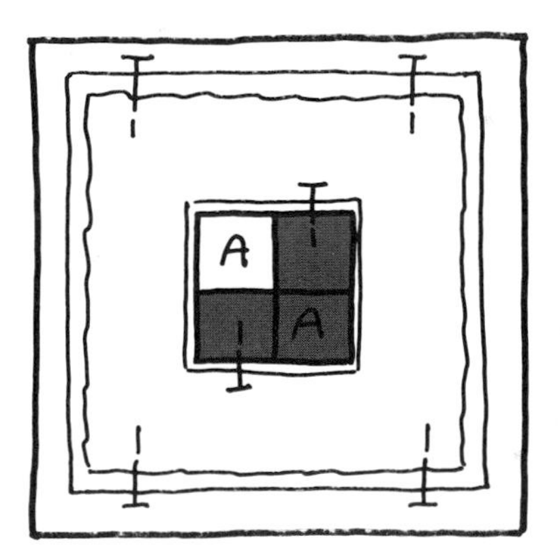

Diagram 5. Sew center unit to block inside penciled center square.

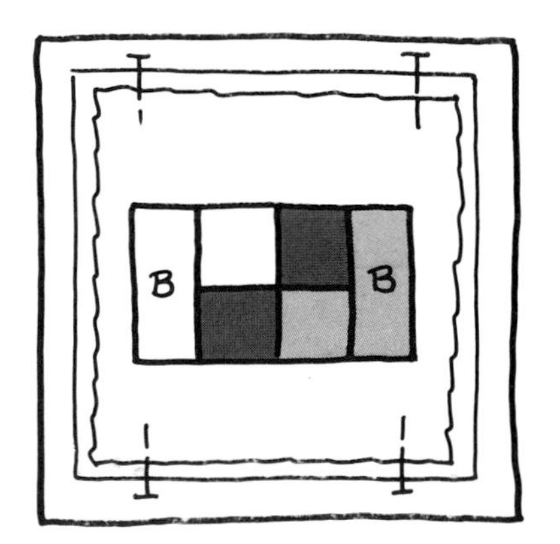

Diagram 6. Sew one **B** to each side of center unit.

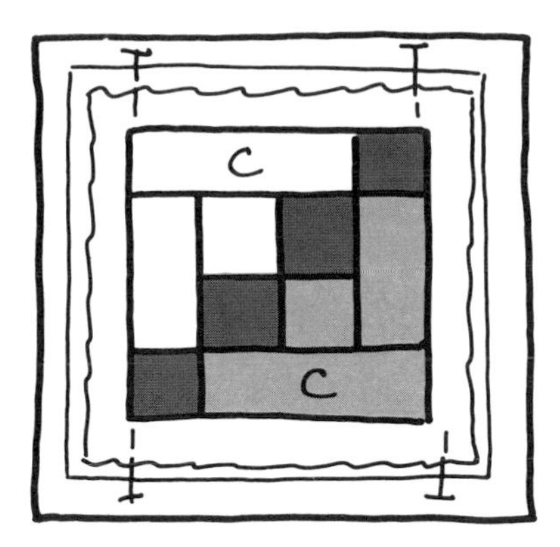

Diagram 7. Sew one **C** (with cornerstone) to top and bottom.

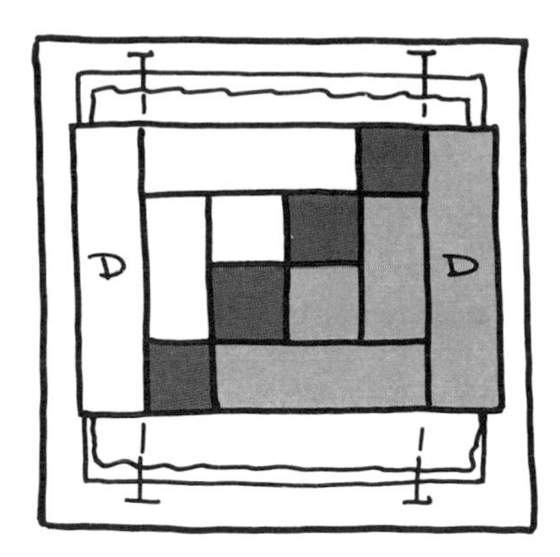

Diagram 8. Sew one **D** to each side.

10. By now you have ten blocks. Do ten more another day, and so on until you have what you need. Once you've decided on an overall pattern, arrange the blocks accordingly on the floor and begin to sew them together to make the quilt top.

Assembly

11. I like to assemble four blocks at a time into larger squares rather than sewing blocks together in rows. Long rows seem harder to handle than square or rectangular sections of four or eight blocks (Diagram 10). Press each seam open after sewing.

12. For the back of the quilt, cut the length of fabric in half to make two pieces. Remove selvages and sew the two pieces together along one long side. Press seams open.

Diagram 9. Sew one **E** (with cornerstone) to top and bottom.

Diagram 10. Assemble blocks in four-block units according to desired design.

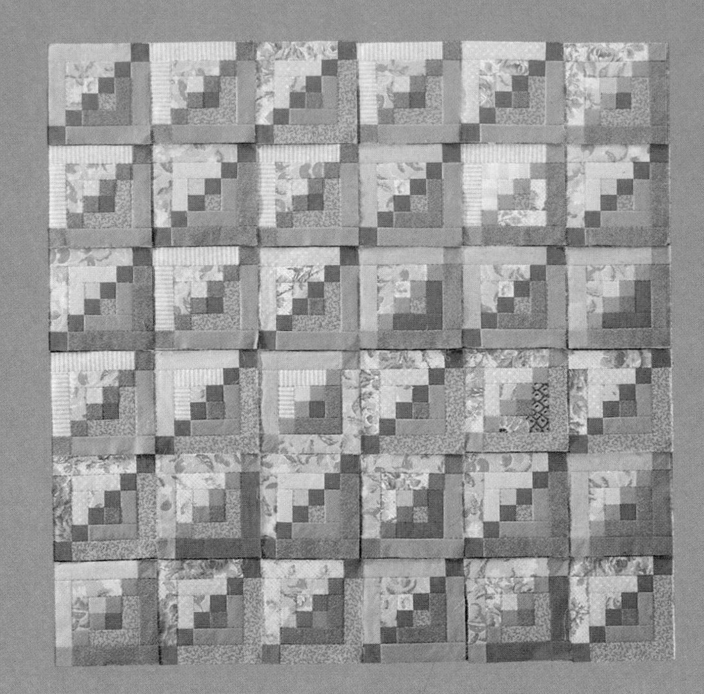
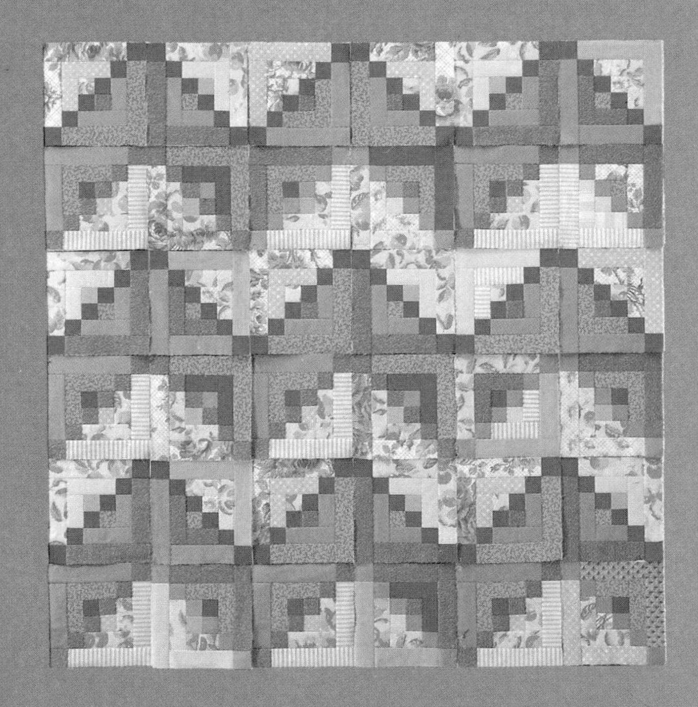
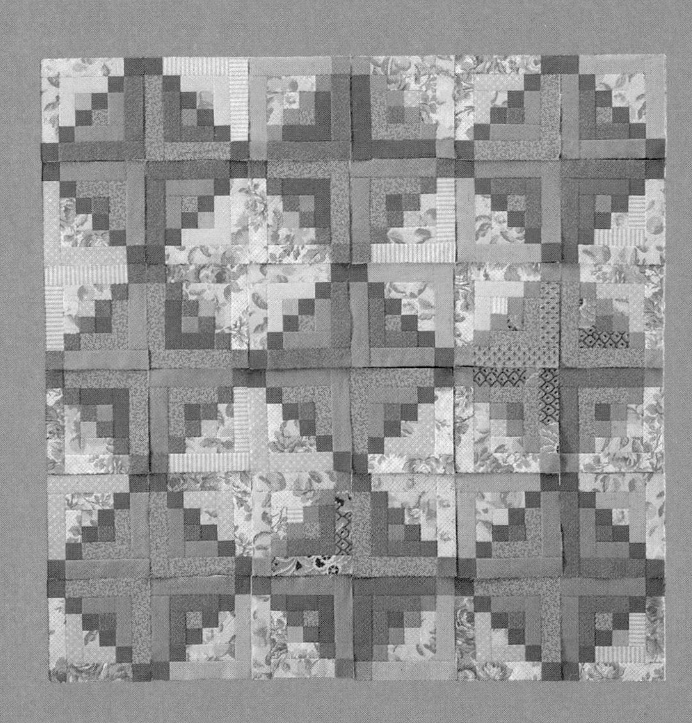

13. With right side down, spread the back out on the floor, making sure that it's free of wrinkles. With right side up, carefully center the quilt top on top of the back without wrinkling it (Diagram 11). Pin in place and baste the top to the back.

14. To make the borders, fold over one edge of the quilt back and pin it to the quilt top (see Diagram 12).

15. Fold over adjacent edge of the quilt back and pin it to the quilt top. Fold the end under to miter the corner (see Diagram 13). Repeat for all four sides.

Note: You may wish to trim away some of the excess fabric at each corner to eliminate bulk. Machine stitch or hand stitch the edges of the borders to the quilt top.

16. The quilt can be finished in one of two ways. Either tack the top to the back at each corner of every square, or make a grid pattern by machine stitching "in the ditch" along the seam lines.

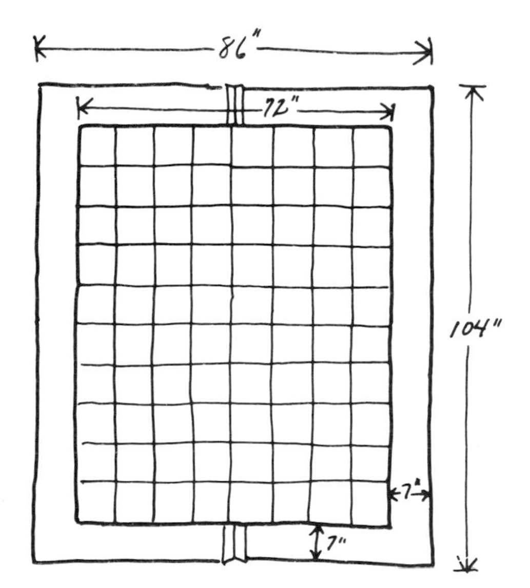

Diagram 11. Place quilt top on top of quilt back.

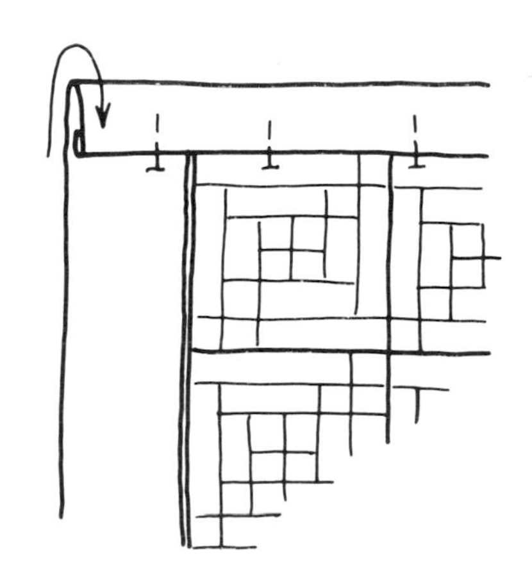

Diagram 12. Fold over one edge of quilt back and pin to quilt top.

Diagram 13. Fold over adjacent edge of quilt back and miter the corner.

LOG CABIN PILLOW

A

B

C

D

E

COMPANION PILLOWS FOR THE LOG CABIN WITH CORNERSTONES QUILT

There were a lot of strips left over after I finished all the blocks for the Log Cabin with Cornerstones, and I thought about using them in room accessories. Not that I feel obligated to use up all the leftover scraps, I enjoy coming up with new uses for leftovers. I always over-cut in case I change my mind about the colors while I'm working—and I almost always do.

The following designs incorporate the leftover 2-inch strips (1½-inch finished size). Two of them are made only with strips; the other two include a few other pattern pieces. Colors have not been indicated in the instructions because you may wish to use your own. The finished pillows have ruffles or piped edges, and you will find instructions for these finishes on pages 26 to 28.

Size: The finished pillows measure 12 × 12 inches, except for Zigzag, which is ½ inch larger. They require a 12½ × 12½-inch square of fabric for the back, a 12-inch pillow form, and a 12-inch zipper. The Zigzag pillow will require a 13 × 13-inch back. You may wish to use a larger pillow form (14 × 14 inches) for a snug fit.

Crossroads Pillow

MATERIALS

Fabric

Pattern piece	Number of pieces
A	1
B	4
C	4
D	8
E	4
F	4

Note: The 2-inch strips can be used with pattern pieces **B, C,** and **D**.

SEWING INSTRUCTIONS

1. Sew all the pieces together in five horizontal rows according to the order indicated in Diagram 1. Press all seams open.

2. Matching seams at intersections, sew these rows together into the finished square.

CROSSROADS PILLOW

F	D	E	D	F
D	B	C	B	D
E	C	A	C	E
D	B	C	B	D
F	D	E	D	F

Piecing Diagram

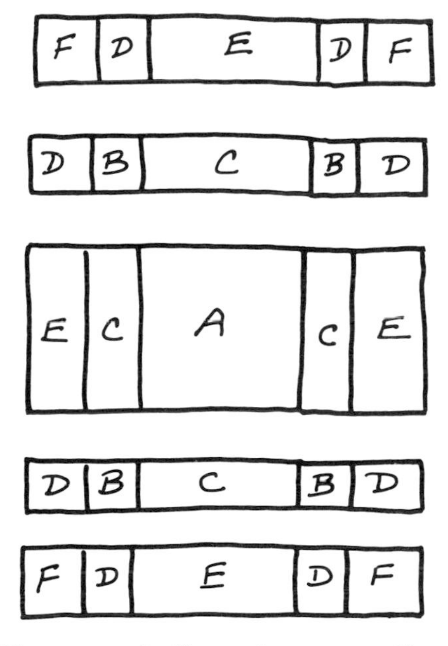

Diagram 1. Sew pieces together in rows.

CROSSROADS PILLOW

A

D

B

C

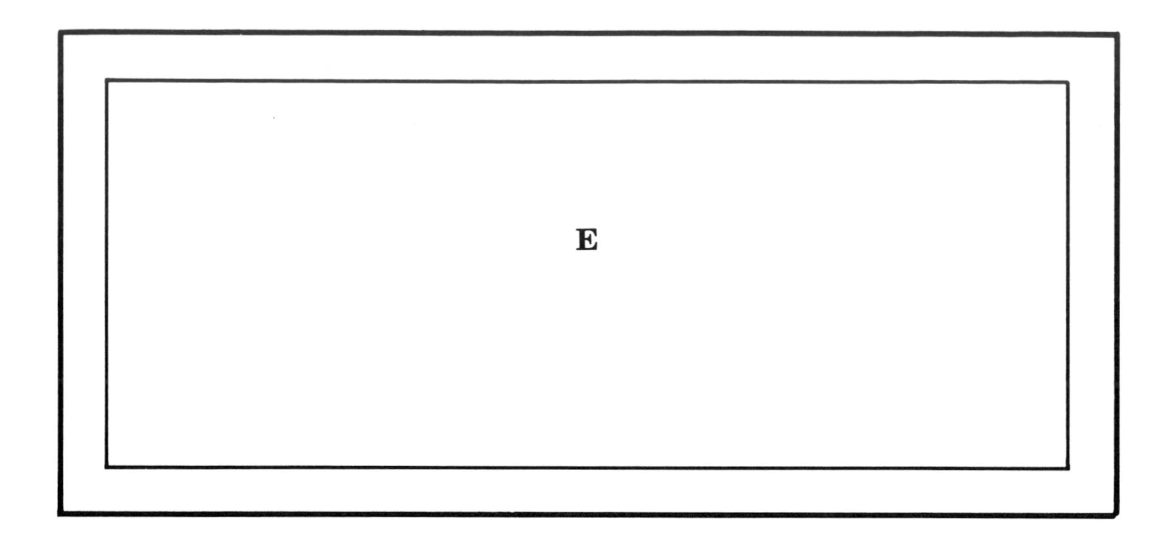
E

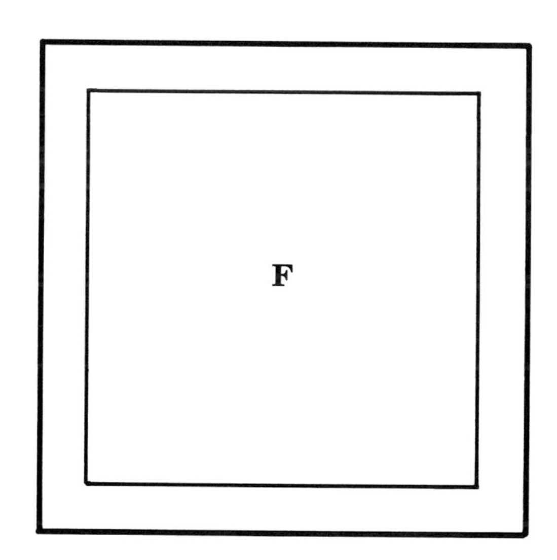
F

Staircase Pillow

MATERIALS

Fabric

Four 2 x 8 inch strips each of four different colors, ranging from dark to light.

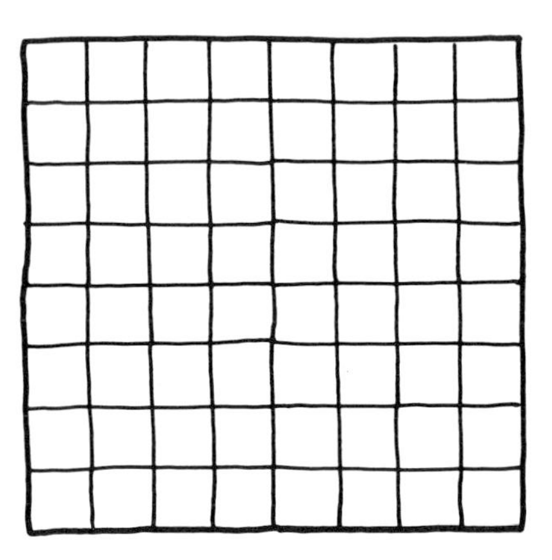

Piecing Diagram

SEWING INSTRUCTIONS

1. Sew the strips together to make four units with four strips in each unit. In the first unit (A), start with the darkest color on the top and the lightest on the bottom. Change the position of the colors in the following units (B, C, D), moving them down one row in each unit. By the time you get to unit D, the darkest color will be the bottom row and the lightest will be just above it (Diagram 1). Press seams open.

2. Using a rotary cutter, cut across the strips in each unit, dividing each unit into four 2-inch strips.

3. Arrange the strips into eight rows with two strips in each row (Diagram 2). Both rows 1 and 5 will be made of two strips from unit A; rows 2 and 6 will be made of two strips from unit B; rows 3 and 7 will be made of two strips from unit C; and rows 4 and 8 will be made of two strips from unit D. Sew together the two strips in each row end to end. Press seams open.

4. Matching seams at intersections, sew all the rows together to make a square. Press seams open. The top and bottom of these rows are now even, and the colors are staggered.

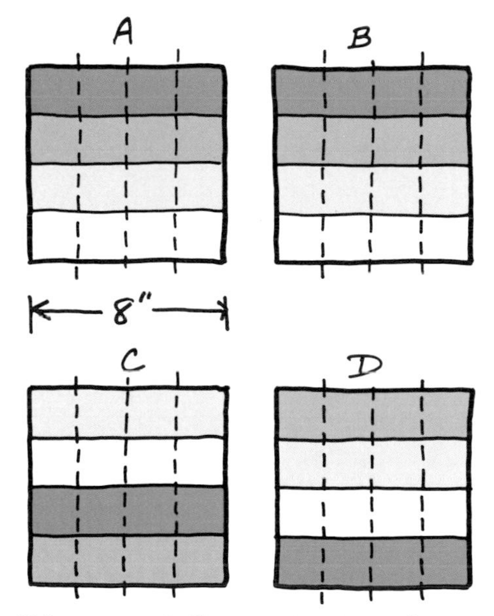

Diagram 1. Sew strips together into four units, changing the position of the colors in each unit.

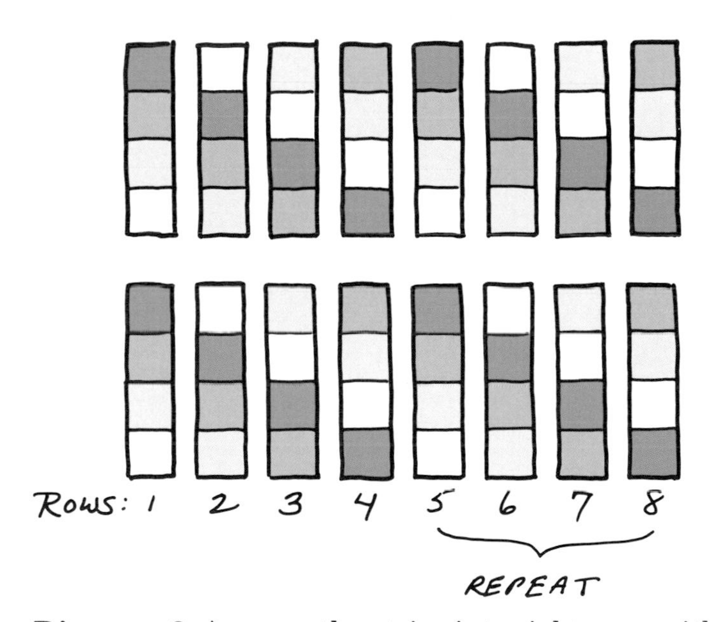

Diagram 2. Arrange the strips into eight rows with two strips in each row.

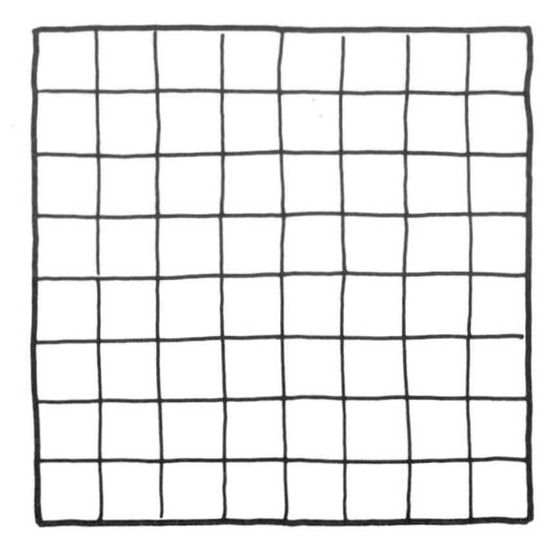

Piecing Diagram

Checkerboard Pillow

The Checkerboard is the same as the Staircase, except that two colors are used instead of four (see the red-and-white pillow on page 110), and only two strips of each color are required instead of four.

MATERIALS

Fabric

Two 2 x 36-inch strips of two contrasting colors

SEWING INSTRUCTIONS

1. Sew the four strips together, alternating colors, into one 36-inch band (Diagram 1). Press seams open.

Cut the band in half and sew the two halves together so the colors alternate (Diagram 2). Press seams open.

2. Cut across this band into eight 2-inch-wide strips. (The remaining 2 inches is wastage to allow for possible error.) To alternate colors, turn every second strip around so the dark square is at the bottom, while on strips 1, 3, 5, and 7, it remains at the top (Diagram 3). Matching seams at intersections, sew the eight rows together to make a square. Press seams open.

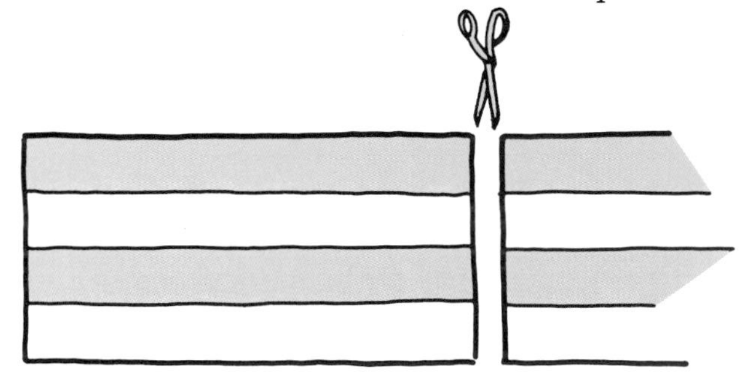

Diagram 1. Sew four strips together into one band. Cut band in half.

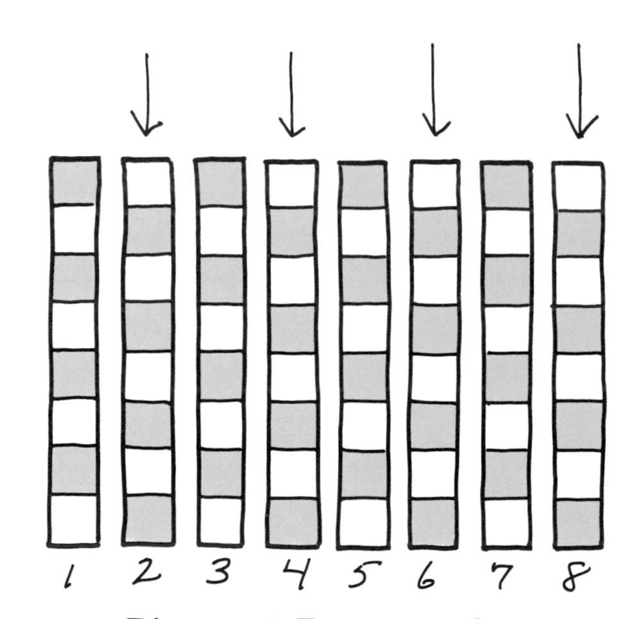

Diagram 3. Turn every other strip to alternate colors.

Diagram 2. Sew the two halves together.

Puss-in-the-Corner Pillow

Except for piece **A**, all the pieces in this design can be cut from 2-inch strips.

MATERIALS

Fabric

Pattern piece	Number of pieces
A	1
B	12
C	4
D	4
E	4

Piecing Diagram

SEWING INSTRUCTIONS

1. Sew one **C** to right and one to left side of **A**. Sew one **B** to right and left ends of the remaining two **C** pieces (Diagram 1). Press seams open.

2. Matching seams at intersections, sew one **B-C-B** strip to the top and one to the bottom of the **C-A-C** unit. Press seams open.

3. Sew one **D** to right and left sides of the center unit just completed. Sew one **B** to the right and one to the left end of the remaining **D** pieces (Diagram 2). Press seams open.

4. Matching seams at intersections, sew one **B-D-B** strip to the top and bottom of the center unit. Press seams open.

5. Sew one **E** to left and right sides of the center unit just completed. Sew one **B** to opposite ends of the remaining **E** pieces (Diagram 3). Press seams open and, matching seams at intersections, sew the **B-E-B** strips to the top and bottom of the center unit. Press seams open.

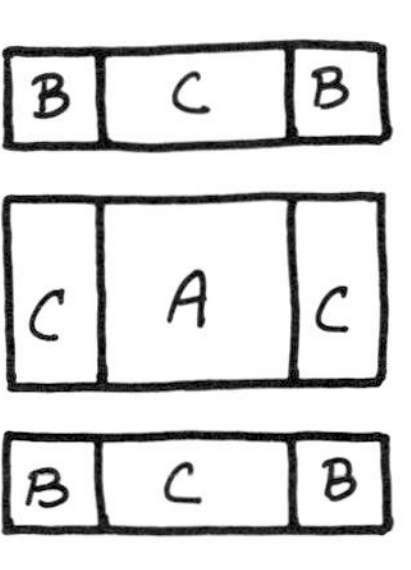

Diagram 1. Sew one **C** to right and one to left side of **A**.

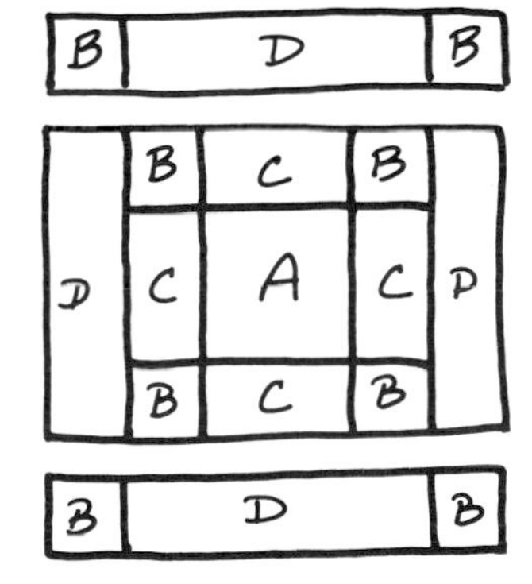

Diagram 2. Sew one **D** to right and one to left side of center unit.

Diagram 3. Sew one **E** to left and one to right side of center unit.

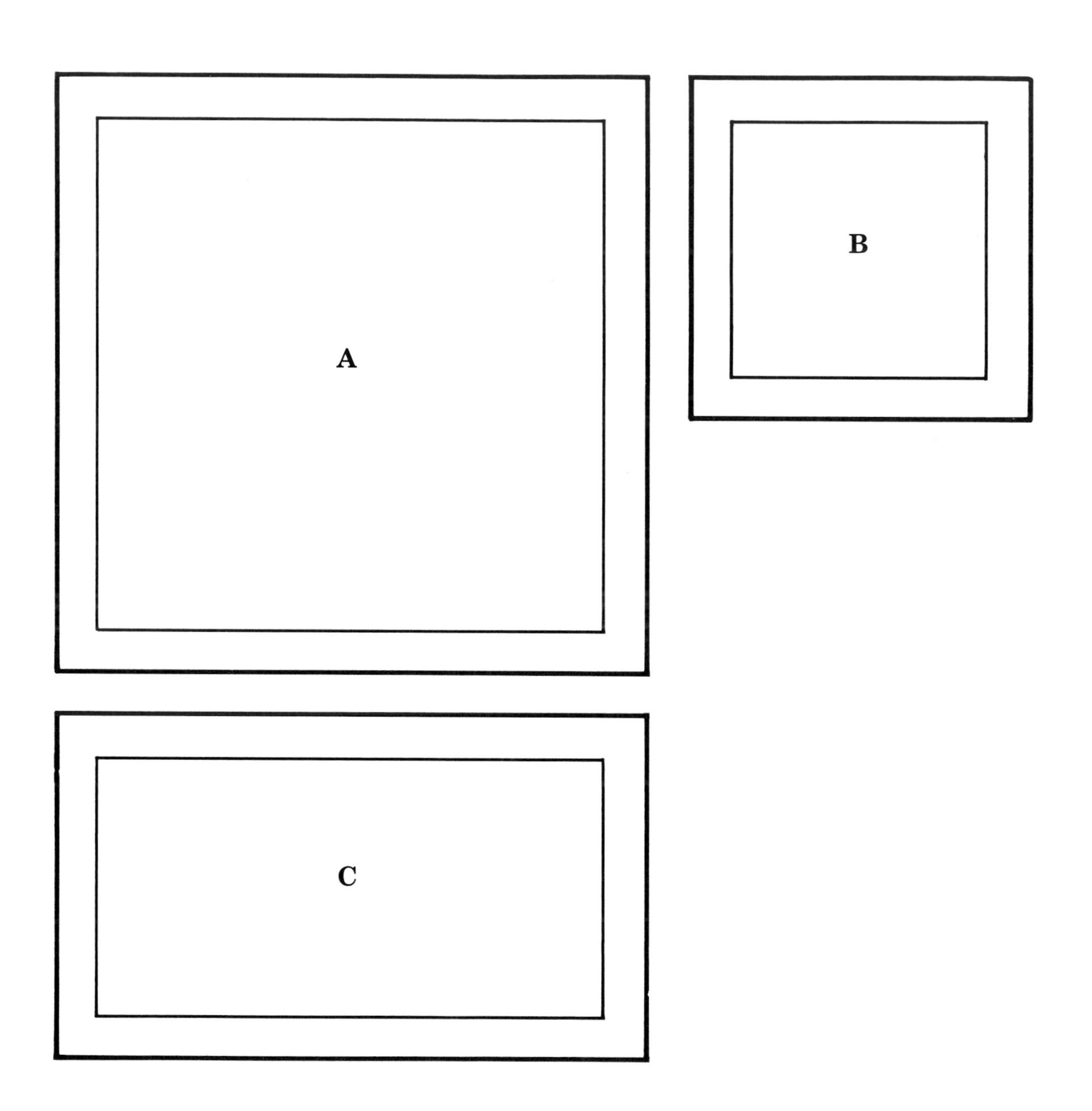
A
B
C

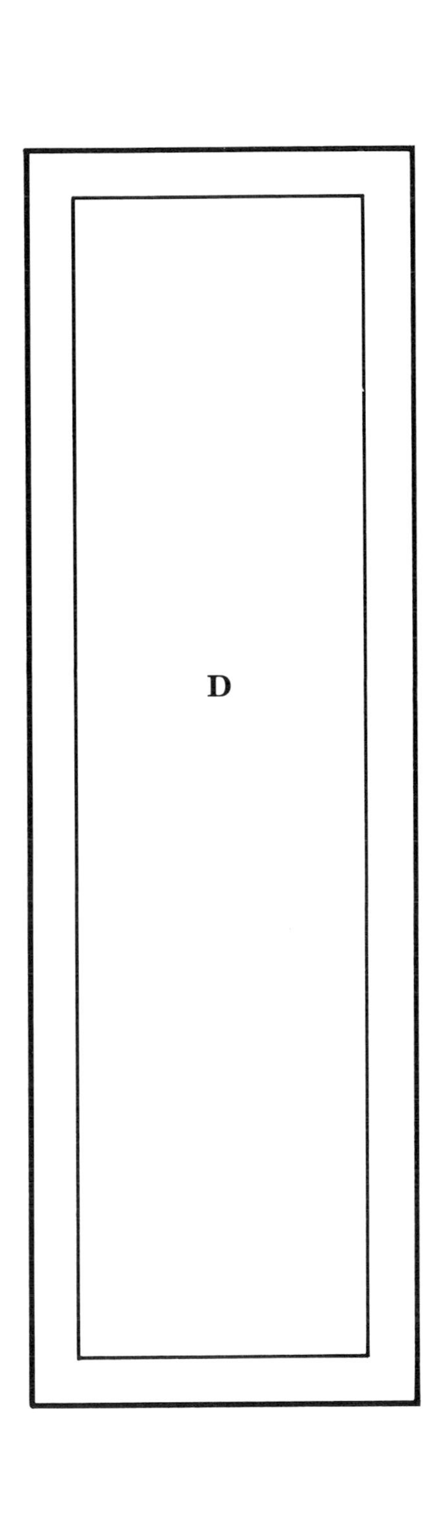
D

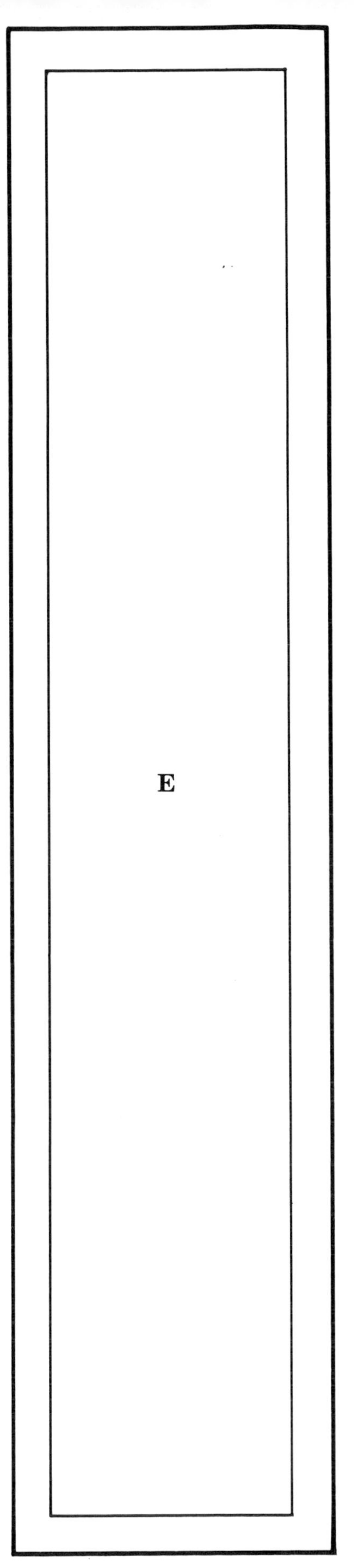
E

Piecing Diagram

Zigzag Pillow

This design is made entirely of 2-inch strips.

MATERIALS

Fabric

Seven 2 × 41-inch strips: four in a light color and three in a darker, contrasting color

SEWING INSTRUCTIONS

1. Alternating the colors, with the lighter color on the two outside edges, sew the seven strips together into one band. Press seams open.

2. Cutting across the band at a 45-degree angle, cut three 2-inch strips. Cutting across at a 45-degree angle in the opposite direction, cut three more 2-inch strips (Diagram 1).

3. Arrange these strips in rows to create a zigzag pattern, as indicated in Diagram 2. Matching seams at intersections, sew these rows together. Press seams open. To make a square, trim the top and bottom (Diagram 2).

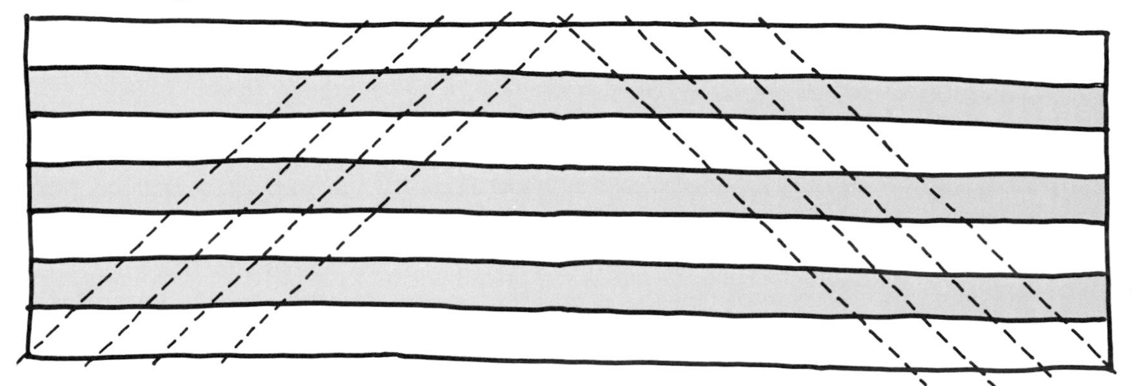

Diagram 1. Sew seven strips together into a single band. Cut across at a 45-degree angle into three 2-inch strips. Cut across at a 45-degree angle in the opposite directionand make three more 2-inch strips.

Diagram 2. Arrange strips in rows to make zigzag pattern.

REVERSIBLE LOG CABIN

This reversible Log Cabin quilt was inspired by "Mt. St. Helens," a Barn-Raising Log Cabin quilt, by Louise O. Townsend, which appeared in *Log Cabin Quilts,* by Bonnie Leman and Judy Martin. Until that time I had never seen a quilt with a pattern on both sides. It wasn't made, as you might think, by sewing the front and back separately and joining them afterward. The front and back of *each block* were sewn simultaneously. That is, as each strip was sewn to the front, another strip was sewn simultaneously to the back of each block. Although the fabrics were different on each side, the positioning of the light and dark pieces was the same. This may sound tricky but it's really quite easy.

As soon as I saw "Mt. St. Helens" I knew that I wanted to make a reversible Log Cabin of my own, but one in which the designs on the front and back, instead of being the same, would be different—for example, a Straight Furrow on one side and a Streak o' Lightning on the other. As far as I knew, no one had ever tried this, and I wondered if it could be done. I made some drawings and started working on some test pieces.

Another idea came from the same book. On the cover was a quilt by Judy Martin with "cornerstones," little squares that run across the blocks diagonally. Why not double the challenge and add cornerstones? I was meeting regularly with Emiko Toda Loeb, who was my student at the time, and when I told her of my plan we were both so excited that we dropped everything else to see if it would work. The result is the quilt you see on pages 58 and 59. To my knowledge, it's the first of its kind.

When we were about halfway through, Emiko had some other ideas for Reversible Log Cabin quilts that she wanted to try out on quilts of her own. Since then Emiko has made quite a few, each different from the last. Her use of this concept demonstrates the versatility of the Log Cabin design, and how a simple, basic idea can be stretched as far as you're willing to take it. Someday soon I plan to return to making more Reversible Log Cabin quilts, inspired by someone who once looked to me for ideas.

If you've never made a reversible Log Cabin, take a look at the following description of the basic technique and make at least one block—the Reversible Log Cabin Potholder, perhaps—to familiarize yourself with the process. You could sew a lot of blocks and make a quilt in which the designs are the same on both sides. Then you might go on to make one in which the designs are different (as is mine, with the Streak o' Lightning and Straight Furrow designs).

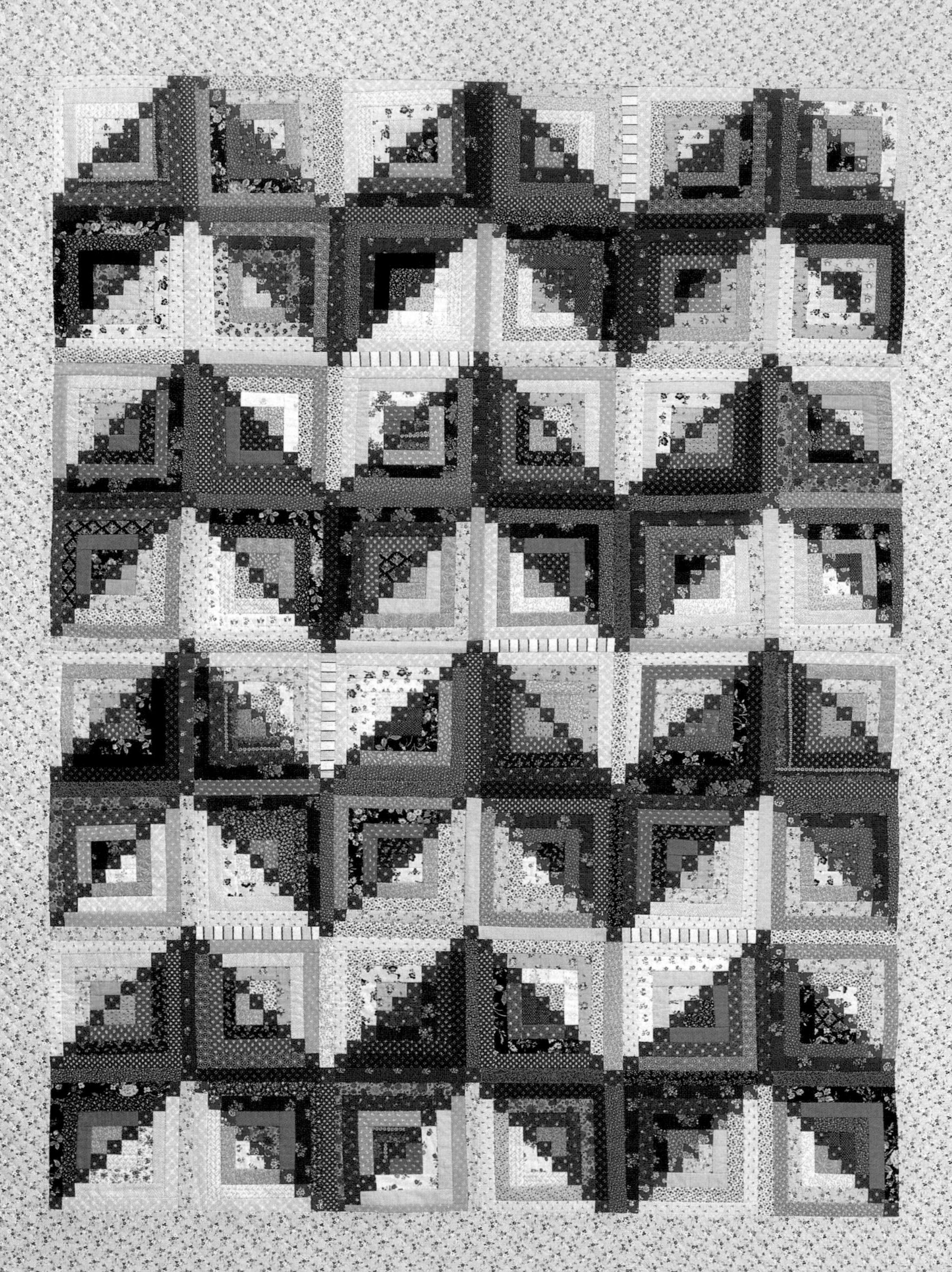

REVERSIBLE LOG CABIN

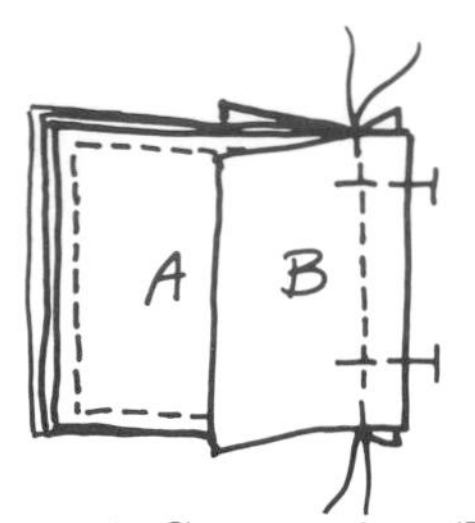

Diagram 1. Sew strips (**B**) to front and back of **A** at the same time.

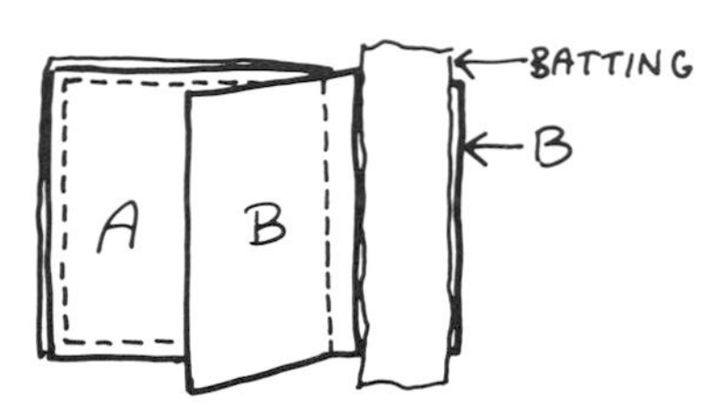

Diagram 2. Fold **B** away from **A**. Insert batting strip.

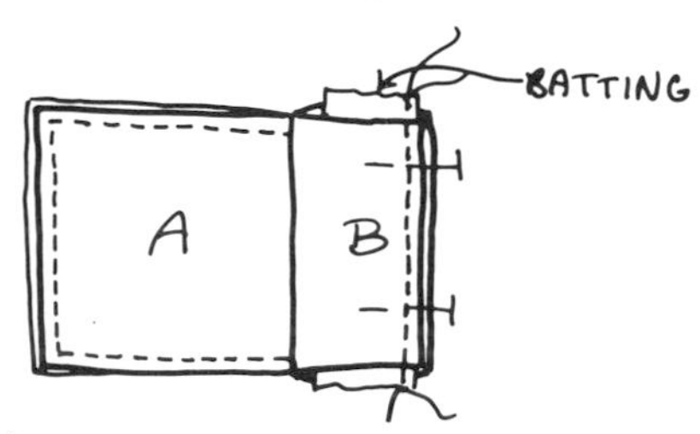

Diagram 3. Fold top **B** over to match bottom **B**. Stitch outside edge.

SEWING INSTRUCTIONS

1. Cut two **A** pieces and two **B** pieces.

2. Except for the center squares, which require a piece of batting of the same size, cut strips of batting ¼ inch narrower than the fabric pieces.

3. Sew a light **C** to the front and back on the *left* side of the block (Diagram 3). Press or fold both **C** pieces away from the center. Insert a strip of batting between the two **C** pieces, and sew the three layers together along the outside edge.

4. Press or fold the bottom **B** away from **A**, and insert batting (Diagram 2). Although pressing will flatten the batting slightly, it gradually fluffs up again. Because pressing produces neater and more accurate work, I prefer to press even if this may mean losing some of the loft.

5. Fold the top **B** away from **A** and pin the two **B** pieces together with the batting in between (Diagram 3). Sew the **B** pieces together along their outside edges. Proceed in the same manner for all other pieces.

REVERSIBLE LOG CABIN BLOCK POTHOLDER

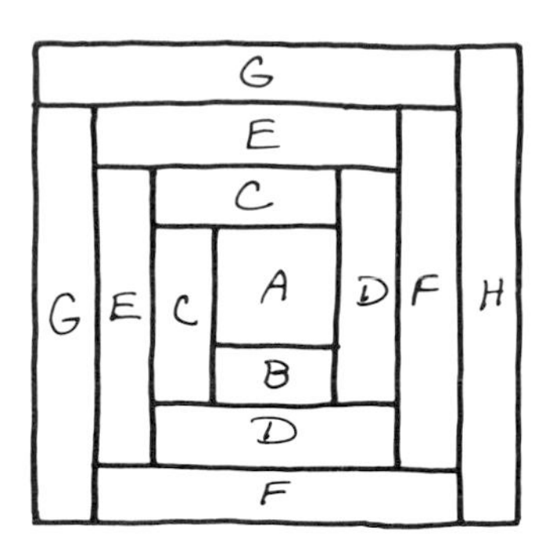

Piecing Diagram

The following instructions are for a reversible block in which the design on both front and back is the same. Make at least one of these blocks to become familiar with the process. If you go on to make a quilt, think about using various color schemes—for a summer/winter quilt, perhaps, which could be turned over as the seasons change or to suit your mood.

MATERIALS

Pattern piece	Number of pieces
A	2 (any color)
B	2 dark
C	4 light
D	4 dark
E	4 light
F	4 dark
G	4 light
H	2 dark

This 8 × 8-inch block is made with 1½-inch strips and requires ¾-inch strips of batting, except for piece **A** (center square), the batting for which should be the same size as the square.

Note that except for piece **A**, which you will find at the end of these instructions, the patterns for this block are the same for the Reversible Log Cabin on pages 71 and 72.

Diagram 1. With a strip of batting between the layers, sew two **A** pieces together.

SEWING INSTRUCTIONS

Piecing

1. Sew the two center square pieces (**A**) together with their right sides facing out and a piece of batting in between (Diagram 1).

2. Sew a dark **B** to the front and back of the *bottom* side of **A** (Diagram 2). Press or fold the **B** pieces away from the center piece (**A**). Insert a strip of batting between the two **B** pieces, and sew the three layers together along the outside edge.

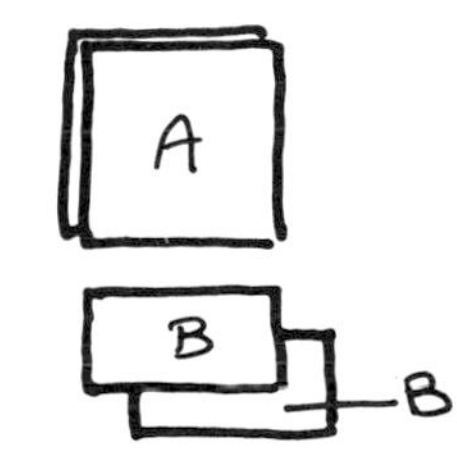

Diagram 2. Sew a **B** to the front and back of the bottom of piece **A**.

3. Sew the batting between the two center squares (**A**), stitching the square on all four sides. With right sides facing, sew a **B** to the front and back of **A** along the right side of the square (Diagram 1).

4. Sew a light **C** to the front and back on the *top* of the block (Diagram 4). Press or fold both **C** pieces away from the center. Insert a strip of batting between the two **C** pieces, and sew the three layers together along the outside edge.

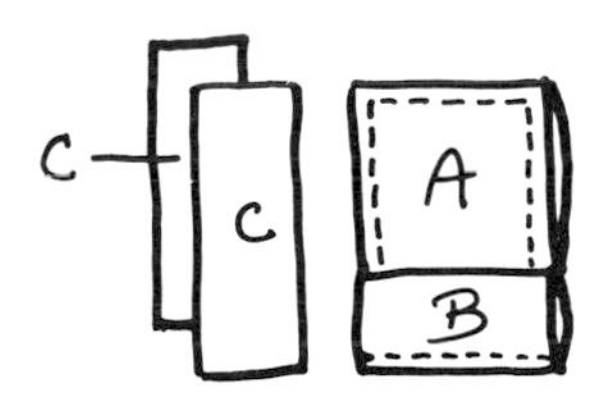

Diagram 3. Sew one **C** to the front and one **C** to the back on the left side of the block.

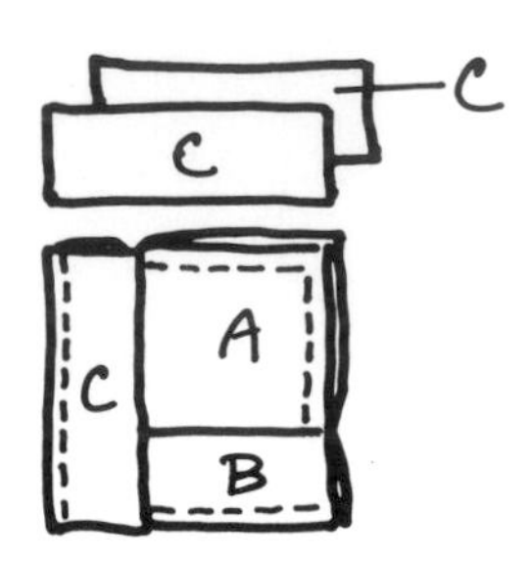

Diagram 4. Sew one **C** to the front and one **C** to the back on the top of the block.

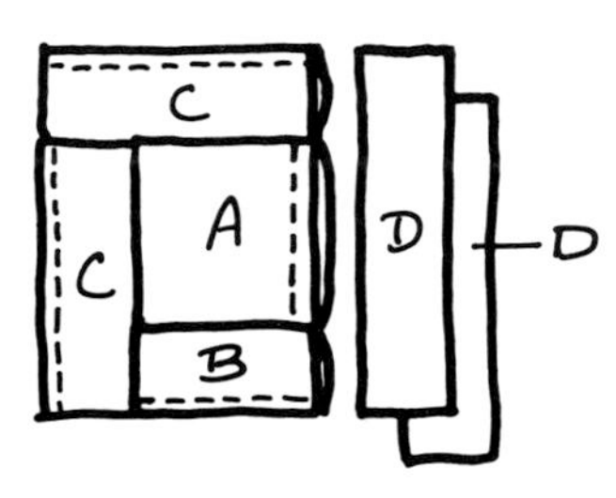

Diagram 5. Sew one **D** to the front and one **D** to the back of the right side of the block.

5. Sew a dark **D** to the front and back of the *right* side of the block (Diagram 5). Press or fold the **D** pieces away from the center. Insert a strip of batting between the two **D** pieces, and sew the three layers together along the outside edge.

6. Proceed in this manner until the block is completed. Finish the outside edge with a 2-inch × 1-yard strip of bias binding, with a loop for hanging at one corner. For detailed instructions on bias bindings, see page 19.

LOG CABIN POTHOLDER

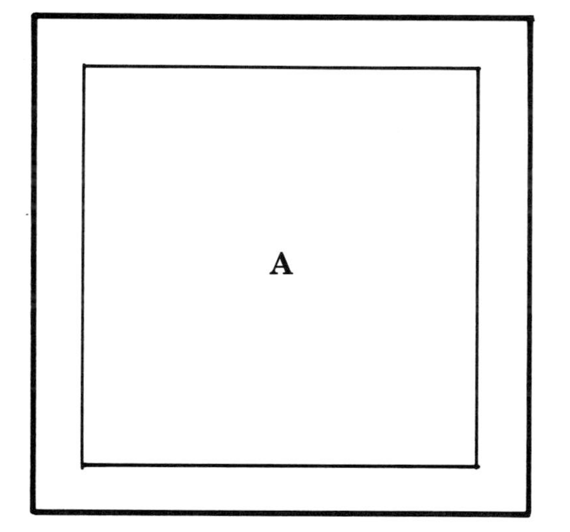

REVERSIBLE LOG CABIN WITH CORNERSTONES: STREAK O' LIGHTNING FRONT AND STRAIGHT FURROW BACK

Although it seems unlikely, this quilt isn't technically difficult to make, even with the cornerstones. The tricky part is knowing where to place the dark and light pieces without losing your place. I got mixed up a few times before I got the hang of it, but the process soon became almost automatic, as for any other quilt block. I wish I'd had the instructions and diagrams I've prepared for you here while I was working on my first quilt of this sort!

There are two basic blocks, 24 of each.

Size: A single block measures 9 × 9 inches. The finished size of this quilt is 77 × 97 inches, perfect for a queen-size bed.

MATERIALS

Fabric

Each side of this quilt requires approximately ½ yard of fabric for the cornerstones, 7½ yards of assorted colors (half light, half dark), and 2⅓ for the borders.

Pattern piece	Number of pieces
A	2 light, 2 dark, 9 red, 9 yellow*
B	2 light, 2 dark
C	2 light, 2 dark
D	2 light, 2 dark
E	2 light, 2 dark
F	2 light, 2 dark
G	2 light, 2 dark
H	2 light, 2 dark

All of the above pattern pieces are required to construct either ***Block A*** or ***Block B***.

Connecting strips, or sashes, for joining blocks

Streak o' Lightning*

Pattern piece I   44 dark, 38 light
Pattern piece A   35 red (zigzag)

Straight Furrow*

Pattern piece I   41 dark, 41 light
Pattern piece A   35 yellow

Four 9¼ × 79¼-inch strips of fabric for the side borders

Four 9¼ × 77¼-inch strips of fabric for the top and bottom borders

One continuous 2-inch × 9¾-yard strip of bias binding for the outside edge

REVERSIBLE LOG CABIN: STREAK O' LIGHTNING AND STRAIGHT FURROW

Block A (Streak o' Lightning side up)

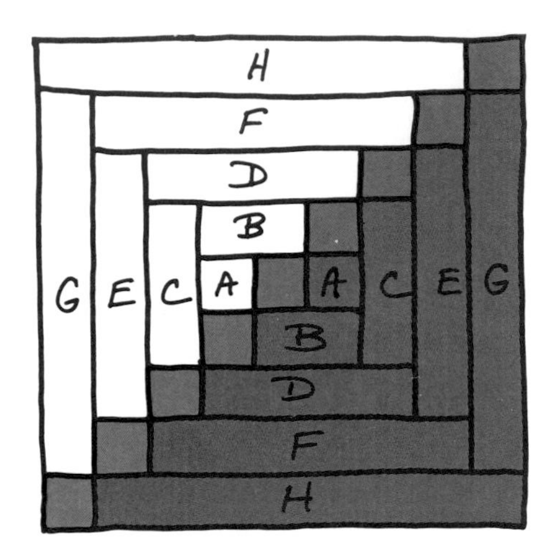

Piecing Diagram
Make 24

*I chose red cornerstones for the Streak o' Lightning and yellow for the Straight Furrow. To make the instructions easy to follow, I've indicated the colors of the cornerstones. However, any colors can be used. You can even vary the colors within one block. Just keep track of the substitutions you wish to make.

Other Materials

Batting cut into ¾-inch strips, two 9 × 79¼-inch strips for the side borders, and two 9 × 77¼-inch strips for the top and bottom borders

SEWING INSTRUCTIONS

Piecing

Block A

1. With their right sides facing out and a piece of batting in between, sew two cornerstones (**A**) together: one red on top and one yellow underneath. Machine stitch ⅛ inch from the outside edge around all four sides (Diagram 1).

2. Sew one light **A** to the left side of the center cornerstone with one dark **A** behind it. Reverse for the right side (Diagram 2). Insert a square of batting between the layers on both sides and sew the outside edges together ⅛ inch from the edge. This will hold the edges in place until the **C** pieces are attached.

3. Sew one red cornerstone to one end of one light **B** and one dark **B**,

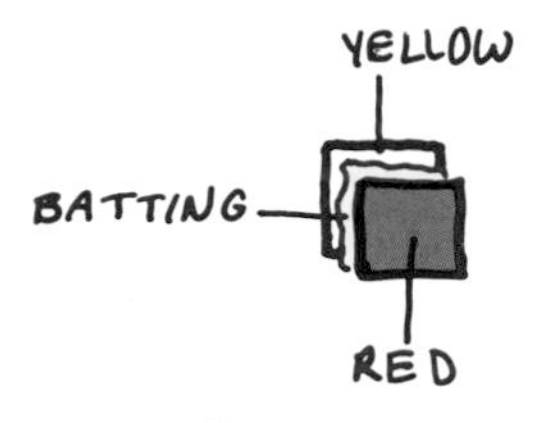

Diagram 1. Sew two cornerstones (**A**) together with batting in between.

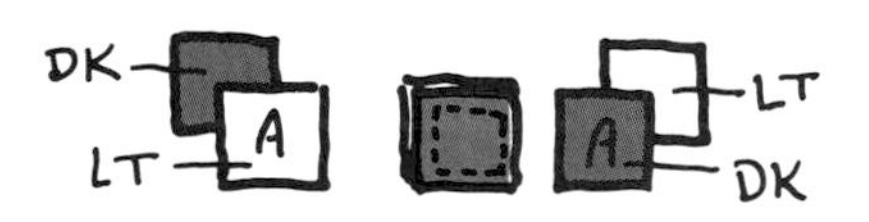

Diagram 2. Sew one light **A** to left side with one dark **A** behind it. Reverse for right side.

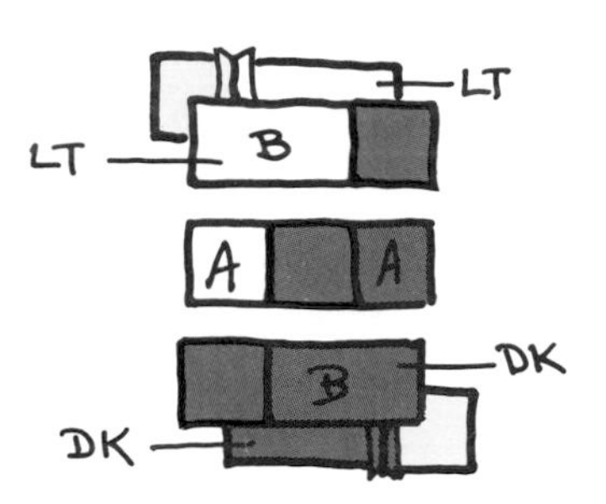

Diagram 3. With cornerstones on opposite ends, sew two light **B** pieces to the top and two dark **B** pieces to the bottom of the block.

Diagram 4. Sew one light **C** to the left side of the block with one dark **C** behind it. Reverse for right side.

and one yellow cornerstone to one end of one light **B** and one dark **B**. Press seams open.

4. With the red cornerstone facing to the right, sew one light **B** to the top of the center unit; at the same time, sew the other light **B** with the yellow cornerstone facing to the left behind it (Diagram 3). With the red cornerstone facing to the left, sew one dark **B** to the bottom of the center unit; at the same time, sew the other dark **B** with the yellow cornerstone facing to the right behind it (Diagram 3). Match seams at all intersections. Press or finger press the **B** pieces away from the center. Insert a strip of batting between the layers and sew the outside edges of the **B** pieces together ⅛ inch from the edge.

5. Sew one light **C** to the left side of the block with one dark **C** behind it. Reverse for the right side (Diagram 4). Press or finger press the **C** pieces away from the center. Insert a strip of batting between the layers and sew the outside edges of the **C** pieces together.

6. Sew one red cornerstone to one end of one light **D** and one dark **D**, and one yellow cornerstone to one end of one light **D** and one dark **D**. Press seams open.

7. With the red cornerstone facing to the right, sew one light **D** to the top of the block; at the same time, sew the other light **D** with the yellow cornerstone facing to the left behind it (Diagram 5). With the red cornerstone facing to the left, sew one dark **D** to the bottom of the block; at the same time, sew the other dark **D** with the yellow cornerstone facing to the right behind it (Diagram 5). Press or finger press the **D** pieces away from the center. Insert a strip of batting between the layers and sew the outside edges of the **D** pieces together.

8. Sew one light **E** to the left side of the block with one dark **E** behind it. Reverse for the right side (Diagram 6). Press or finger press the **E**

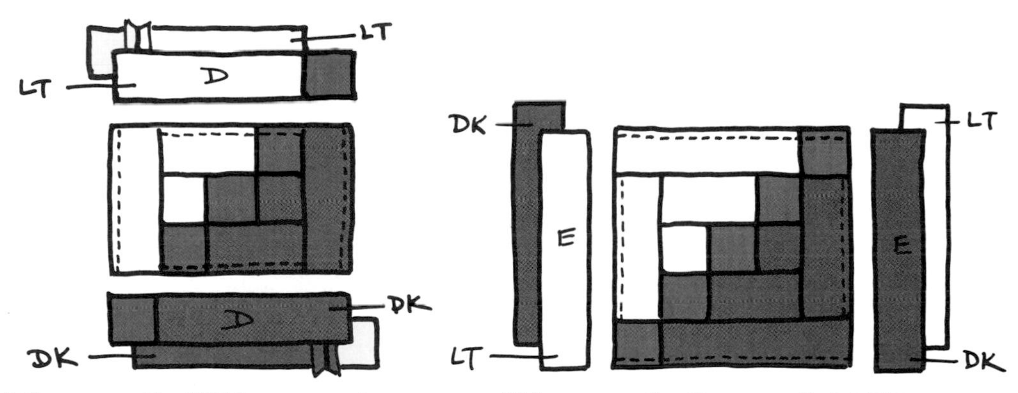

Diagram 5. With cornerstones on opposite ends, sew two light **D** pieces to the top and two dark pieces to the bottom of the block.

Diagram 6. Sew one light **E** to the left side of the block with one dark **E** behind it. Reverse for the right side.

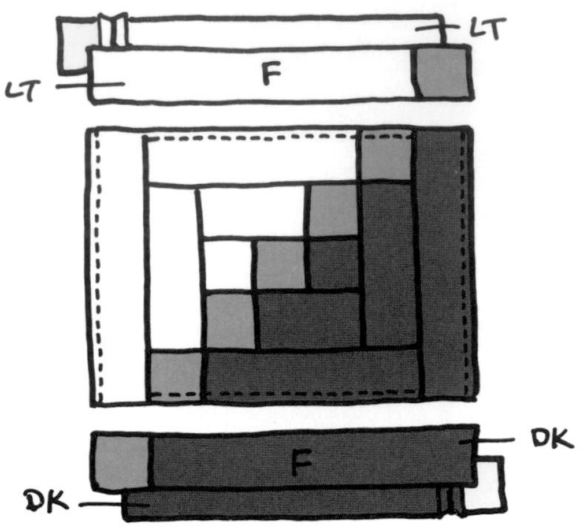

Diagram 7. With cornerstones on opposite ends, sew two light **F** pieces to the top and two dark **F** pieces to the bottom of the block.

pieces away from the center. Insert a strip of batting in between and sew the outside edges of the **E** pieces together.

9. Sew one red cornerstone to one end of one light **F** and one dark **F**, and one yellow cornerstone to one end of one light **F** and one dark **F**. Press seams open.

10. With the red cornerstone facing to the right, sew one light **F** to the top of the block; at the same time, sew the other light **F** with the yellow cornerstone facing to the left behind it (Diagram 7). With the red cornerstone facing to the left, sew one dark **F** to the bottom of the block; at the same time, sew the other dark **F** with the yellow cornerstone facing to the right behind it (Diagram 7). Press or finger press the **F** pieces away from the center. Insert a strip of batting between the layers and sew the outside edges of the **F** pieces together.

11. Sew one light **G** to the left side of the block with one dark **G** behind it. Reverse for the right side (Diagram 8). Press or fold the **G** pieces away from the center. Insert a strip of batting between the layers and sew the outside edges of the **G** pieces together.

12. Sew one red cornerstone to one end of one light **H** and one dark **H**, and one yellow cornerstone to one end of one light **H** and one dark **H**. Press seams open.

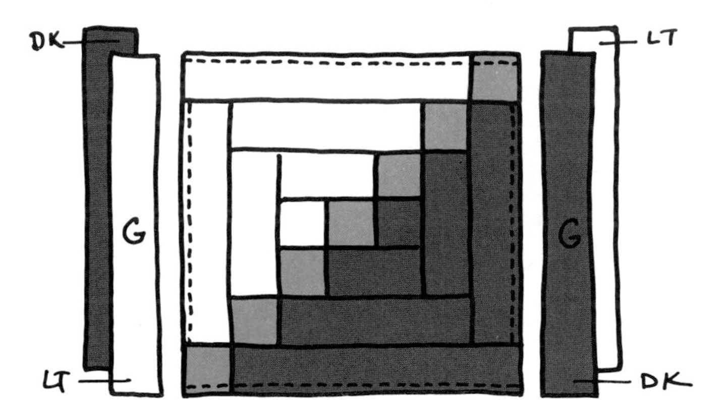

Diagram 8. Sew one light **G** to the left side of the block with one dark **G** behind it. Reverse for the right side.

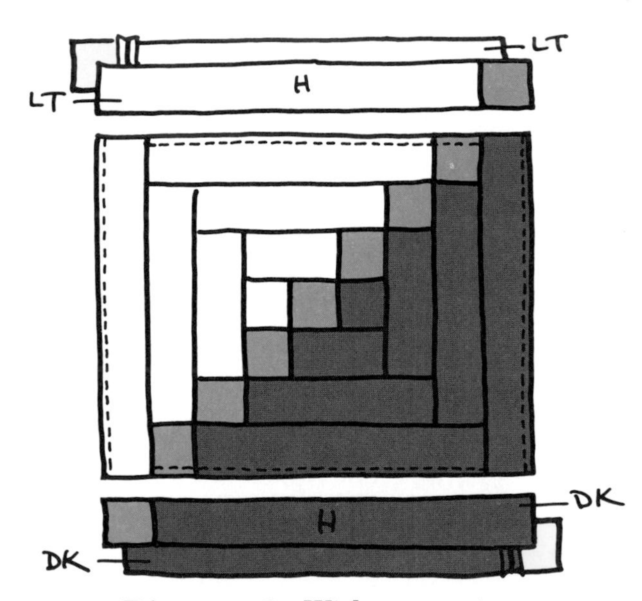

Diagram 9. With cornerstones on opposite ends, sew two dark **H** pieces to the top and two dark **H** pieces to the bottom of the block.

13. With the red cornerstone facing to the right, sew one light **H** piece to the top of the block; at the same time, sew the other light **H** with the yellow cornerstone facing to the left behind it (Diagram 9). With the red cornerstone facing to the left, sew one dark **H** to the bottom of the block; at the same time, sew the other dark **H** with the yellow cornerstone facing to the right behind it (Diagram 9). Press or finger press the **H** pieces away from the center. Insert a strip of batting between the layers and sew the outside edges of the **H** pieces together.

Repeat for a total of 24 of Block A.

Block B

1. With their right sides facing out and a piece of batting between them, sew two cornerstones (**A**) together, one red on top and one yellow behind it. Machine stitch 1/8 inch from the outside edge around all four sides (Diagram 1).

2. Sew one light (**A**) to the top of the center cornerstones with one dark **A** behind it. Reverse for the bottom (Diagram 2). Insert a square of batting between the layers on both sides and sew the outside edges together 1/8 inch from the edges.

3. Sew one red cornerstone **A** to one end of one light **B** and one dark **B**, and one yellow cornerstone to one end of one light **B** and one dark **B**. Press seams open.

4. With both cornerstones at the top, sew the dark **B** with the red cornerstone to the left side of the center unit, and at the same time, sew the light **B** with the yellow cornerstone behind it (Diagram 3). Reverse for the right side. Match seams at all intersections. Press or finger press the **B** pieces away from the center. Insert a strip of batting between the layers on both sides and sew the outside edges of the **B** pieces together 1/8 inch from the edges.

Block B
(Straight Furrow side up)
Piecing Diagram

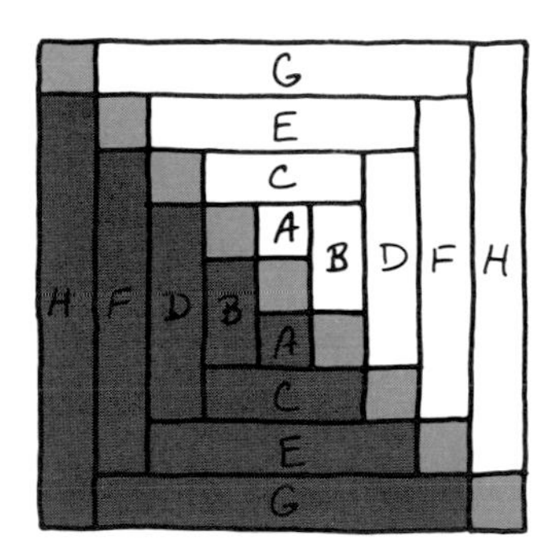

Make 24

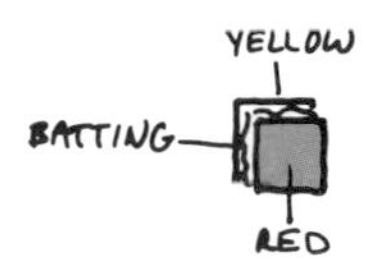

Diagram 1. Sew two cornerstones (A) together with batting in between.

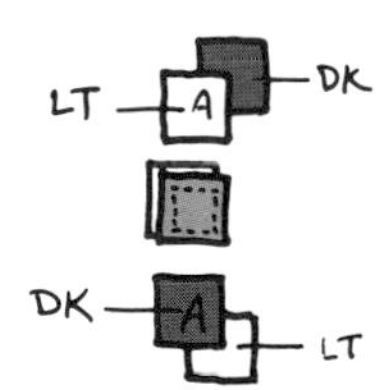

Diagram 2. Sew one light **A** on top of the block with one dark **A** behind it. Reverse for bottom.

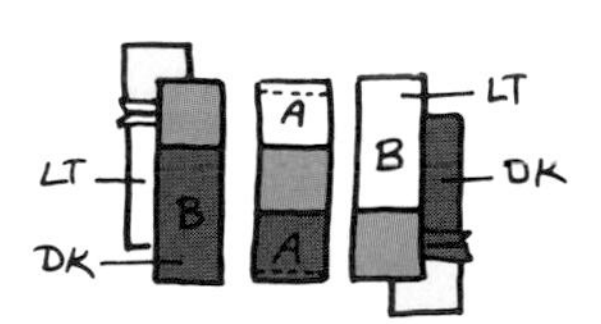

Diagram 3. With both cornerstones at the top, sew one dark **B** to the left side with one light **B** behind it. Reverse for right side.

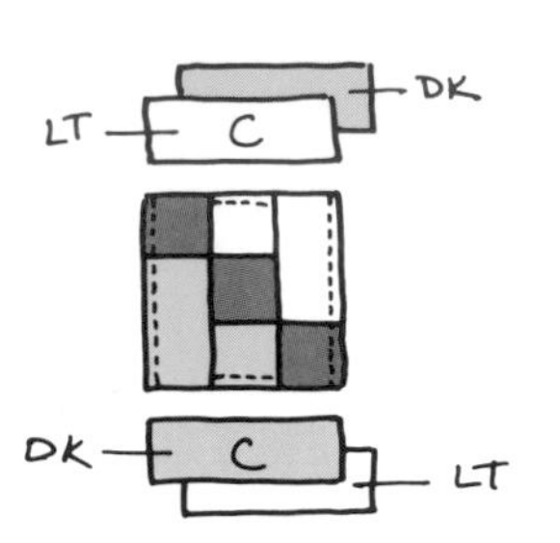

Diagram 4. Sew one light **C** to the top of the block with one dark **C** behind it. Reverse for bottom.

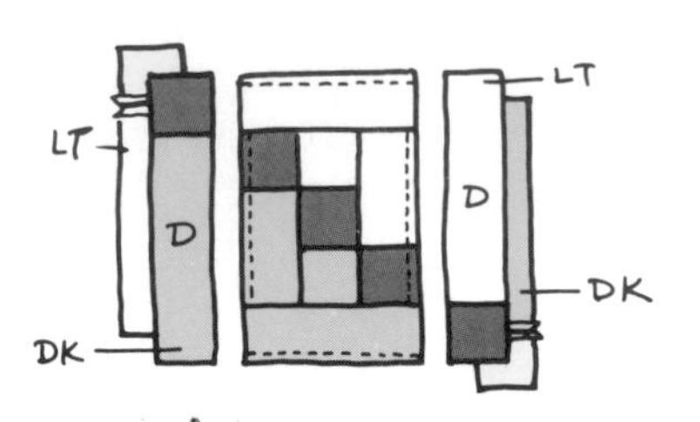

Diagram 5. With both cornerstones at the top, sew one dark **D** to the left side of the block with one light **D** behind it. Reverse for right side.

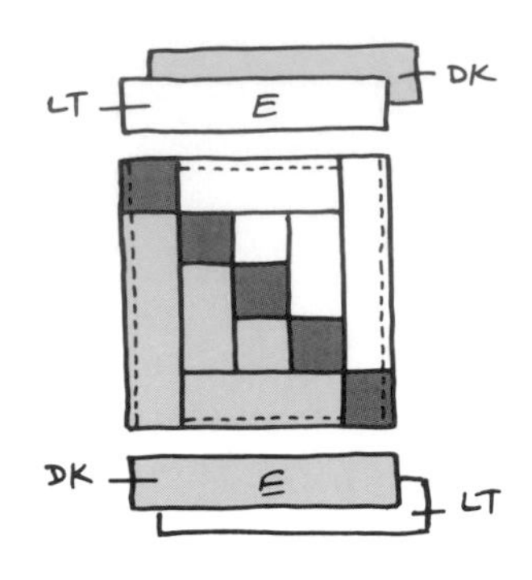

Diagram 6. Sew one light **E** to the top of the block with one dark **E** behind it. Reverse for bottom.

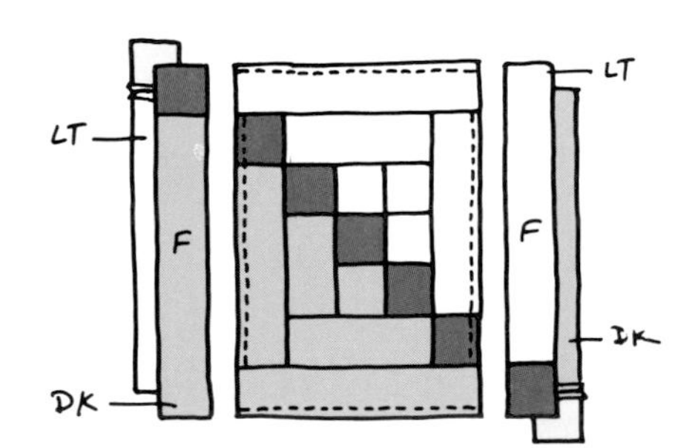

Diagram 7. With both cornerstones at the top, sew one dark **F** to the left side of the block with one light **F** behind it. Reverse for right side.

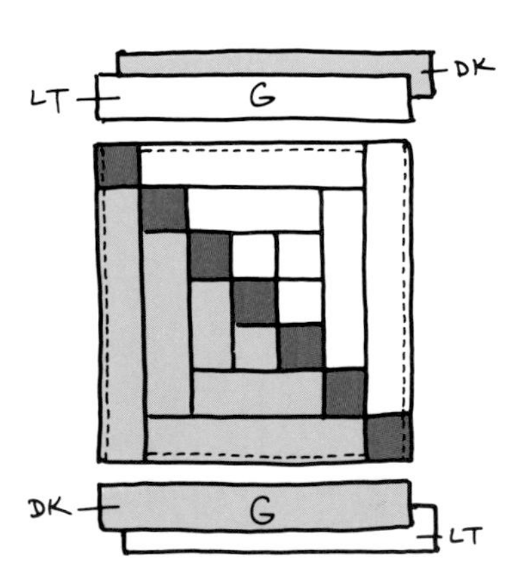

Diagram 8. Sew one light **G** to the top of the block with one dark **G** behind it. Reverse for bottom.

5. Sew one light **C** to the top of the block with one dark **C** behind it. Reverse for the bottom (Diagram 4). Press or finger press the **C** pieces away from the center. Insert a strip of batting between the layers on both top and bottom and sew the outside edges of the **C** pieces together ⅛ inch from the edges.

6. Sew one red cornerstone to one end of one light **D** and one dark **D**, and one yellow cornerstone to one end of one light **D** and one dark **D**. Press seams open.

7. With both cornerstones at the top, sew the dark **D** with the red cornerstone to the left side of the block, and at the same time, sew the light **D** with the yellow cornerstone behind it (Diagram 5). Reverse for the right side. Match seams at all intersections. Press or finger press the **D** pieces away from the center. Insert a strip of batting between the layers on both sides and sew the outside edges of the **D** pieces together ⅛ inch from the edges.

8. Sew one light **E** to the top of the block with one dark **E** behind it. Reverse for the bottom (Diagram 6). Press or finger press the **E** pieces away from the center. Insert a strip of batting between the layers on both top and bottom and sew the outside edges of the **E** pieces together ⅛ inch from the edges.

9. Sew one red cornerstone to one end of one light **F** and one dark **F**, and one yellow cornerstone to one end of one light **F** and one dark **F**. Press seams open.

10. With both cornerstones at the top, sew the dark **F** with the red cornerstone to the left side of the block, and at the same time, sew the light **F** with the yellow cornerstone behind it (Diagram 7). Reverse for the right side. Match seams at all intersections. Press or finger press the **F** pieces away from the center. Insert a strip of batting between the layers on both sides and sew the outside edges of the **F** pieces together ⅛ inch from the edges.

11. Sew one light **G** to the top of the block with one dark **G** behind it. Reverse for the bottom (Diagram 8). Press or finger press the **G** pieces

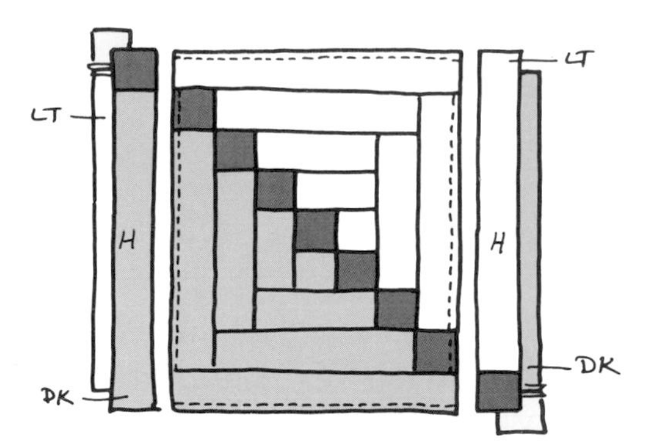

Diagram 9. With both cornerstones at the top, sew one dark **H** to the left side of the block with one light **H** behind it. Reverse for right side.

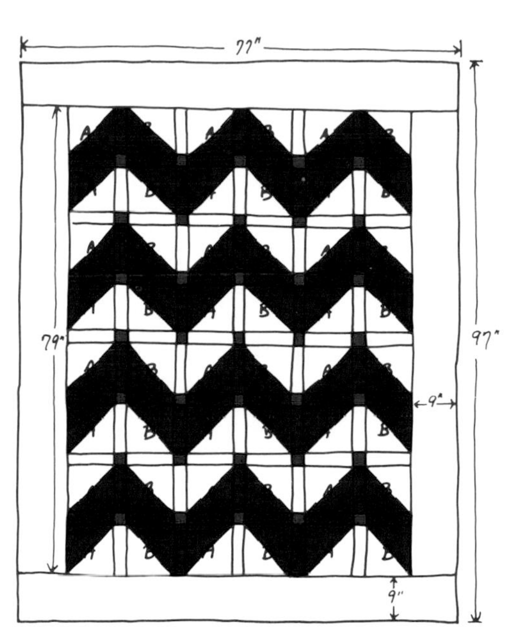

Diagram 10. Streak o' Lightning layout: Connecting strips (piece **I**) with cornerstones.

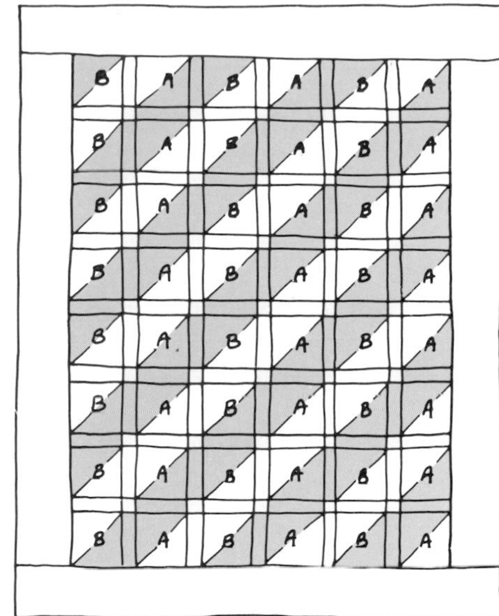

Straight Furrow layout: Sashes (piece **I**) with cornerstones.

away from the center. Insert a strip of batting between the layers on both top and bottom and sew the outside edges of the **G** pieces together ⅛ inch from the edges.

12. Sew one red cornerstone to one end of one light **H** and one dark **H**, and one yellow cornerstone to one end of one light **H** and one dark **H**. Press seams open.

13. With both cornerstones at the top, sew the dark **H** with the red cornerstone to the left side of the block, and at the same time, sew the light **H** with the yellow cornerstone behind it (Diagram 9). Reverse for the right side. Match seams at all intersections. Press or finger press the **H** pieces away from the center. Insert a strip of batting between the layers on both sides and sew the outside edges of the **H** pieces together ⅛ inch from the edges.

Repeat for a total of 24 of Block B.

Assembly

14. The next step is to arrange the blocks to create the Streak o' Lightning on one side of the quilt and the Straight Furrow on the other. Concentrate on one side at a time, starting with the Streak o' Lightning, and set out the blocks in columns, alternating the A and B blocks (Diagram 10). The blocks are then sewn together with sashes, or connecting strips (I), and a cornerstone at each intersection.

15. To join two blocks (A and B), sew one **I** to the front and one **I** to the back of one side of Block A (Diagram 11). Press or finger press **I** away from the block.

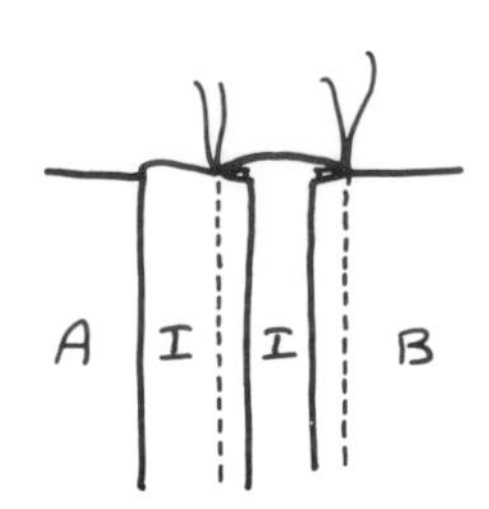

Diagram 11. Sew an **I** to top and back of Block A. Sew the other side of one **I** to Block B.

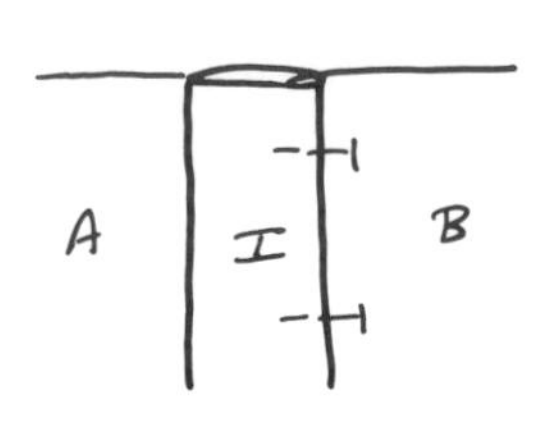

Diagram 12. Pin and sew remaining side of one **I** to Block B.

Make 12.

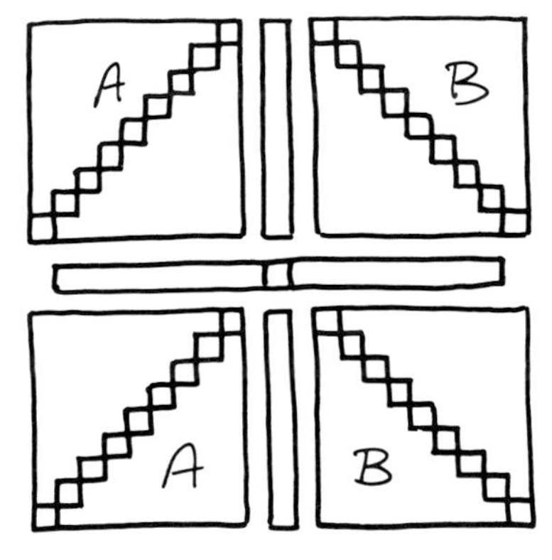

Diagram 13. Basic four-block unit.

16. Sew the other side of the **I** to one side of Block B. Press or finger press the **I** away from Block B. Insert a strip of batting and fold over the free edge of the second **I** ¼ inch and pin the edge to Block B. Blindstitch the edge of **I** to Block B (Diagram 12).

17. After joining the blocks together in pairs in this manner, join the pairs to create four-block units (Diagram 13) for a total of twelve units. With a cornerstone **A** in between, sew two **I** pieces (alternating one light and one dark) together into a strip. Repeat to make two sets. Press seams open.

18. Join one pair of blocks (A and B) to another pair with this strip so that the cornerstone falls at the intersection. They are joined in exactly the same manner as described above. Repeat to make twelve sets of four blocks each.

19. Join the twelve sets of blocks, three across and four down, to complete the pattern.

Borders

20. Sew one 9¼ × 79¼-inch border to the top left side of the quilt top, with another border underneath. Repeat for the right side. Press or fold borders away from the quilt top. Insert one 9 × 79¼-inch strip of batting between the two layers of both borders. Machine baste the outside edges of both borders.

21. Sew one 9¼ × 77-inch border to the top of the quilt top with another border underneath. Repeat for the bottom. Press or fold borders away from the quilt top. Insert one 9 × 77¼-inch strip of batting between the two layers of both borders. Machine baste the outside edges of both borders.

22. Finish the edge with 2-inch (½-inch finished size) bias seam binding. For instructions on bias binding, see page 19.

A

B

C

D

E

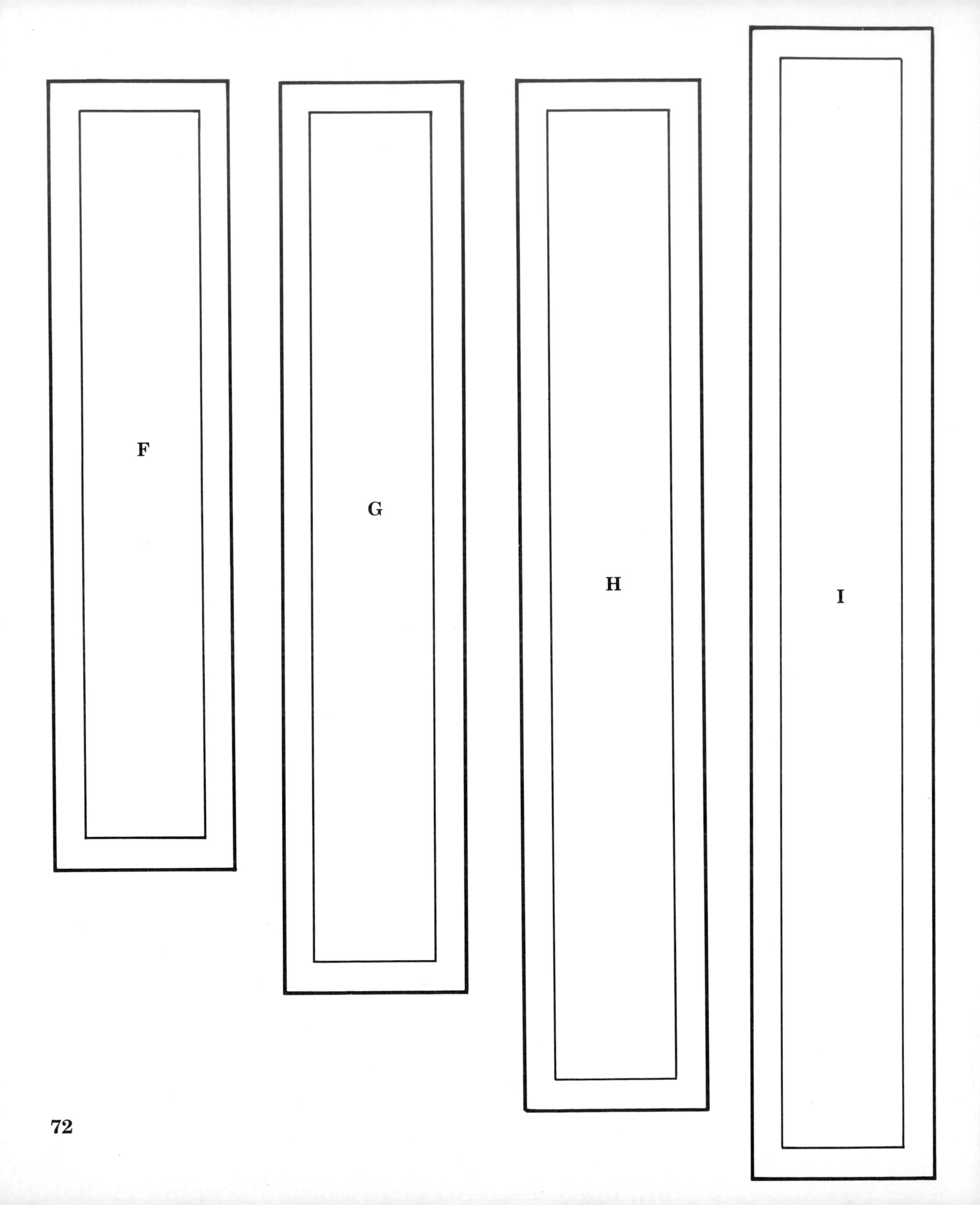
F
G
H
I

FLYING BOXES

Have you ever tried to make a Baby Blocks quilt? I haven't. I made a 12 × 12-inch block for a sampler quilt and discovered how hard it is to piece, partly because the pieces were so small. I'm sure that if I had made them larger, the piecing would have been easier. I remember how glad I was that I hadn't committed myself to making a quilt.

I assembled the pieces the way most quilters do, by turning corners. I now think that using the English technique of pinning paper diamonds on fabric, turning the seam allowance over to the back of the paper, basting the edges, and whipstitching them together by hand is probably the best way to handle a large Baby Blocks project with small pieces, even though this method is more time-consuming.

Someday I may go on to make a quilt using one of these techniques. In the meantime, I made the process easier for myself by adding two triangles to the basic block. This isn't my invention; it has been done before. I recommend this method if you're new to making Baby Blocks and to turning corners in general. Even though you'll be turning one corner to make each block, you won't lose your mind because you'll be able to sew them together with straight seamlines.

Flying Boxes is a lovely introduction to Baby Blocks. It's fairly easy to sew, and the addition of the triangles, while making the blocks easier to assemble, doesn't alter the three-dimensional impact of the cubes.

The most interesting thing about this pattern is the way color can affect its appearance. In the quilt we see boxes, in the pillow we see stars with cubes in the middle (try squinting if you have trouble seeing the stars), yet they're both the same design. To give you the opportunity to play with color before you cut your fabric, I've included a drawing of a diamond grid for you to photocopy and color to test your ideas.

I made my quilt as a throw or wall hanging. You could make yours any size you like by adding or subtracting blocks. You could also make enough to use in a pillow or as part of a garment.

FLYING BOXES QUILT

Size: One nine-block unit is 9 × 10½ inches. I used twelve units to make a pieced top measuring 27 × 42 inches. The finished size of the quilt with 10½-inch borders is 47 × 62 inches.

MATERIALS

Fabric

One nine-block unit

Pattern piece	Number of pieces
A	27
B	18

Quilt: twelve nine-block units

Pattern piece	Number of pieces
A	342
B	232

The quilt requires a few extra A and B pieces to even up the rows once they're assembled (see Diagram 5).

Two 10½- × 42-inch borders for the sides

Two 10½- × 47½-inch borders for the top and bottom

Note: For the borders, remove the selvages from a 1½-yard length of fabric and cut lengthwise into four 10½-inch strips. Trim to appropriate lengths.

Other Materials

48 × 63-inch piece of batting

2⅔ yards of fabric for the back

SEWING INSTRUCTIONS

1. Sew two **A** pieces together (Diagram 1). Press seam open.

2. With right sides together, place the third **A** underneath the top **A** of the **A-A** unit. Starting at the top, sew the two **A** pieces together, stopping with the needle down precisely in the middle of the seamline (Diagram 2). Leaving the needle down, lift the presser foot and clip the threads in the seam up to the needle. Slide the **A** underneath so that its next side lines up with the side of the other **A** on top. Lower the presser foot and continue sewing off the end. Press seam open from each end.

3. Sew a **B** to the top right side of the block. Sew a **B** to the bottom left side of the block (Diagram 3). Press seams open. Repeat this process for 108 blocks (or as many as you need). Eighteen **A** pieces and 16 **B** pieces will be left over.

FLYING BOXES

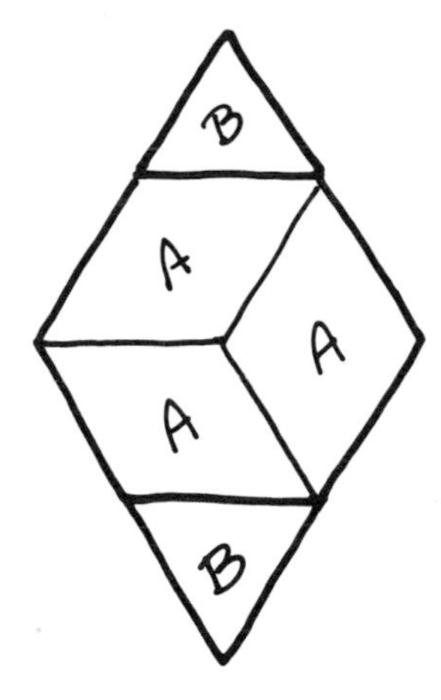

Piecing Diagram

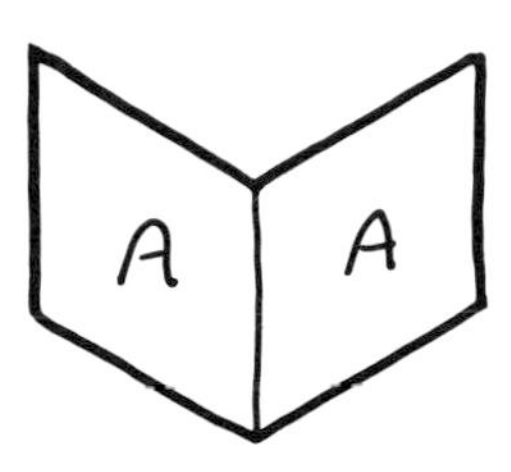

Diagram 1. Sew two **A** pieces together.

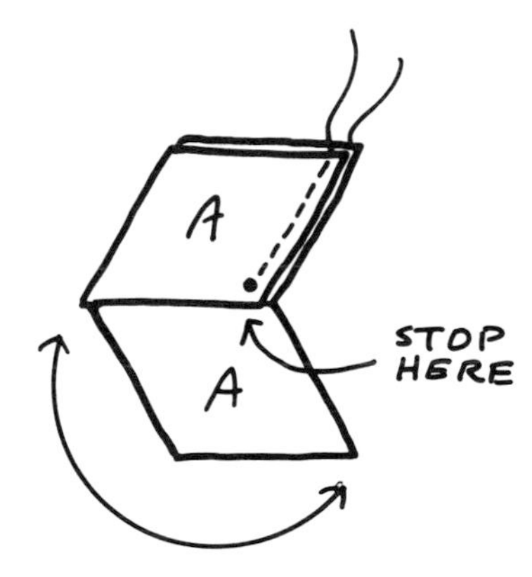

Diagram 2. Sew together the two top pieces.

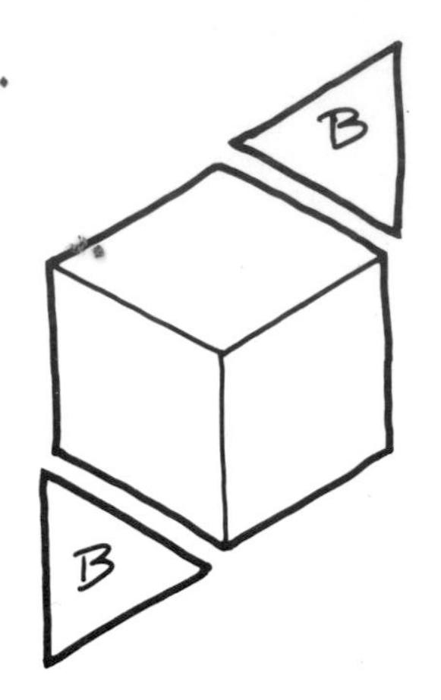

Diagram 3. Sew a **B** to opposite sides of the hexagon.

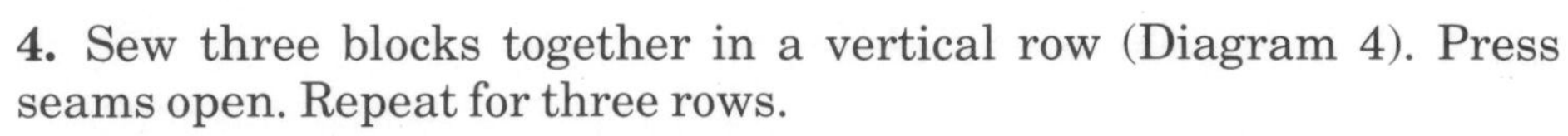

4. Sew three blocks together in a vertical row (Diagram 4). Press seams open. Repeat for three rows.

5. Matching seams at intersections, sew the three rows together to make a nine-block unit. Repeat for a total of 12 units. Sew the units together in three vertical rows of four units per row (Diagram 5). Press seams open.

6. Sew the leftover **A** pieces into six blocks. Sew the blocks together with the remaining **B** pieces to make the extra units shown in Diagram 5. Press seams open. By attaching these units to the ends of the rows, you will be able to trim off the top and bottom of the quilt top without losing too much from some of the units.

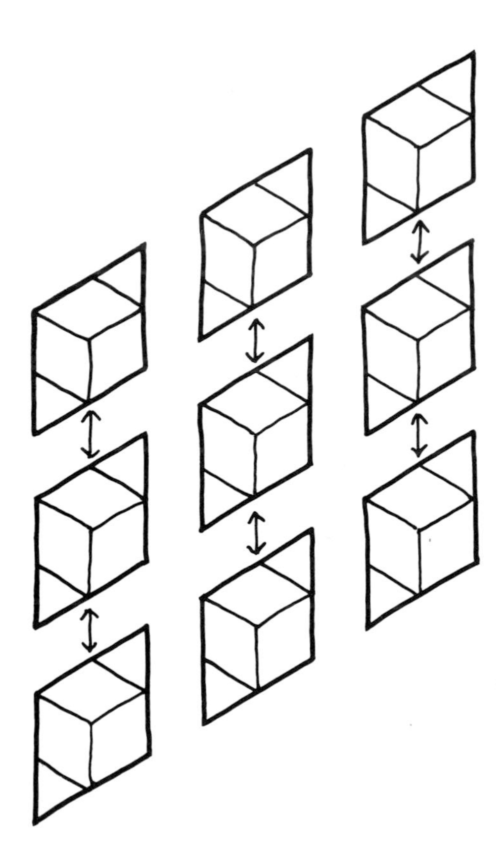

Diagram 4. Sew three blocks together in three vertical rows.

Diagram 5. Sew nine-block units into three rows of four blocks. Sew extra pieces together to make extra units for the ends of the rows.

7. Matching seams at intersections, sew the three rows together to make the quilt top. Press seams open. Trim off the jagged edges of the top and bottom of the quilt top (Diagram 6).

Assembly

8. Sew one 10½ × 42-inch border to each side of the quilt top. Press seams toward border.

9. Sew one 10½ × 47½-inch border to the top and bottom of the quilt top. Press seams toward border. Assemble the quilt as described under Assembling the Quilt Top, page 14.

Quilting

I would quilt in one of two ways: by hand, ¼ inch inside each diamond or cube; or by machine "in the ditch" (in the seamlines), stitching in three directions, joining all the blocks in an overall hexagonal pattern.

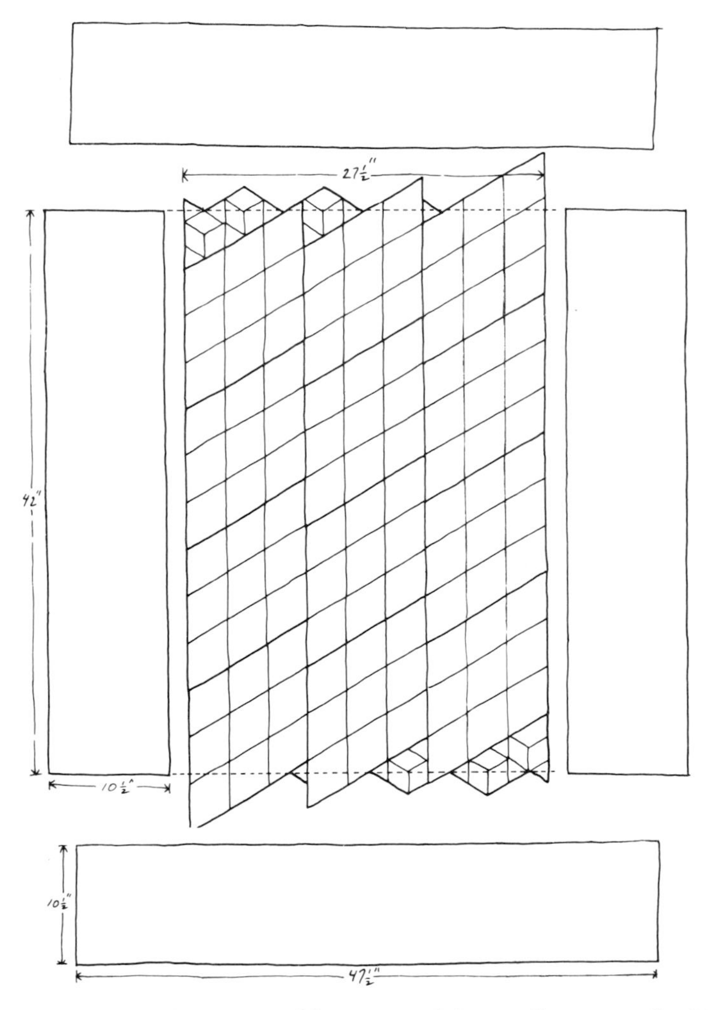

Diagram 6. Trim the top and bottom of the quilt top and add borders.

Coloring Chart

Pattern for Machine Quilting

FLYING BOXES

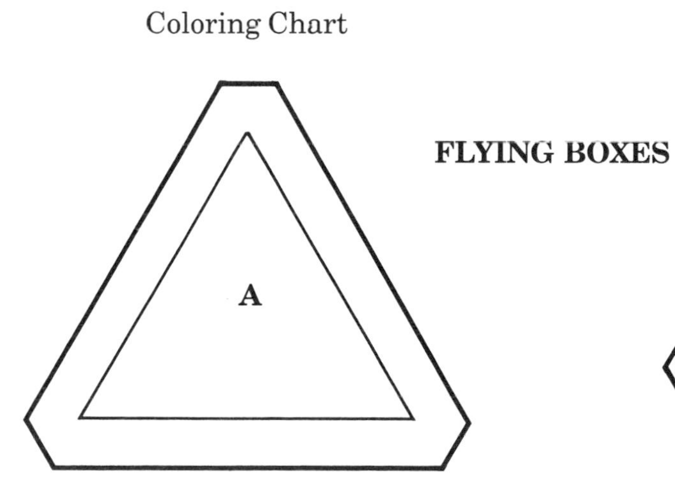

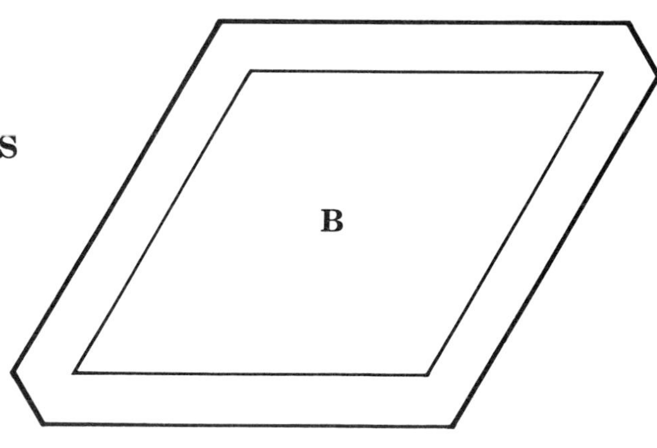

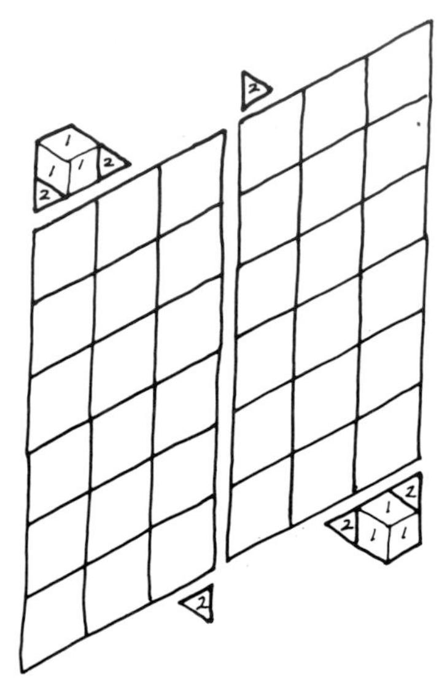

Diagram 1. Sew nine-block units into vertical rows. Add extra blocks and triangles (**B**) to the corners of the rows.

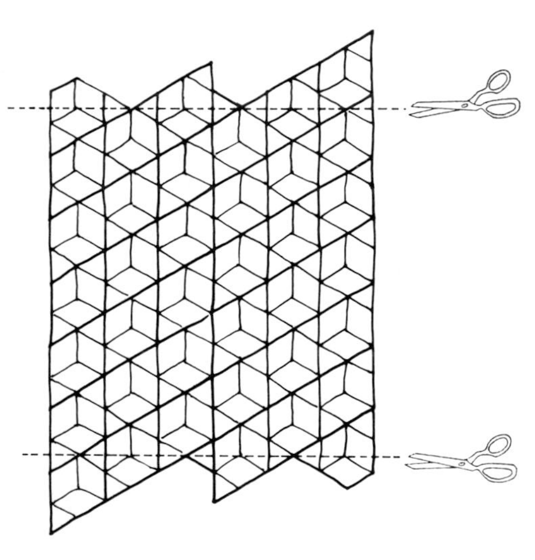

Diagram 2. Trim the top and bottom edges.

FLYING BOXES PILLOW

I made this pillow top with four nine-block units in exactly the same way as the quilt top, except for the colors, which I arranged to create stars on a green field.

MATERIALS

Fabric

Pattern piece	Number of pieces
A	114
B	78

18 × 18-inch fabric square for the back

Other Materials

18 × 18-inch pillow form

16-inch zipper

SEWING INSTRUCTIONS

1. Following the preceding instructions for the Flying Boxes quilt (pages 75 to 79), make and assemble 36 basic blocks

2. Assemble the blocks into four nine-block units.

3. Sew the units together into two vertical rows (Diagram 1).

4. Assemble two more blocks in the same way as the others, except for the placement of the **B** pieces, which should be sewn to the sides of the hexagons as shown in Diagram 1.

5. Sew these two blocks to the upper left corner of the first row and the lower right corner of the second row. Sew one **B** to the lower right corner of the first row and the upper left corner of the second row. Press seams open.

6. Sew the two rows together, matching seams at intersections. Press seams open.

7. Trim the top and bottom edges for a finished size of 18 × 18 inches (Diagram 2).

FLOWER
BASKET
MEDALLION

FLOWER BASKET MEDALLION

Most quilts have only one decorative border—if they have any at all. This one, which was inspired by a quilt by Jane Noble, is based on the idea that you can make a centerpiece and build out around it, using as many borders as you like.

The other important feature in this quilt is a printed flower basket medallion. It seems that medallions and other printed motifs are now being re-introduced in celebration of the fabrics of earlier days. When I come across exciting new prints, I try to take advantage of any special features they may have and incorporate them into designs that show them off.

This medallion, and another just like it, were pre-printed on a one-yard panel for use as the front and back of a pillow. On the same panel were two sides of a standing flower basket that could be cut out, sewn together, and stuffed. I used one of the medallions for a pillow, substituting a coerdinating fabric for the back, and used the other as the centerpiece for a quilt. I followed the directions, also printed on the panel, to assemble the standing basket. The result is the group you'll find on pages 81 and 84.

If you don't want to use a medallion, or if none are readily available, you can use one of your favorite fabrics cut from piece **A**. You could, in fact, substitute the entire center section (pieces **A** through **G**) with any 20-inch square that's pieced, cross-stitched, or appliquéd.

Fabrics change from season to season, so don't let it throw you if you discover that the one you've had your heart set on is no longer available. Remember that the nice thing about making quilts is that you can always find another way to interpret a design, and the changes you make could produce a design that's more interesting than the original.

Although this design appears to be complex, the centerpiece and the borders, if considered separately, are not difficult to construct. The instructions for the central medallion and the borders are broken down into separate sections to make them easier to follow. You may wish to substitute a border, or subtract one, as I did, from the design that inspired me, or add a few more. Investigating the possibilities is what I enjoy most about designing quilts.

The finished quilt is a 58-inch square.

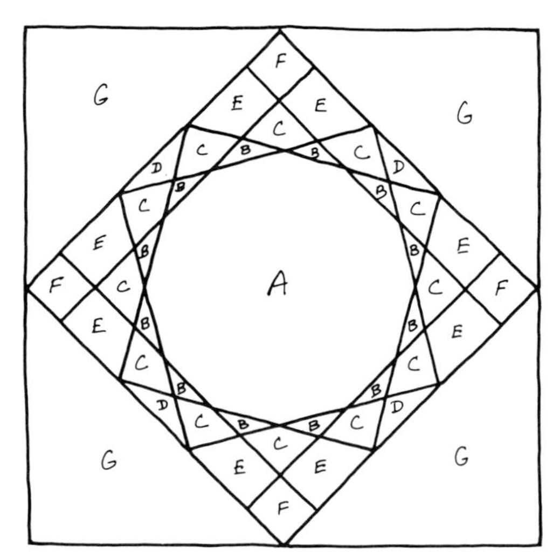

Piecing Diagram

MATERIALS

Fabric

For the top, including borders, I used approximately 2 yards of white fabric, 3 yards of blue, 1 yard of green, ½ yard of pink, and ½ yard of yellow fabric. Please feel free to substitute colors of your own choice.

Medallion

Pattern piece	Number of pieces
A*	1 (medallion)
B	12 pink
C	12 blue
D	4 yellow
E**	8 yellow
F	4 green
G†	4 white

* Cut **A** from fabric folded into quarters.

** Cut the **E** pieces from fabric folded with right sides facing so that half of them face one direction and half face the opposite direction.

† For **G**, cut two 10½-inch squares and fold and cut them in half along the diagonal.

Border A

H	4 white
I††	80 (28 yellow, 24 blue, 28 green)
J	8 blue

†† Cut the **I** pieces from fabric folded with right sides facing so that half of them face in the opposite direction.

Border B

Four green strips, each 1¾ × 29 inches

Border C

J	128 white
K	32 pink
L	56 blue
M	16 blue

Border D

Four green strips, each 2¼ × 40½ inches

Border E

J	272 (136 blue, 136 white)
L	8 green
N	44 (20 blue, 24 yellow)
O	36 (20 blue, 16 green)
P	8 green
Q	8 blue

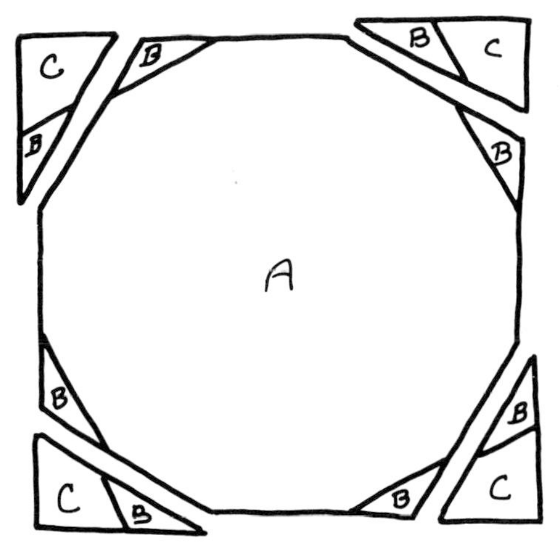

Diagram 1. Sew a **B** to every third side (i.e., skip two sides). Sew one **B** to the right side of four **C** pieces.

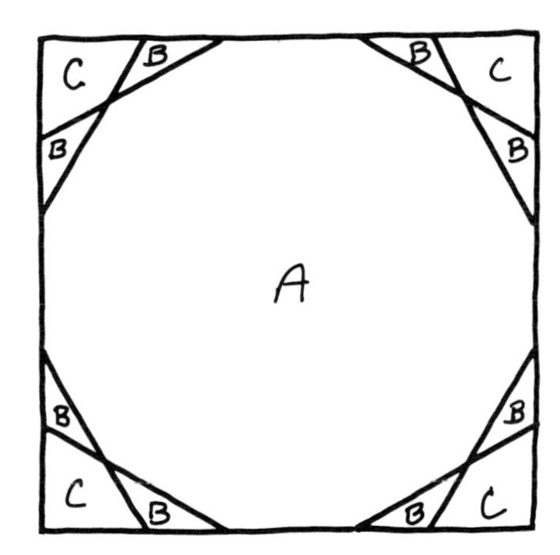

Diagram 2. Sew the **B-C** units to the right and left sides of the first **B** pieces to make a square.

Border F
Four blue strips, each 2½ × 56 inches

Other Materials

Polyester batting

6 yards of 3-inch blue bias binding

3 yards of fabric for the back

SEWING INSTRUCTIONS

Medallion

1. Skipping two sides, sew one **B** to every third side on **A**. Sew one **B** to the top right side of four **C** pieces (Diagram 1). Press seams open.

2. To create a square, sew the **B-C** units to one side of the four **B** pieces sewn to **A**, matching seams at intersections (Diagram 2). Press seams open.

3. Sew one **C** to the diagonal end of each **E**. Four **E** pieces will face in one direction; the other four will face in the other direction (Diagram 3). Press seams open.

4. Sew one **D** to the right end of the four **C-E** units that point to the right and one **B** to the four **C-E** units that point to the left (Diagram 3). Press seams open.

5. Sew the right-facing **C-D-E** unit to the left-facing **B-C-E** units, matching seams at intersections. Press seams open. This will create four strips for each side of the center square.

6. Sew one of these strips to the right and one to the left side of the center square, matching seams at intersections. Press seams open.

7. Sew one **F** to each end of the two remaining strips (Diagram 4). Press seams open. To finish the medallion, sew these strips to the top and bottom of the center square. Press seams open.

8. Sew one **G** to the right and one to the left side of the medallion. Press seams open. Sew one **G** to the top and one to the bottom of the medallion. Press seams open. (See page 83 for **G** dimensions.)

Border A

9. Note that the position of colors changes in opposite borders. Sew two green **I** pieces to the top right and top left sides of two **H** pieces, pressing seams open after each step. Sew two yellow **I** pieces to the top right and left sides of the two remaining **H** pieces in the same way (Diagram 5).

10. Add another **I** to each bottom side of the **H** pieces (blue **I** pieces on two borders and green **I** pieces on the other two borders). Press seams open.

11. Continue to add **I** pieces, alternating the colors until each half of the four borders has ten **I** pieces (Diagram 5). Sew one blue **J** to the bottom end of each border. Press seams open after each step.

Make Four   Make Four

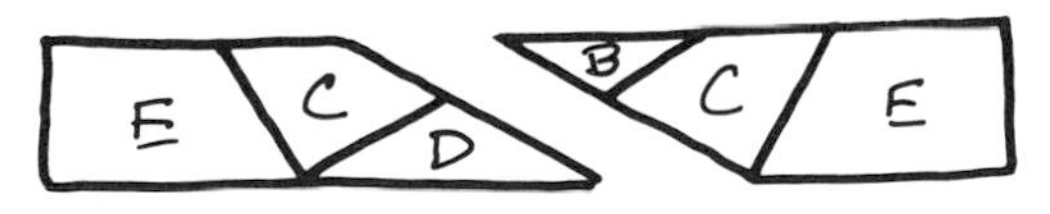

Diagram 3. Sew one **C** to the diagonal end of each **E**. Sew a **D** to the right end of four **E-C** units and one **B** to the left end of the other four units.

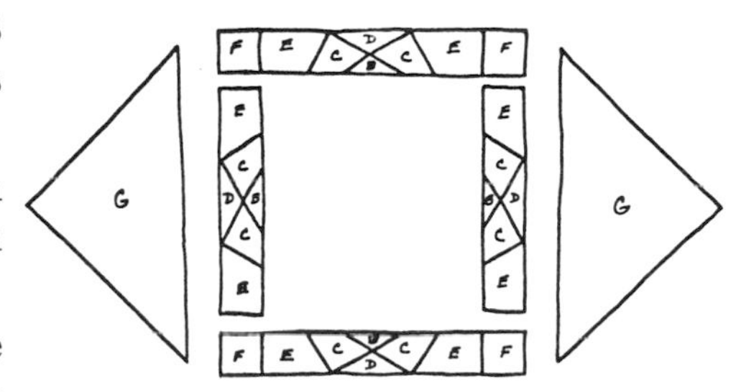

Diagram 4. Sew one **F** to each end of two **B-C-D-E** strips.

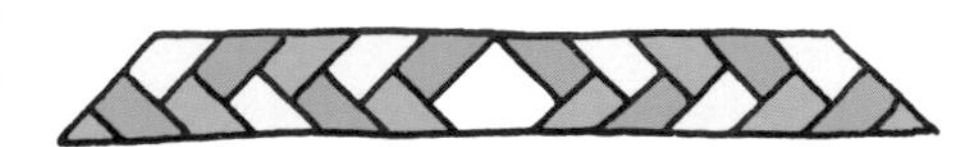

Make Two

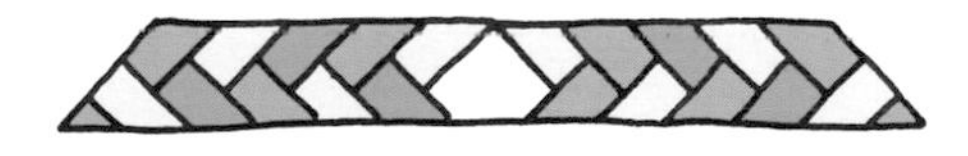

Make Two

Diagram 5. Sew two **I** pieces to the top and bottom of **H** pieces.

Diagram 6. Fold top ends of border over and crease.

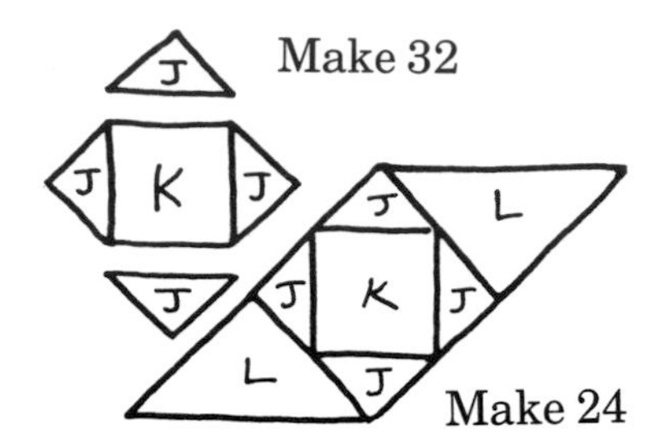

Diagram 7. Sew one **J** to each side of each **K**. Sew one **L** to the upper right and another **L** to the lower left side of twenty-four **J-K** units.

Border C: Make Two

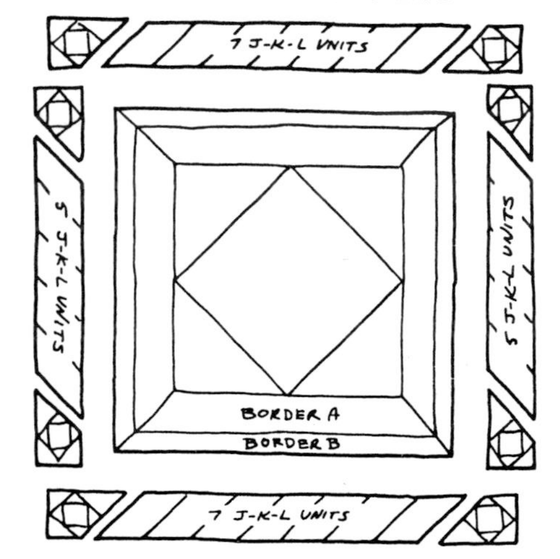

Diagram 8. Assembly and placement of eight end sections for Border C Piecing Diagram.

End Section Make Eight

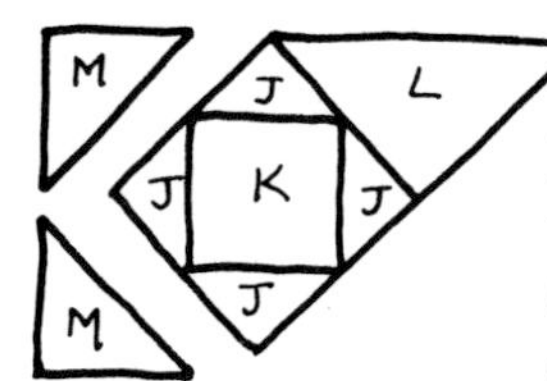

Diagram 9. Sew one **L** to the top right side of eight **J-K** units. Sew one **M** to the top and bottom sides opposite **L**.

12. Sew one Border A to each side of the quilt top, stopping ¼ inch from the corners. Press seams open or toward center square. Sew the diagonal ends together at each corner, matching seams at intersections. Press seams open.

Border B

13. To miter corners, mark the ends of the strips by folding down the top corners and creasing the folds (Diagram 6). Trim the corners, cutting along the fold line. Press seams open.

14. Sew a 1¾ × 29-inch strip to each side of the quilt top, stopping ¼ inch from the corners. Sew the diagonal ends together at each corner. Press seams open or toward Border B.

Border C

15. Sew one **J** to the right and one **J** to the left side of each **K**. Press seams open. Sew one **J** to the top and one **J** to the bottom of each **K** (Diagram 7). Press seams open.

16. Sew one **L** to the top right and one **L** to the bottom left of twenty-four of the **J-K** units just completed.

17. Each border will need two end sections (Diagram 8). To make eight end sections, sew *one* **L** to the top right of the eight remaining **J-K** units (Diagram 9). Press seams open.

18. Sew one **M** to the top and bottom of the sides opposite the **L** in all eight **J-K-L** units just completed, pressing seams open after each step (Diagram 9).

19. Sew five **J-K-L** units together in a row. Repeat for a second row of five units. Sew seven of the twenty-four **J-K-L** units together in a row. Repeat for a second row of seven units. Sew an end section to both ends of each row (Diagram 10). Press seams open.

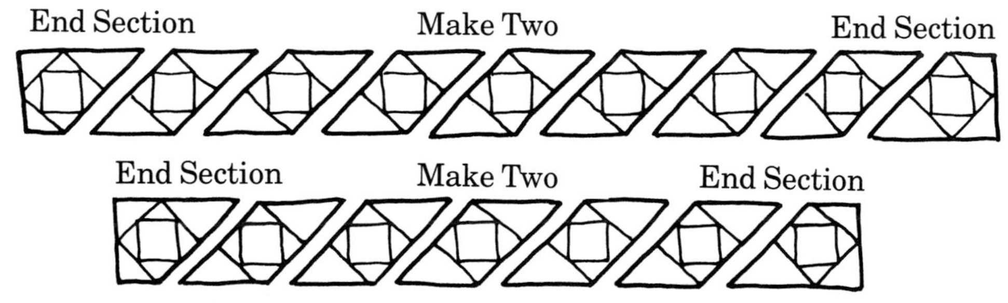

Diagram 10. Sew together seven **J-K-L** units and two end sections. Sew together five **J-K-L** units and two end sections.

Piecing Diagram: Border E

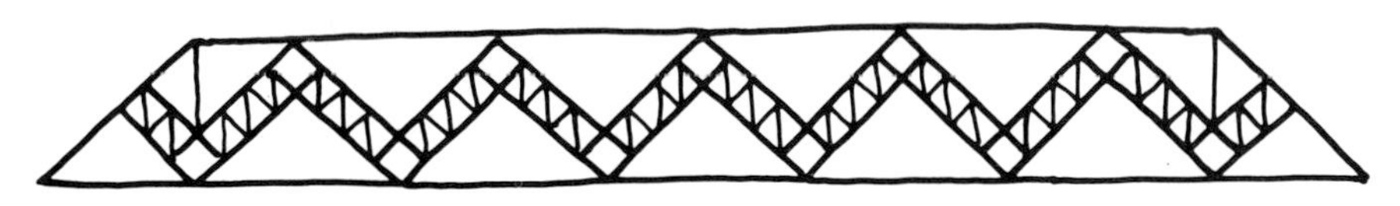

Make Four

20. Sew one Border C with seven diamond units to the right and one to the left side of the quilt top (Diagram 11). Press seams open. Matching seams at intersections, sew one Border C with nine diamond sections to the top and bottom of the quilt top. Press seams open.

Border D

21. Using the 2¼ × 40½-inch strips, miter the corners and sew the strips to the sides of the quilt top in the manner described for Border B. Press seams toward Border D.

Border E

22. Sew one white **J** to one blue **J** along the diagonal to make a square. Continue in this manner until all the **J** pieces are used. Press seams open.

23. With the blue triangles pointing to the left, sew three squares together in a row. Repeat for twenty rows. With the blue triangles pointing to the right, sew three squares together in a row. Repeat for twenty rows (Diagram 12). Press seams open. There will be sixteen squares left over.

24. Sew a yellow **N** to the bottom of twenty rows of squares, with the blue triangles pointing to the left (Diagram 12). Sew a blue **N** to the top end of each of the twenty rows of squares, with the blue triangles pointing to the right (Diagram 12). Press seams open. There will be four yellow **N** pieces left over.

25. Sew the remaining squares together in eight rows of two squares: four rows with the blue triangles pointing to the left and four rows with the blue triangles pointing to the right. Sew a yellow **N** to the bottom of each of the four rows of two squares, with the blue triangles pointing to the left (Diagram 12). Press seams open. There will be four rows left over.

26. With the yellow **N** on the lower right, sew a row of three squares to the right side of the twenty dark **O** pieces (check the position of the **O** pieces in Diagram 13). With the dark **N** on the upper right, sew a row of squares to the right side of the sixteen green **O** pieces. Four rows of squares will be left over. Press seams toward **O**.

27. Sew a blue **J-N-O** unit to the left side of a green **J-N-O** unit, matching seams at intersections. Press seams toward **O**. Sew a blue **J-N-O** unit to the right side of the section just completed. Press seams open. Proceed in this manner until you have a row with nine **J-N-O** units (Diagram 14). Repeat for four rows.

Diagram 11. Sew one Border C with seven diamond units to the right and left sides of quilt top. Sew one Border C with nine diamond units to the top and bottom.

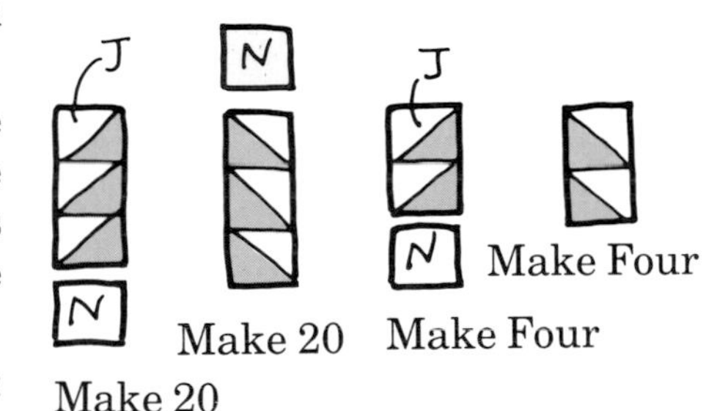

Diagram 12. Sew pieced squares together in rows.

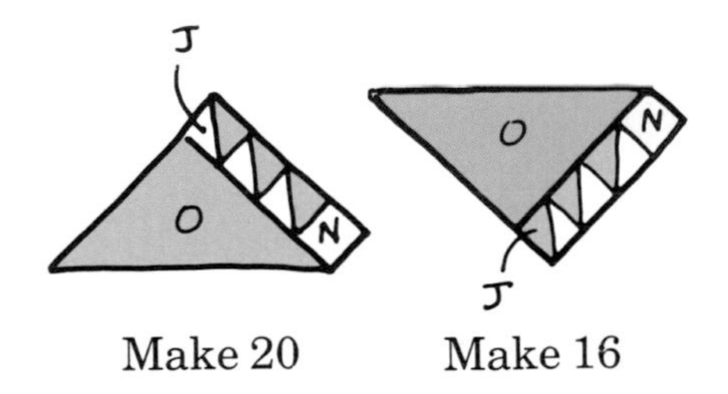

Diagram 13. Sew one row of squares to one side of each **O**.

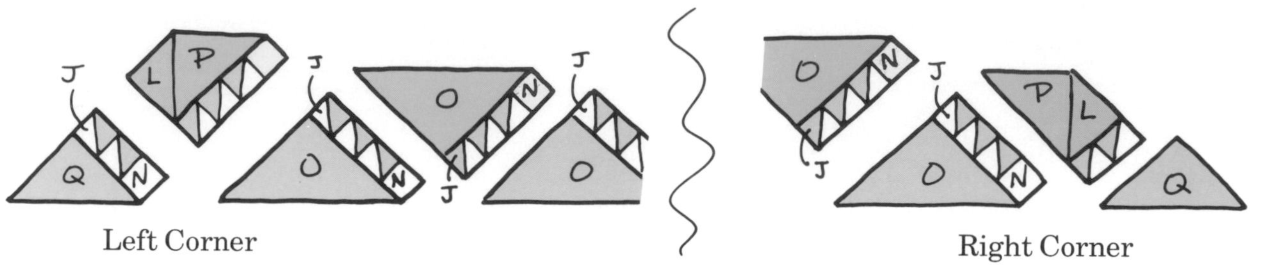

Diagram 14. Sew together five blue and four green **J-N-O** units.

28. To make the corner units, sew one **L** to the left side of four **P** pieces. Sew one **L** to the right side of four **P** pieces (Diagram 14). Press seams open.

29. Sew the rows of two squares with the yellow **N** pieces made in Step 25 to the right sides of four **Q** pieces (left corner of Diagram 14). With the blue **N** on the upper right, sew four rows of squares left over in Step 26 to the diagonal side of **P** in four **L-P** units. See the left corner of Diagram 14. Sew the remaining four rows of two squares left over in Step 25 to the lower right side of **L** in the four remaining **L-P** units (right corner of Diagram 14). Press seams away from squares.

30. For the left corner, sew the **Q** unit to the **L-P** unit. Press toward **L**. Sew this section to the left end of the border. Repeat for four borders.

31. For the right corner, sew the **L-P** unit to the right end of the border. Press seam toward **P**. Sew the remaining **Q** pieces to the right end of each border. Press seams toward **Q**.

32. Sew the borders to each side of the quilt top, stopping ¼ inch from the corners. Press seams away from Border E. Matching seams at intersections, sew the diagonal sides together at each corner. Press seams open.

Border F

33. Using the 2½ × 56-inch strips, miter the corners and sew the strips to each side of the quilt in the manner described for Border B. Press seams toward Border F.

Assembly

34. Cut the 3-yard length of fabric for the back in half across the width. Trim selvages. Sew the two pieces together along their long sides and press seams open.

35. Place the back right side down on the floor. Center the batting and the quilt top, right side up, on top. Baste all layers together. Trim the batting and back to within 1 inch of the quilt top. For further instructions in assembling the quilt top, batting, and back, see pages 14 and 15.

36. After the quilting is finished, the binding can be added. For a 1-inch finished binding, sew the 3-inch bias strip around the edge of the quilt top using a ½-inch seam allowance.

FLOWER
BASKET
MEDALLION

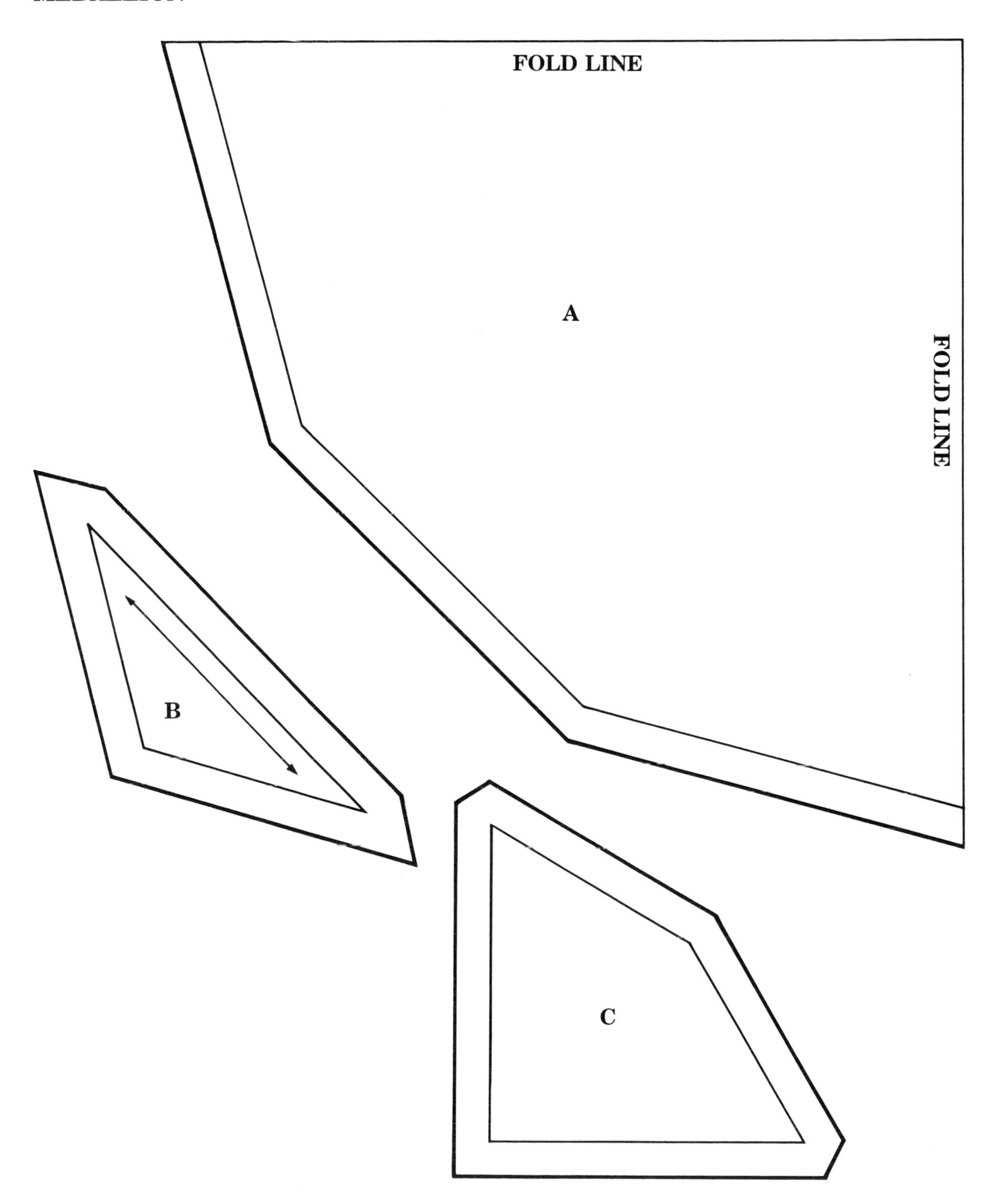

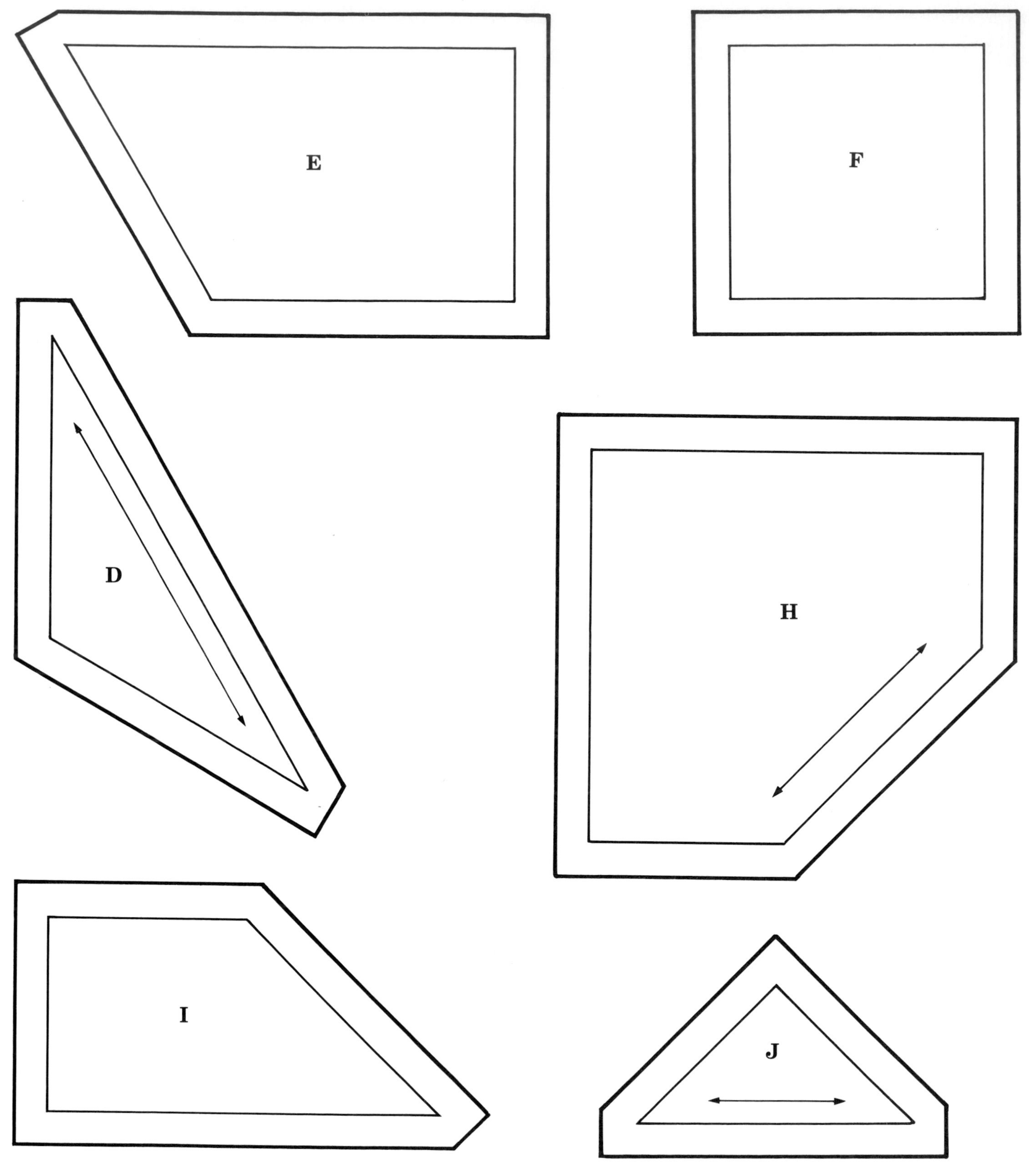
E
F
D
H
I
J

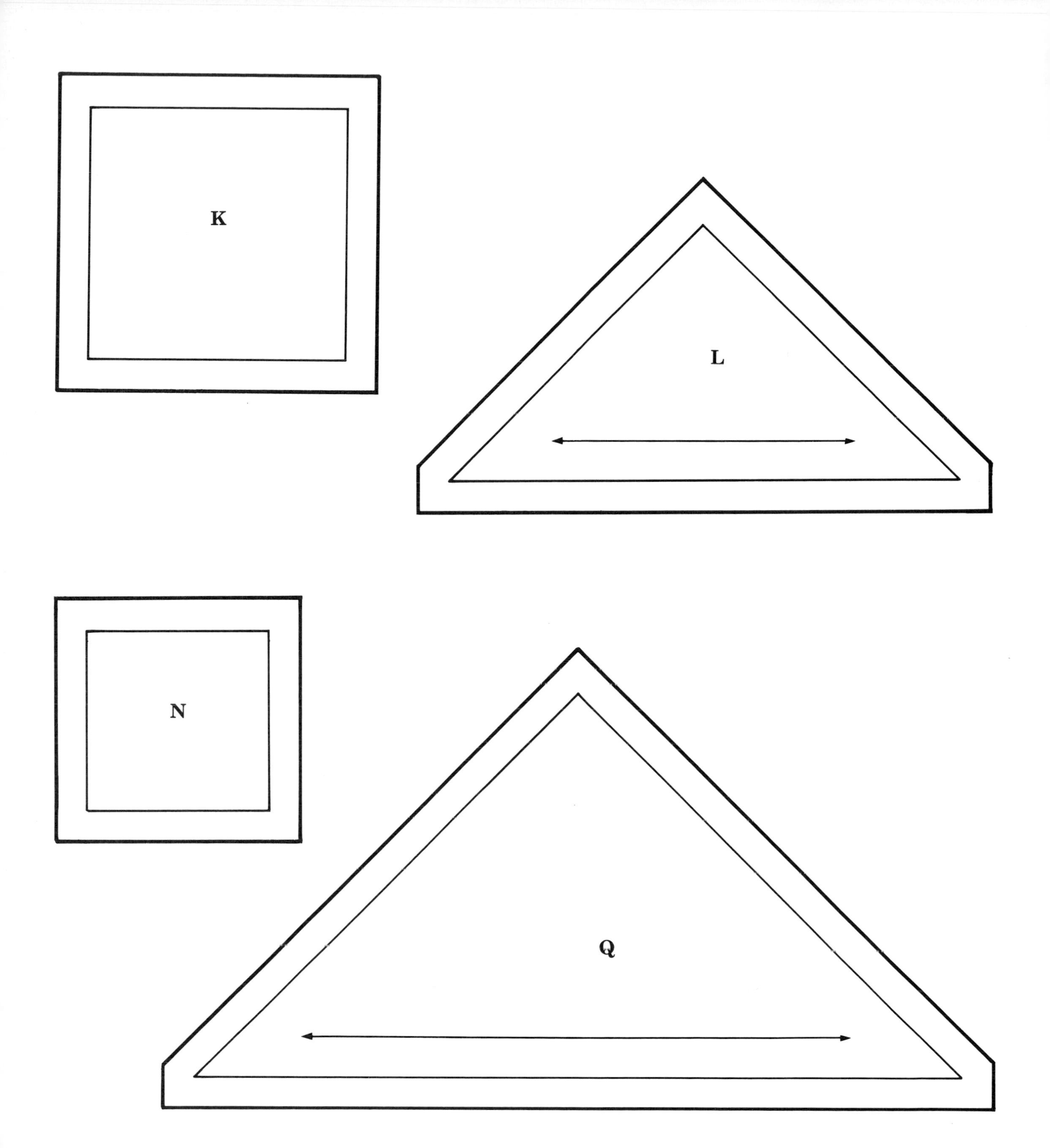
K
L
N
Q

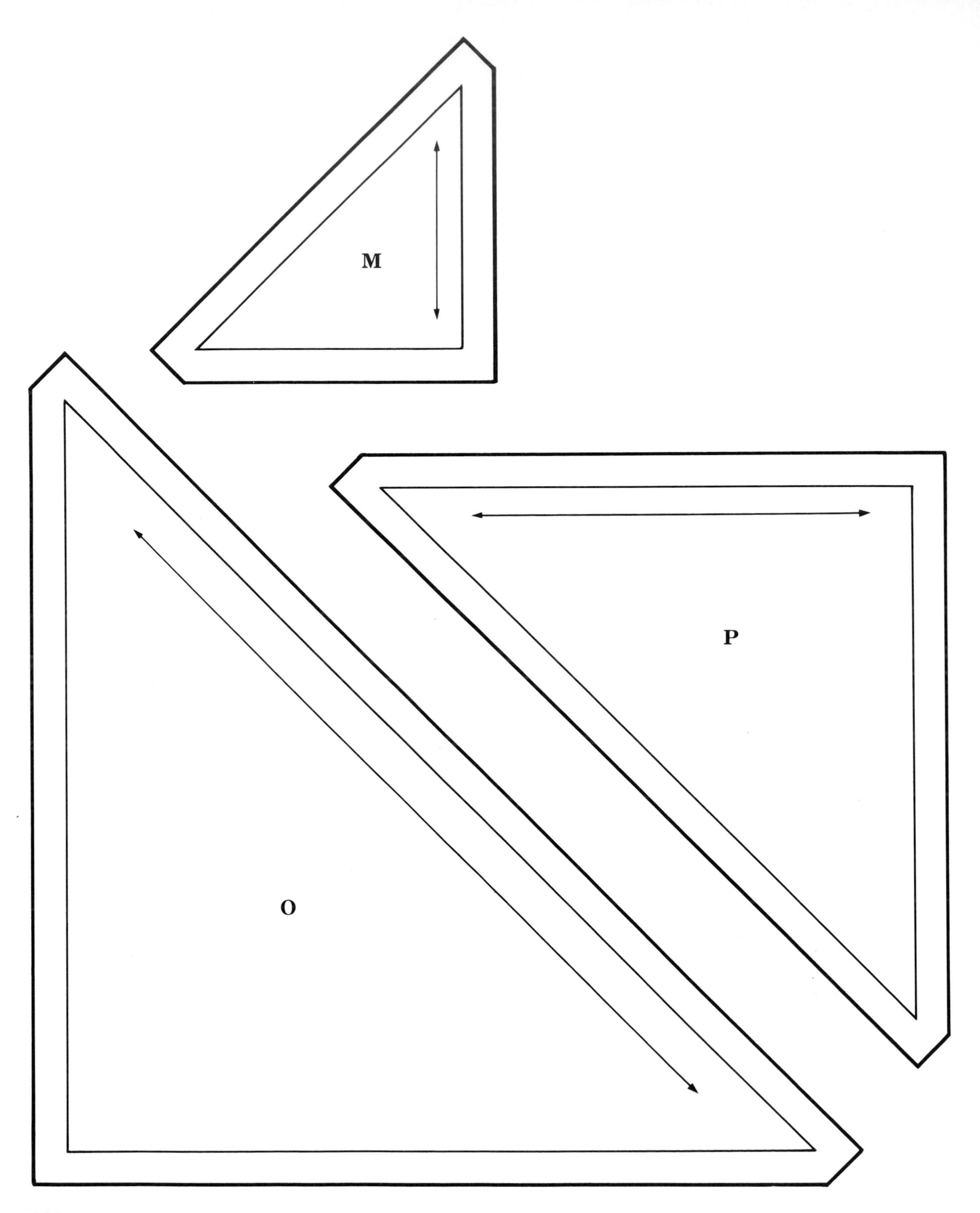
M
P
O

HARVEST APPLIQUÉ

Even though I've been quilting for almost eighteen years, there are some quilts I still regard with awe. I have always believed that certain skills belonging to another century are simply off limits. One example of such an awe-inspiring stitchery is the mid-nineteenth century Baltimore Album quilt, which is probably more highly prized by collectors, curators, and antiques dealers than any other quilt.

But times are changing, and so am I. Today's quilters are turning out work that challenges the best of the past, and I'm just about ready to take on my own Baltimore Album quilt. What makes such an undertaking feasible for me now is a new technique described in an article by Anne J. Oliver in the June 1988 issue of *Quilter's Newsletter.* This technique produces appliqué with the help of freezer paper, a method that takes the intimidation out of appliqué and opens up a world of possibilities to us all. Thank you, Anne!

In the meantime, on my way to Baltimore, I've been amusing myself with a quilt that, on the one hand, is a take-off on the above-mentioned paragon of majestic stitchery and, on the other, is a natural extension of one of my favorite and most satisfying accomplishments, which made its debut in my previous book, *A Patchwork Christmas*.

I refer to a collection of three-dimensional, life-size stuffed fruits and vegetables called Food Stuffs, a basket of which you will find on page 98. They were, and still are, a big hit with me, my family, and friends, and many others from all over the country who have been using the patterns.

I enjoyed designing and making them so much that I was delighted when I was suddenly struck with the idea of making a two-dimensional version of the same thing. This new harvest of home-grown happiness is also life-size but flat, and served up in prints and calicos chosen for their similarity to real fruits and vegetables.

Most album quilts are made with flowers, leaves, birds, hearts, flags, and other more formal subject matter, such as civic buildings, landmarks,and Bibles. I think of mine as down to earth in its use of everyday digestibles — less complicated and high-minded, even funny by comparison.

It's also a bit less ambitious: because the pieces are life-size, they're often larger than many of those in the Baltimore Albums. I've arranged everything in one central wreath with corner clusters rather than in a grid formation with an extensive array of baskets, bouquets, and wreaths, each elaborately decorated with lush detail.

This is not to imply, in comparing my quilt to its predecessors, that I don't think it, too, is wonderful. It is, and I will display it with pride in our dining room during Thanksgiving festivities. My point is that the design was born out of a dual interest in the Baltimore Album quilt and in transferring my funny friends to a flat surface.

Making a quilt is not the only way in which these fruits and vegetables can be used. They can dress up your kitchen and dining room on napkins, place mats, kitchen towels, potholders, tea cozies, toaster and blender covers, aprons, and even a sweatshirt. You could arrange a wreath in the center of a tablecloth and put your finest holiday centerpiece right in the middle of it. Some of these ideas are illustrated on page 98.

One variation on the freezer paper technique involves the use a glue stick to turn under the seam allowance and hold it in place. This works very well. The method that works best for me, however, was shown to me by my friend and colleague, Dee Danley Brown. It omits the glue stick (which means you don't have to be concerned about residue) and produces nice, clean curves without bumps, as well as sharp points on hard-to-turn corners.

It won't be necessary to do much more here than describe the basic technique. Once you cut out your pieces, you can arrange them any way you like on a background. My quilt measures 62 × 66 inches and requires 3½ yards of muslin for the front and the same for the back. Tablecloths, napkins, apron, and towel can all be store-bought.

If you haven't tried this technique before and feel a little unsure of yourself, try just one piece—a pear, for example—and you'll see how easy it is. Patterns for twenty-one designs—eggplant, Blue Moon squash, turnip, orange, pumpkin, plum, grape, pineapple, lettuce or cabbage, two gourds, cucumber, corn, carrot, banana, strawberry, butternut squash, apple, tomato, and summer squash—await your pleasure. There's also a bumble bee.

BASIC FREEZER PAPER APPLIQUÉ

MATERIALS

Fabric

Cotton solids or prints in any colors that suit the fruit and vegetables you have in mind

Other Materials

Freezer paper

Lightweight cardboard or other stable craft paper

Spray glue or rubber cement

SEWING INSTRUCTIONS

Preparation

1. Photocopy the patterns (the slight difference in size that usually results won't matter). Spray the back of the photocopy with spray mount or rubber cement. Mount the pages on oak tag, file folders, or other sturdy paper. Cut out the designs with paper scissors or X-acto knife, taking care to make smooth cuts.

Making a Test Piece

2. Place a pattern on the unshiny side of the freezer paper and trace around it. Cut out the design and place it, shiny side down, on the wrong side of the fabric, leaving enough space for a ¼-inch seam allowance all around. Press with a warm iron: the freezer paper will stick to the fabric.

3. Clip concave curves (Diagram 1). (Be sure not to clip the seam allowance except for concave curves or an inside point, such as the top of a heart, for example. Cuts in other places can cause little bumps along the edge). Place the design, freezer paper side down, on the background fabric and pin it in place.

4. Turning under the seam allowance with your needle, slipstitch the design to the background with tiny, invisible stitches (Diagram 2). Because the freezer paper gives the design stability and a firm edge to work with while turning under the seam allowance, this will go quickly.

5. For sharp points and hard-to-turn corners (such as the point of a carrot), blindstitch one side all the way to the point (Diagram 3). Trim some of the excess seam allowance off the point, leaving enough fabric to turn under (Diagram 4).

6. With your needle, turn under the seam allowance at right angles to the point (Diagram 5). Turn under the seam allowance on the other side of the carrot and continue sewing (Diagram 6).

7. After the design is sewn in place, turn the work over, make a slit, and cut away the background fabric ¼ inch from the stitching all around. Pinch the freezer paper and pull it away from the design (Diagram 7). Note: Some designs require pieces that overlap each

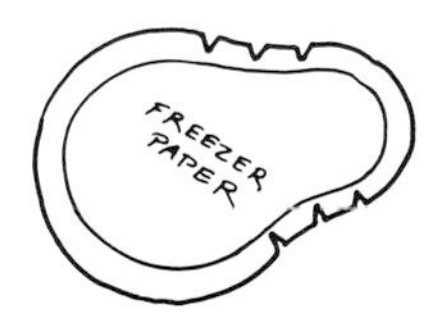

Diagram 1. Clip concave curves.

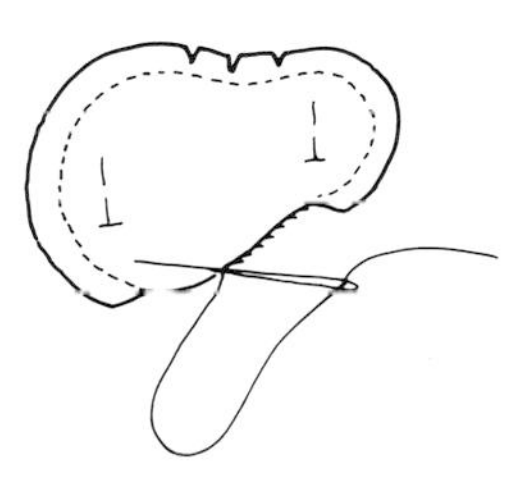

Diagram 2. Blindstitch the design to the background, turning under the seam allowance with your needle as you go.

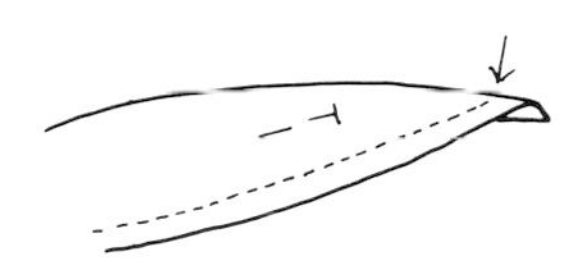

Diagram 3. Turn under the seam allowance and sew to point.

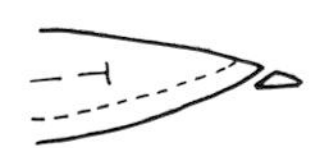

Diagram 4. Trim point.

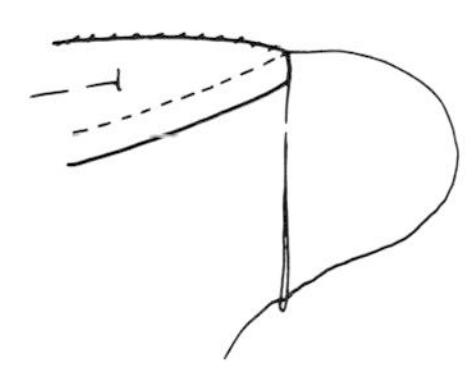

Diagram 5. Tuck point under with needle.

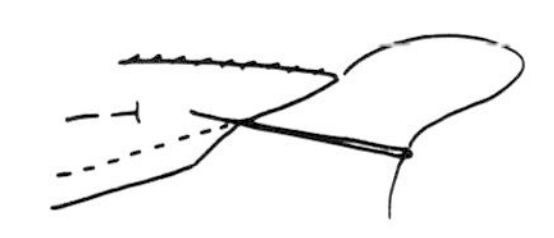

Diagram 6. Turn under seam allowance on other side and continue sewing.

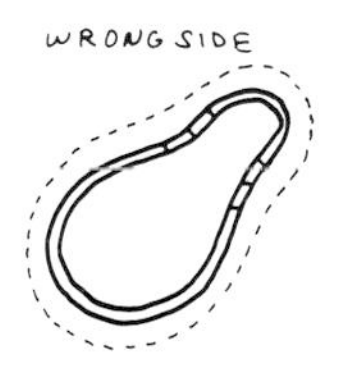

Diagram 7. Trim away background fabric within ¼ inch of stitching. Remove freezer paper.

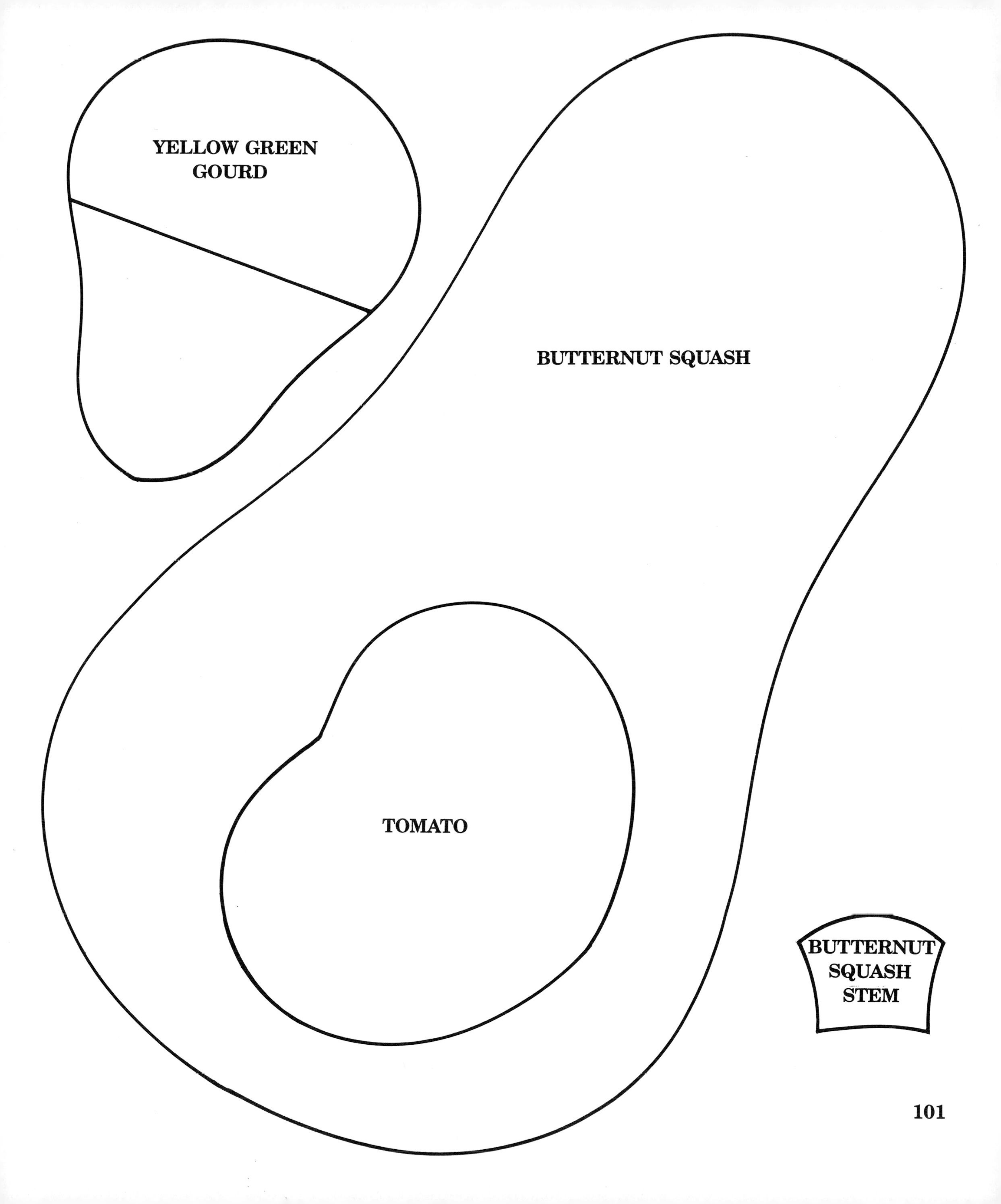
YELLOW GREEN
GOURD
BUTTERNUT SQUASH
TOMATO
BUTTERNUT
SQUASH
STEM

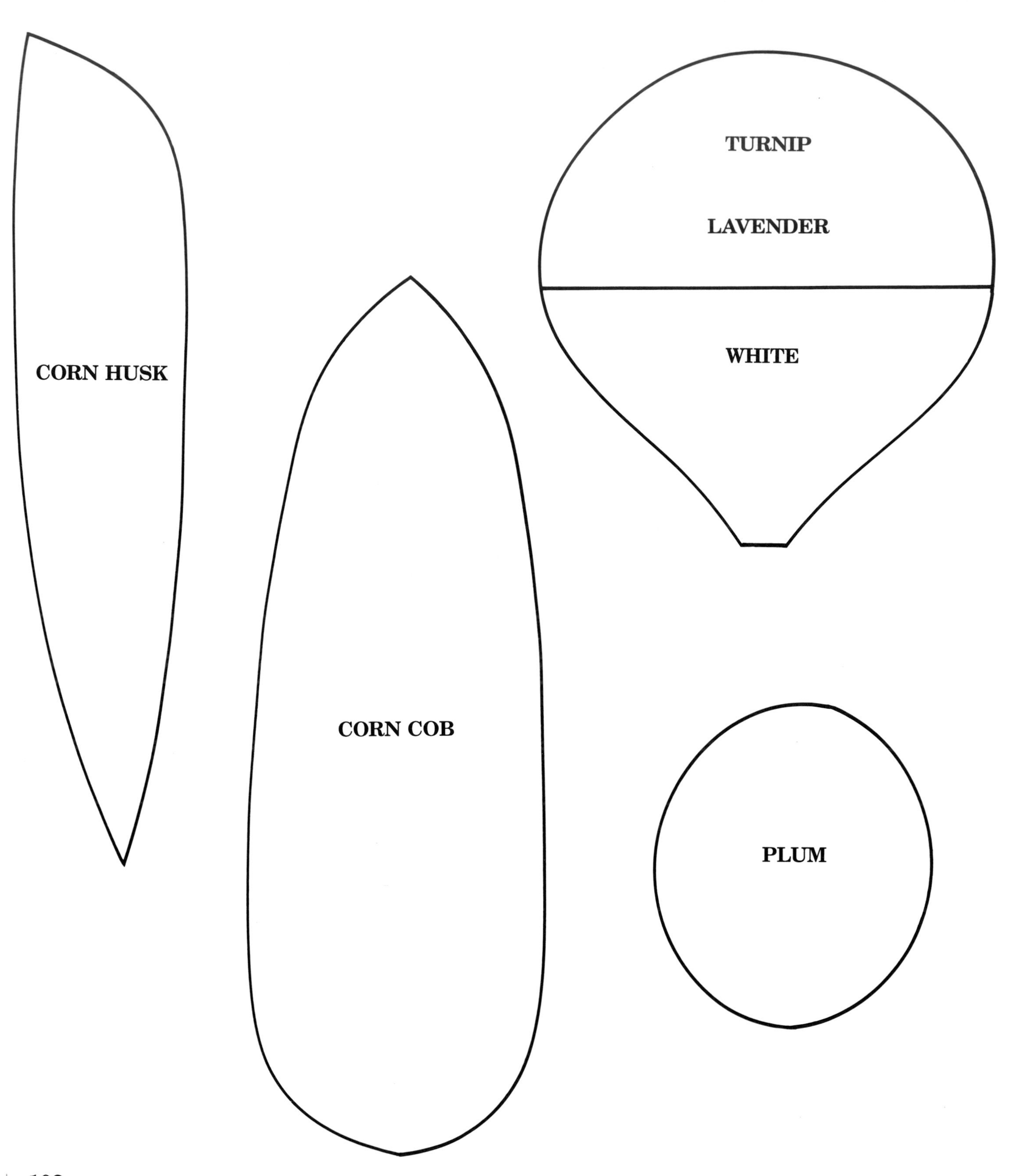
TURNIP
LAVENDER
WHITE
CORN HUSK
CORN COB
PLUM

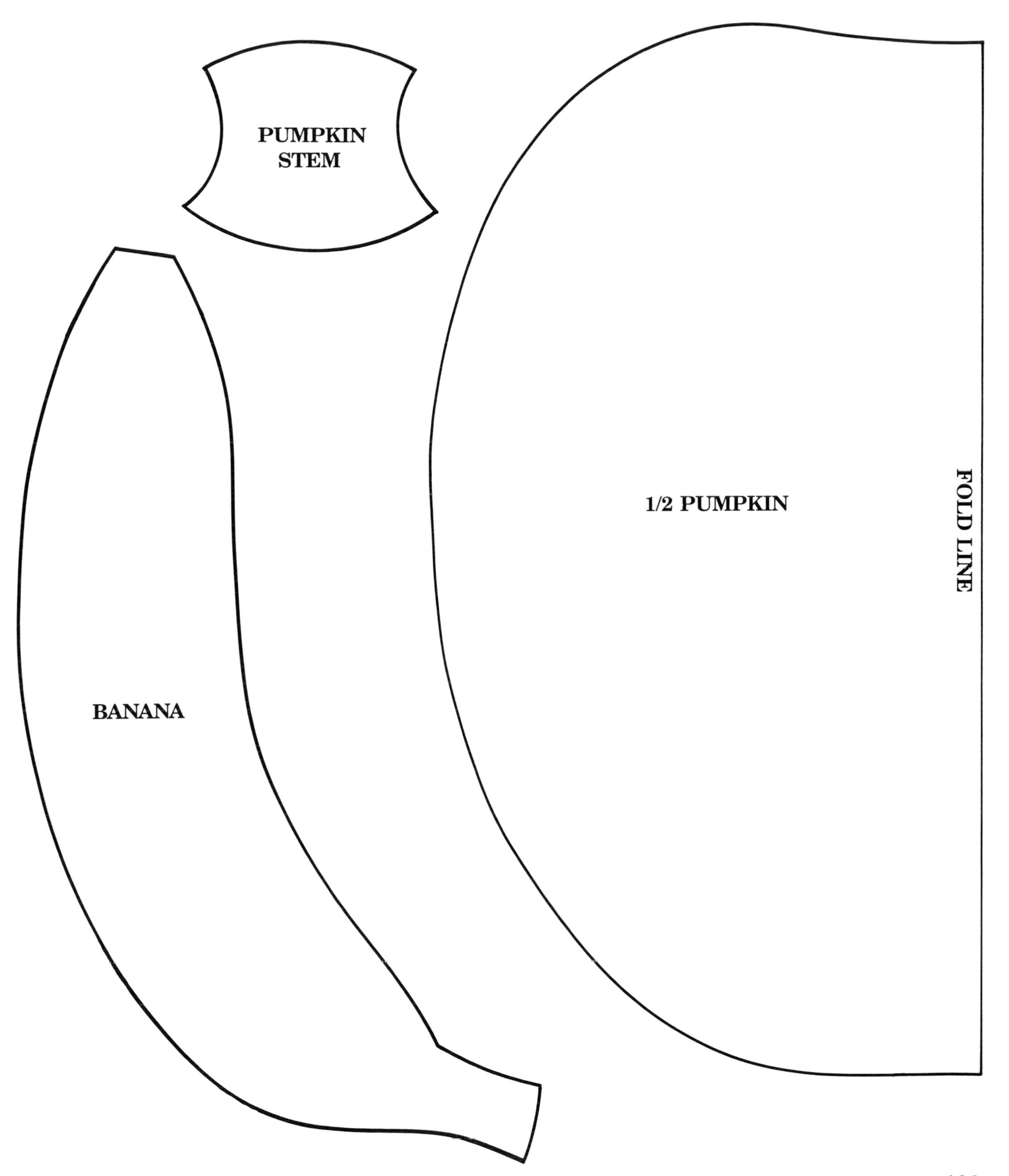
PUMPKIN
STEM
BANANA
1/2 PUMPKIN
FOLD LINE

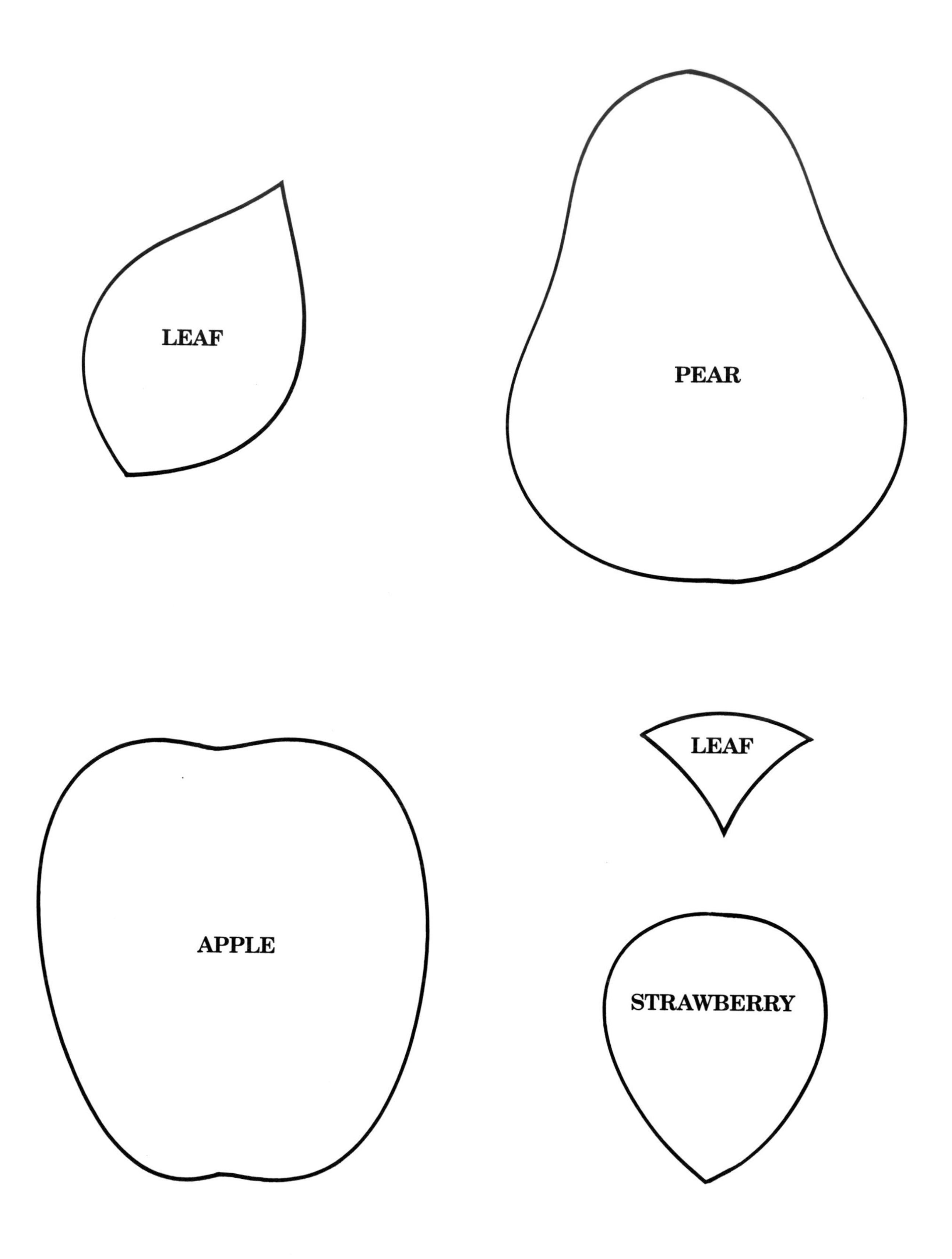
LEAF
PEAR
LEAF
APPLE
STRAWBERRY

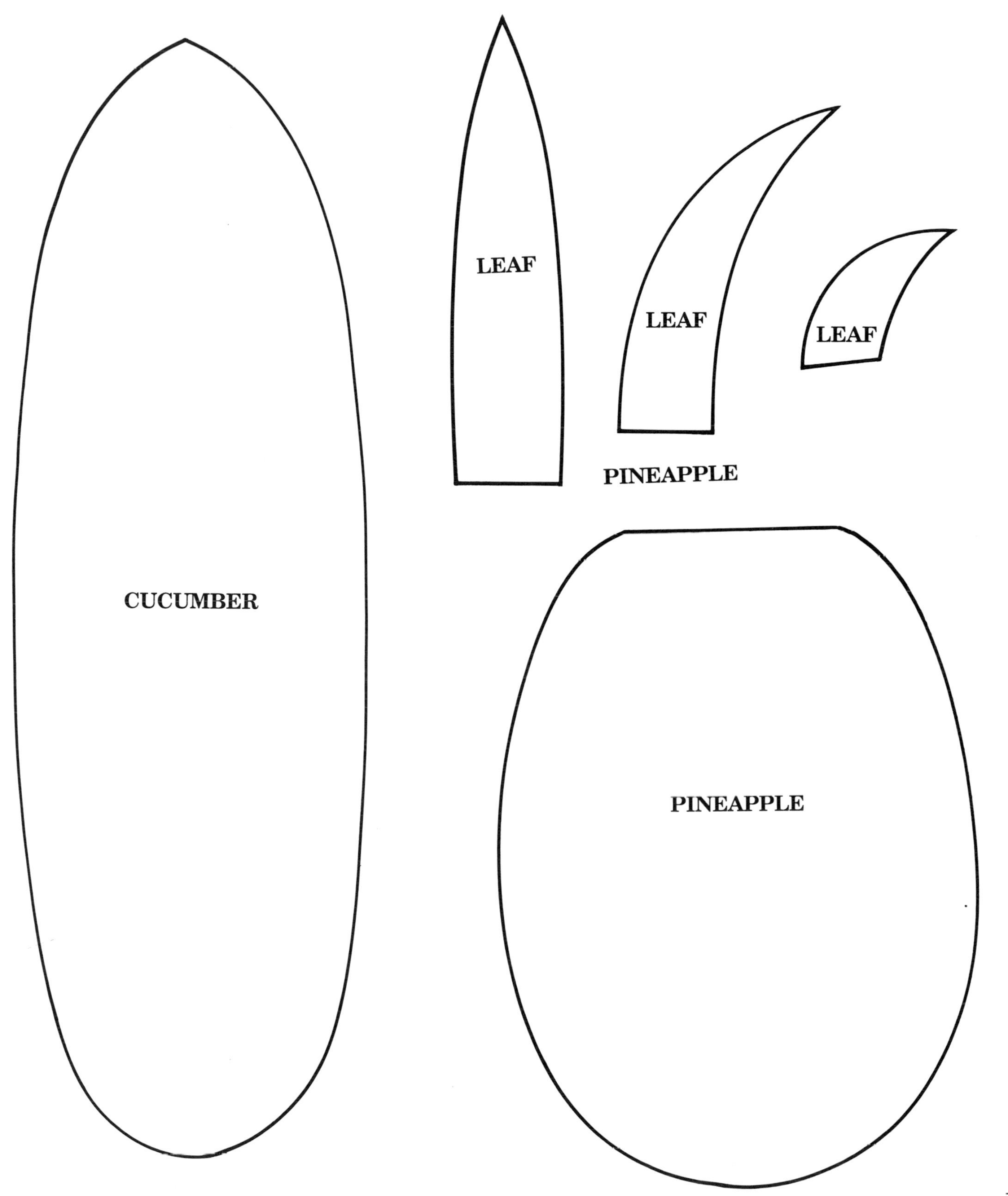
LEAF
LEAF
LEAF
PINEAPPLE
CUCUMBER
PINEAPPLE

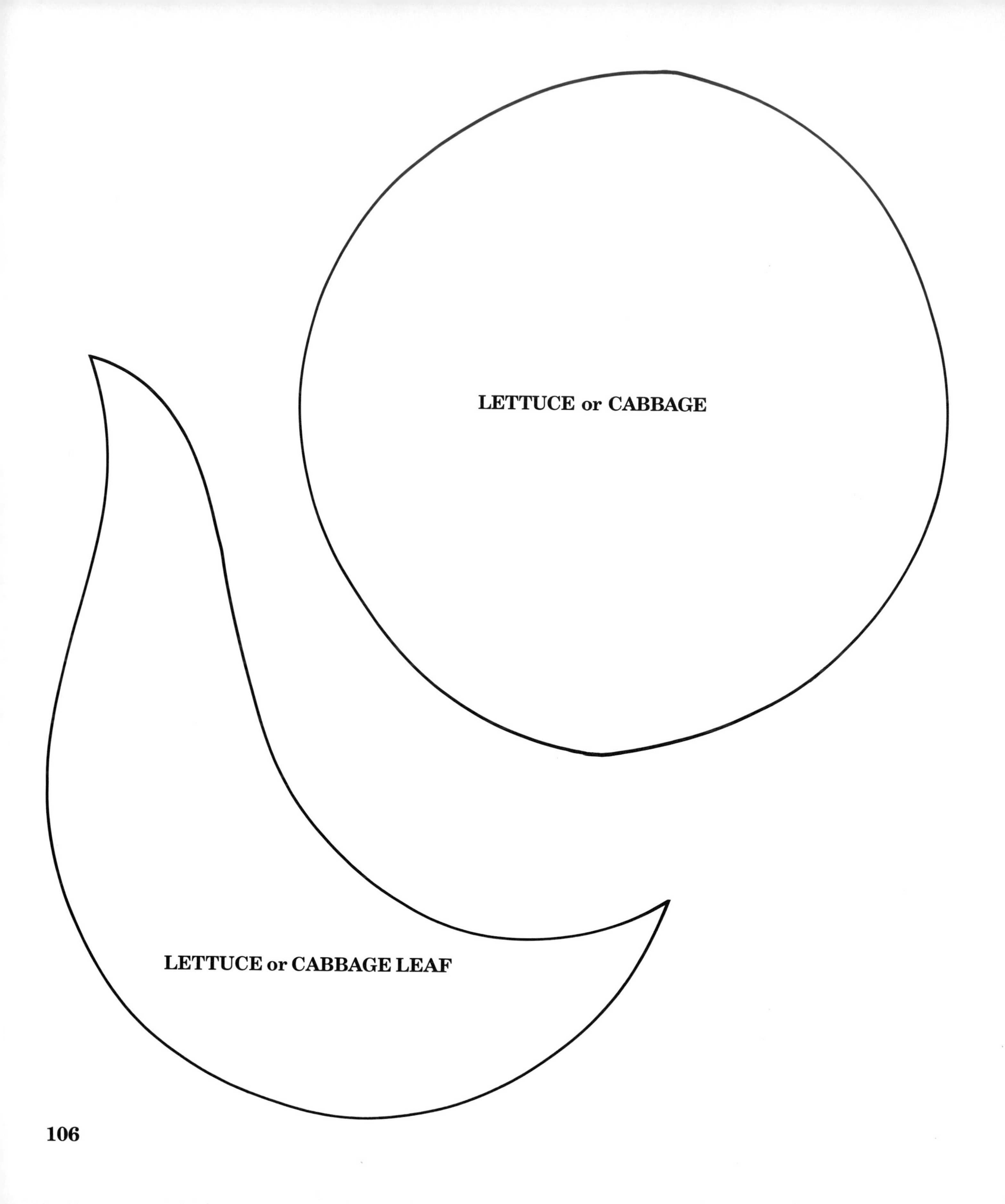
LETTUCE or CABBAGE
LETTUCE or CABBAGE LEAF

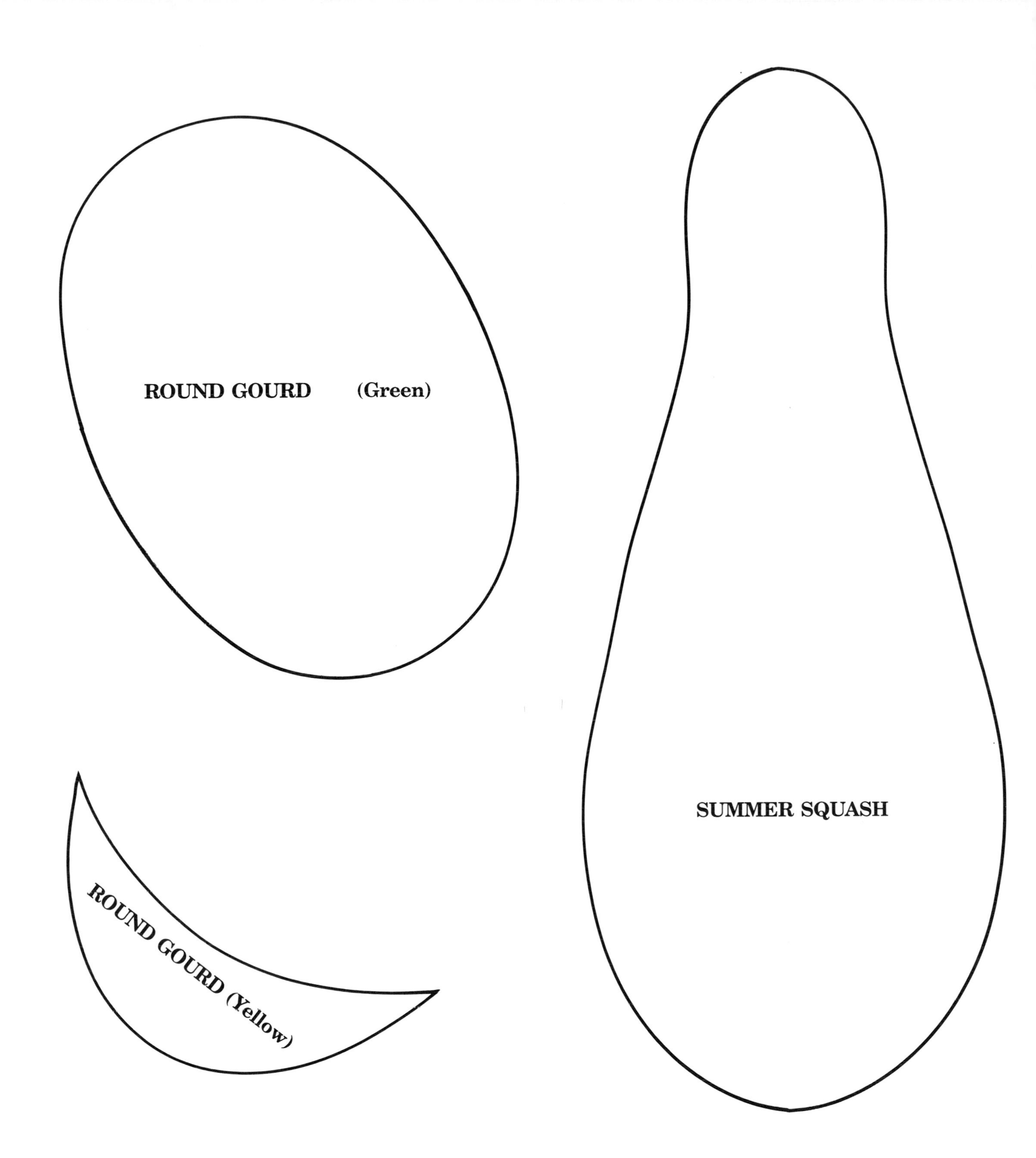
ROUND GOURD (Green)
SUMMER SQUASH
ROUND GOURD (Yellow)

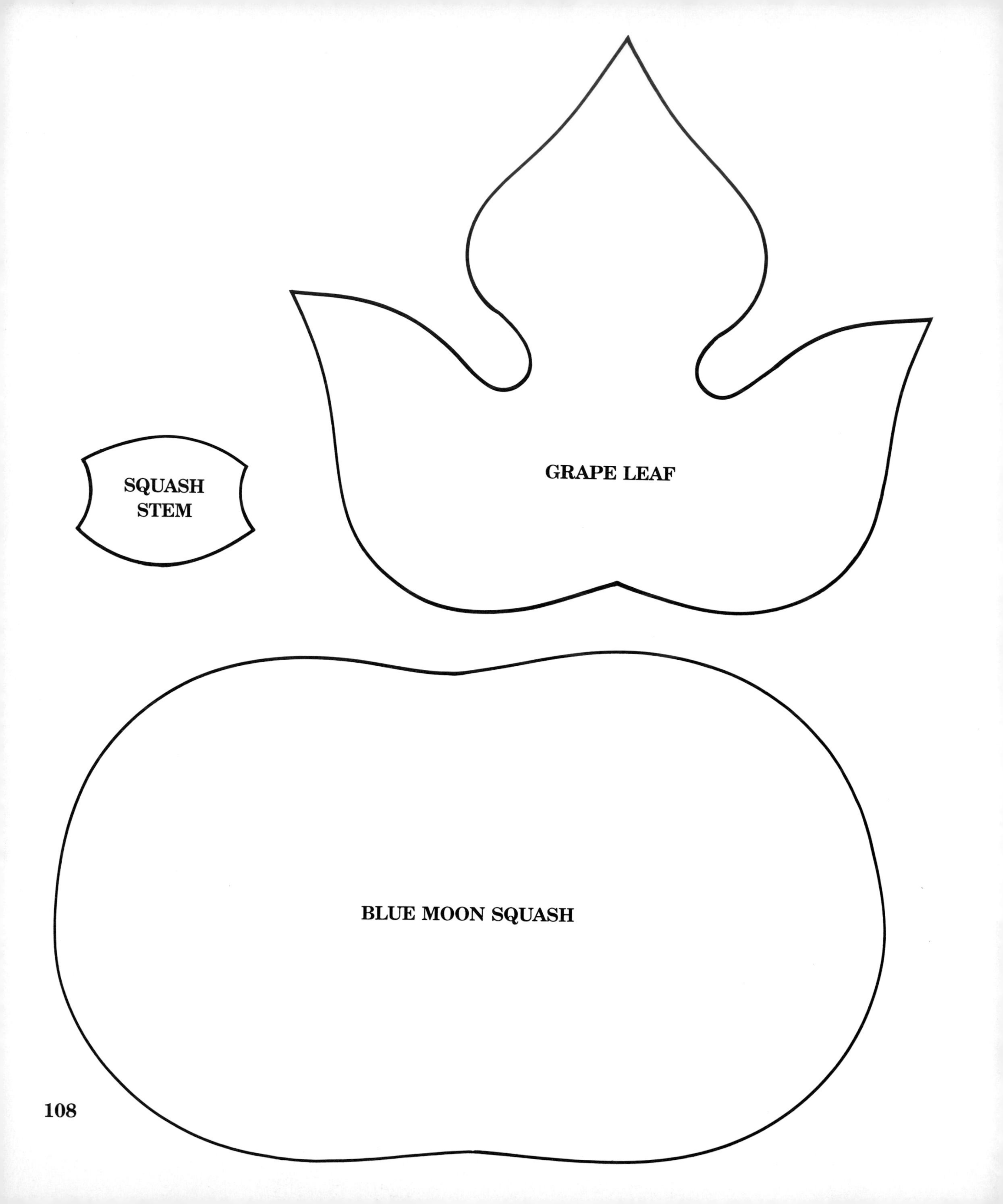
SQUASH
STEM
GRAPE LEAF
BLUE MOON SQUASH

COUNTRY
CHRISTMAS

What's on our Christmas list this year? Some new ornaments—Santa, Mrs. Santa, and their helper; a tree skirt circled in pine trees; a group of red-and-white pillows in sofa and chair sizes, and mini-versions of the same designs to use as tree ornaments—a bright and cheery group to add to your collection of hand-made Christmas treasures.

CHRISTMAS PILLOWS

These beauties are the very same pillows you'll find in the Log Cabin section. The large one is made with four Log Cabin blocks with corner-stones, and the others are the matching pillows made with the leftover strips. The difference is that they're red and white. Bet you didn't recognize the patterns! It's amazing what a change of color will do.

I love red and white, a perfect combination for the holidays. They can be made with any colors, of course, but I like the idea of a white room with touches of red.

No patterns are required for Checkerboard and Zigzag pillows. They're made with 2-inch strips, the mini-version with 1-inch strips. The following patterns are for mini-size Crossroads and Puss-in-the-Corner pillows. The instructions for making them start on page 25.

PUSS-IN-THE-CORNER

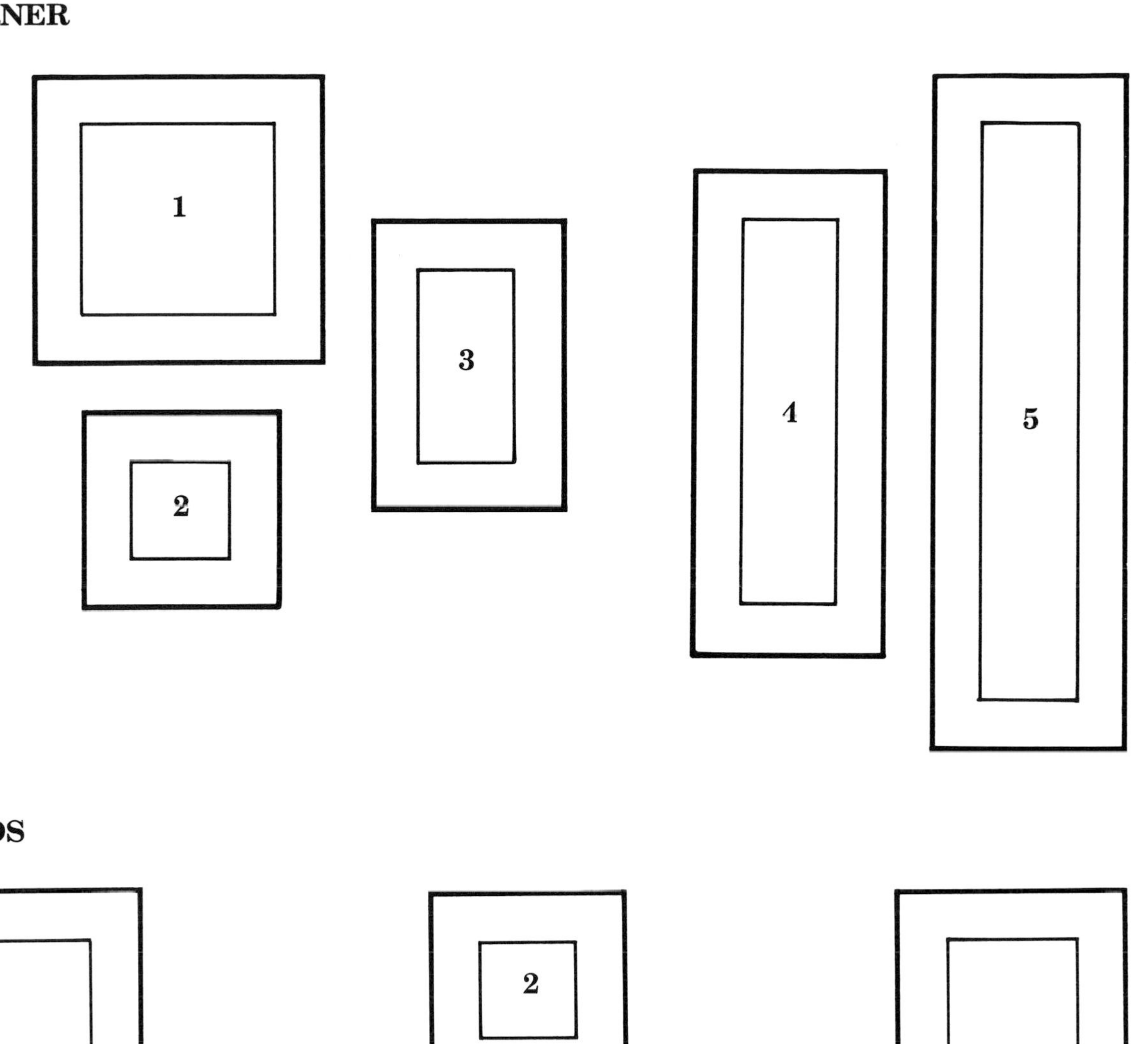

MINI CROSSROADS

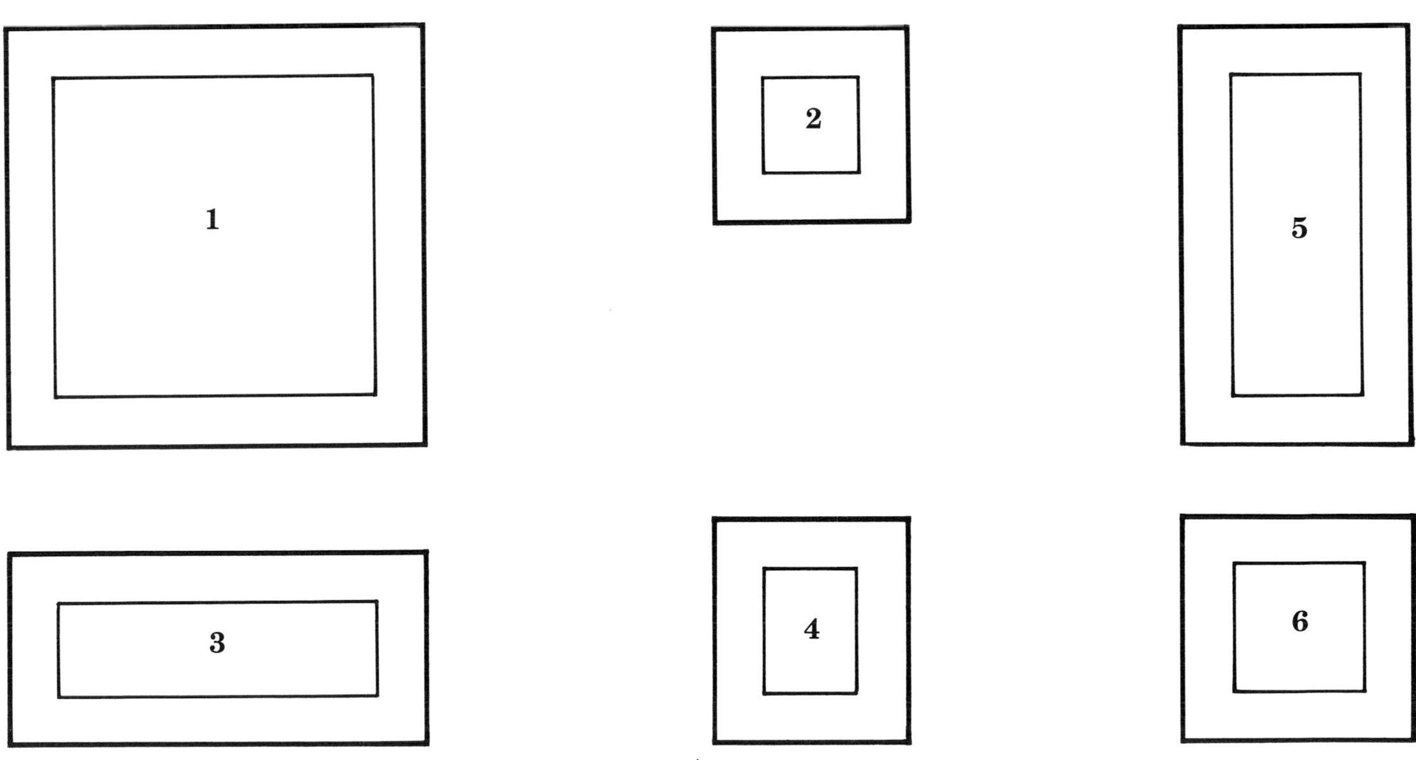

Piecing Diagram

SANTA AND MRS. SANTA

This chubby little couple will look great on your tree; they make safe toys for kids, too. Make them from scraps of red, white, and pink fabric. These ornaments may be somewhat larger than what you're accustomed to, but I find that most branches are sturdy enough to support them, and the ornaments don't get lost in the crowd.

MATERIALS

Fabric (for one Santa *or* Mrs. Santa)

Pattern piece	Number of pieces
A (head)	4 pink
B (head)	4 pink
C (body)	4 red
D (body)	4 red
E (waistband)	1 white
F (sleeve trim)	2 white
G (sleeves)	2 red
H (jacket trim)	1 white
I (skirt: Mrs. Santa)	2 red
J (skirt trim)	2 white
K (collar)	1 white
L (cap trim)	1 white
M (cap)	2 red
N (mittens)	4 white

Note: Besides the lace trim for the beard and hat, the only difference between Santa and Mrs. Santa is her skirt.

Other Materials

Polyester stuffing

Small amount of polyester quilt batting cut into ½-inch strips

Buttons for noses

White yarn for pom-poms

½ yard of ½-inch gathered white cotton eyelet lace

Hook or nylon filament for hanging

SEWING INSTRUCTIONS

To make sewing curves easier and more accurate, set a short stitch length on your sewing machine. Use normal setting for straight seams.

1. With right sides facing, sew the four **A, B, C,** and **D** pieces together in two sets of two (Diagram 1). To turn Santa right side out, leave an opening of about 1½ inches in the seam joining two of the **D** pieces (center-back). Back-stitch at both ends of the opening for strength. Trim all seams to within ⅛ inch of stitch line.

Diagram 1. Sew the **A, B, C,** and **D** pieces together in sets of two.

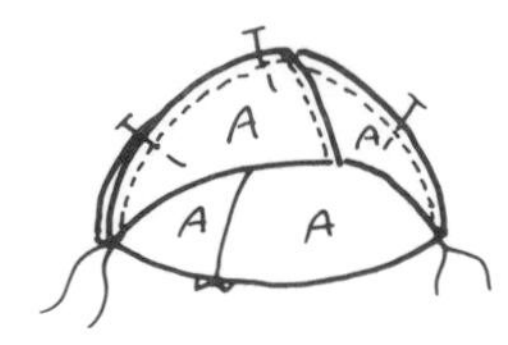

Diagram 2. Sew two **A** units together.

2. With right sides facing, sew the two **A** units together, matching seams at intersections (Diagram 2). Repeat for the two **C** units. Trim seams.

3. To prepare the trim for jacket and cap, fold **F, H, K,** and **L** in half lengthwise, and insert a piece of ½-inch polyester strip into the fold. Sew the sides of each piece together ¼ inch from the edge.

4. Lightly press the seams open on **H** and **K** so that they lie open down the center. Pin **H** in place on the right side on top of the seam line between the two **D** pieces (the **D** unit *without* the opening). Tack in place at both ends. This is the trim for the center front of the jacket.

5. Sew the **F** pieces (sleeve trim) to the **G** pieces along the bottom edge of the sleeve (Diagram 3). Lightly press seams toward sleeve.

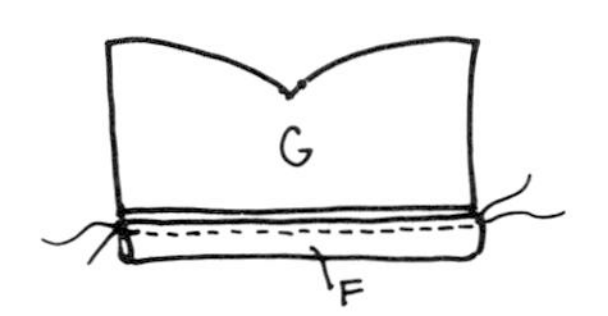

Diagram 3. Sew the sleeve trim (**F**) to the sleeve (**G**).

6. With right sides facing, fold the sleeves in half along the fold line and sew. Turn the sleeves right side out and press.

7. Sew the sleeves in place between the notches on the jacket front ⅛ inch from the edge (Diagram 4).

8. Sew both ends of **E** (waistband) together. Press seam open. With right side out, fold in half and insert a ½-inch strip of batting into the fold. Sew the sides together ⅛ inch from the edge.

9. With right sides together, pin and sew the waistband to the bottom half of the body (the four **C** pieces) ⅛ inch from the edge.

10. For Mrs. Santa's skirt, sew the two **I** pieces together end to end. Sew the two **J** pieces together in the same way. Press seams open.

11. Sew **I** and **J** together along their long sides. Press seam toward **J**. Fold **J** over ½ inch to the wrong side and fold edge under ¼ inch. Hemstitch by hand.

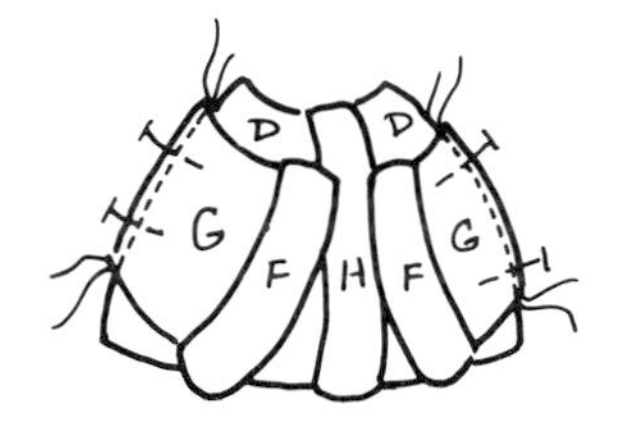

Diagram 4. Sew the sleeves in place on the jacket front between the notches.

12. Using a long stitch, sew two rows of stitching along the top edge of the skirt. Pull the threads to gather. Using a normal stitch length, sew the skirt to the bottom half of the body (the **C** unit pieces). Attach the waistband and proceed as for Santa.

13. With right sides facing, sew a **B** unit to a **D** unit around the concave curve of the neckline, matching seams at intersections (Diagram 5). Repeat for the other **B** and **D** units. Trim seams.

14. With right sides facing, pin and sew both **B-D** units together along one side, matching the notches (with sleeves) and the seams at intersections (Diagram 6). Repeat for other side. Trim seams.

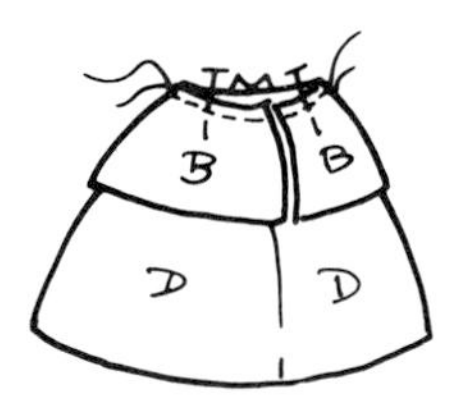

Diagram 5. Sew **B** unit to **D** unit around neckline.

15. With right sides facing, pin and sew the top half of the head (**A** unit) to the bottom half (**B** unit), matching seams at intersections (Diagram 7). Trim seams.

16. Repeat for the bottom half of the body by sewing the **D** unit to the **C** unit (Diagram 8). Trim seams.

17. Turn right side out through center-back opening between the two **D** pieces, stuff firmly with polyester stuffing, and sew opening closed by hand.

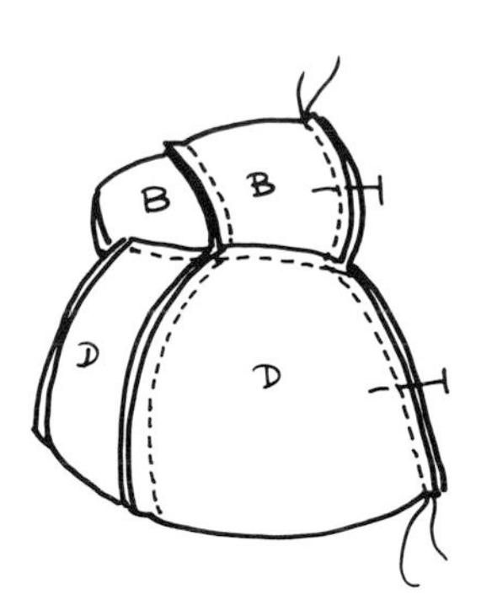

Diagram 6. Sew both **B-D** units together.

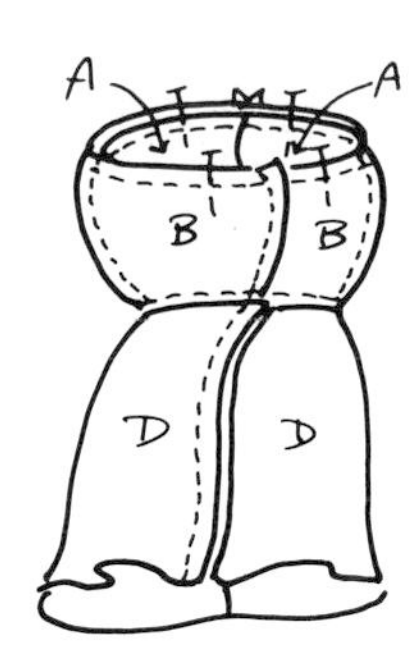

Diagram 7. Sew **A** unit to **B** unit pieces.

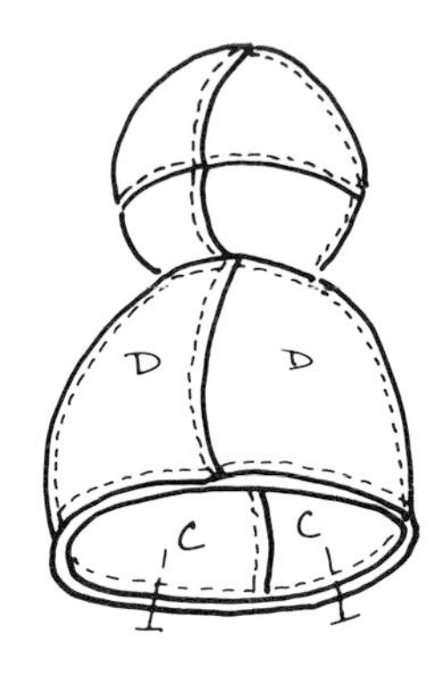

Diagram 8. Sew **C** unit to **D** unit around waistline.

18. With the seam on the inside, wrap **K** around the neck and fold one end over the other at the center-back. Tack in place by hand.

Sew a button at the center-front intersection of the head for the nose.

To make the cap, sew two **M** pieces together along one curved side. Trim seam.

Sew **L** (with the strip of batting inside) to the bottom edge of the cap. Press seam toward cap.

Using a long stitch, machine baste two rows along the top edge of the cap. Using a normal stitch length, sew the other two curved sides of the cap together. To gather the top edge of the cap, pull both ends of each row of stitching as tightly as possible. Tie off and knot. Backstitch across the gathered stitches a few times to secure in place. Turn cap right side out.

To make pom-pom, wind yarn around three fingers about twenty-five times. Pull yarn off fingers and tie tightly in the middle with a strand of yarn. Clip the loops at both ends. Pull all the strands away from the knot and pinch tightly with your fingers. Trim off the ends evenly. Attach pom-pom to the gathered end of the cap.

Place the cap on Santa or Mrs. Santa. With the ends at the center-back, pin a piece of the lace in place around the bottom of the face for Santa's beard, or just under the edge of the cap for Mrs. Santa. Remove the cap and tack the lace in place by hand. Replace the cap and tack in place over the ends of the beard or just over the gathered edge of Mrs. Santa's lace. Twist the end of the cap around to the side of the head and tack in place.

To make the mittens, sew two sets of **N** pieces together around the curved side, leaving the straight side open for turning. Trim the seams, turn right side out, and stuff lightly with polyester batting. At the seam line, hand-tack each mitten in place inside the sleeve, joining the sleeve to the sleeve trim.

For hanging Santa or Mrs. Santa on the tree, make a a thread loop for a hook on the top of the head.

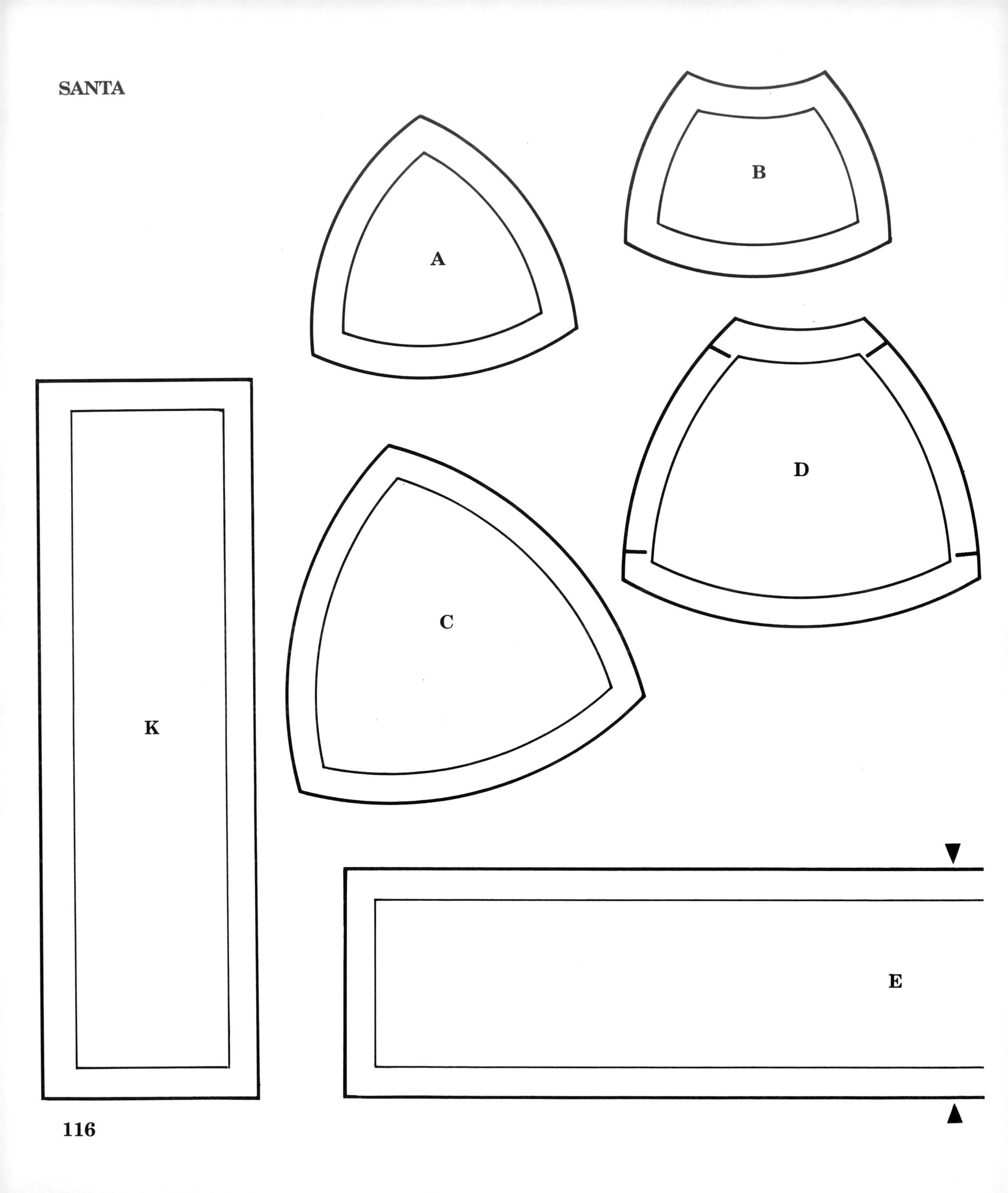
A
B
D
C
K
E

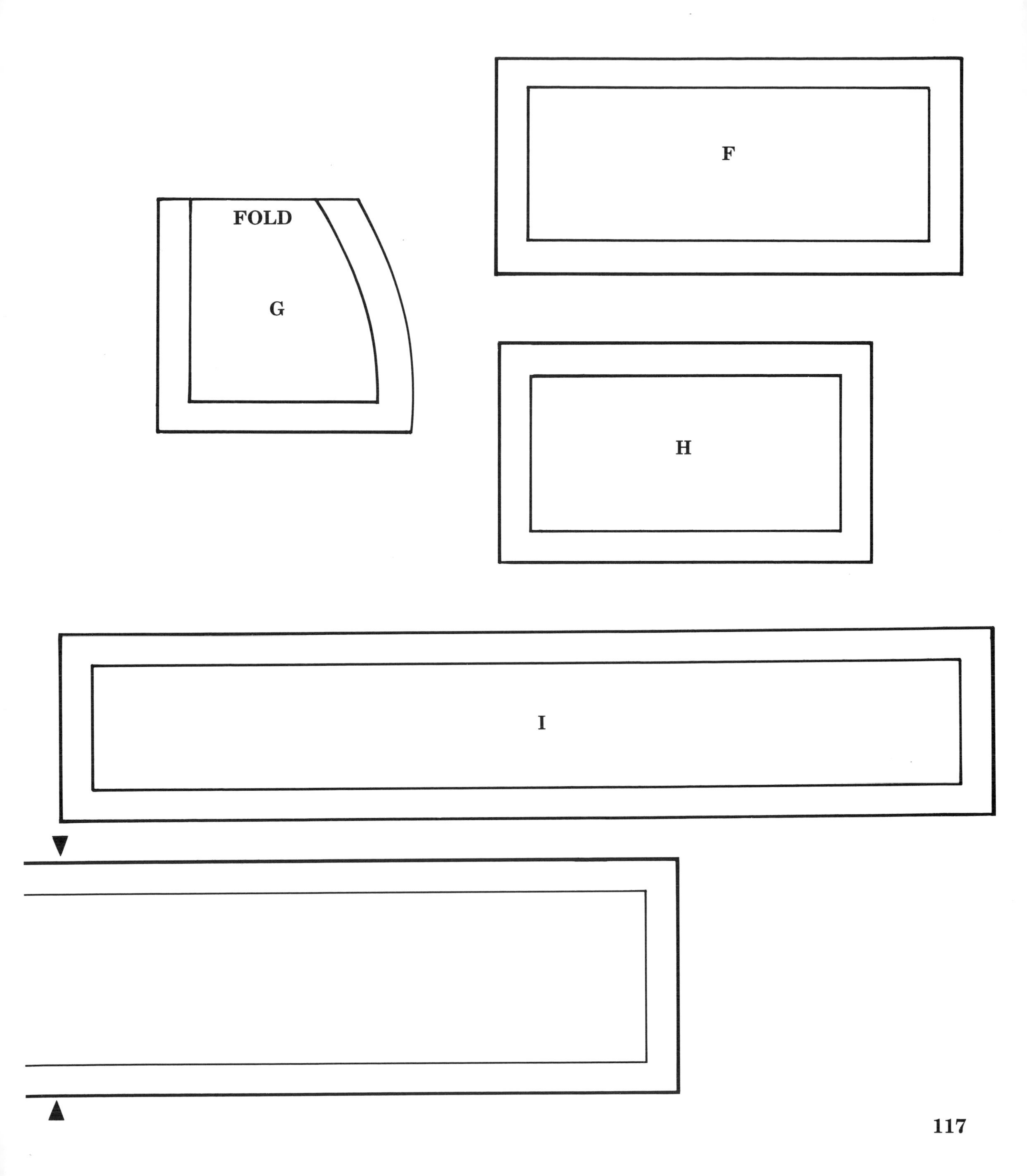
F
FOLD
G
H
I

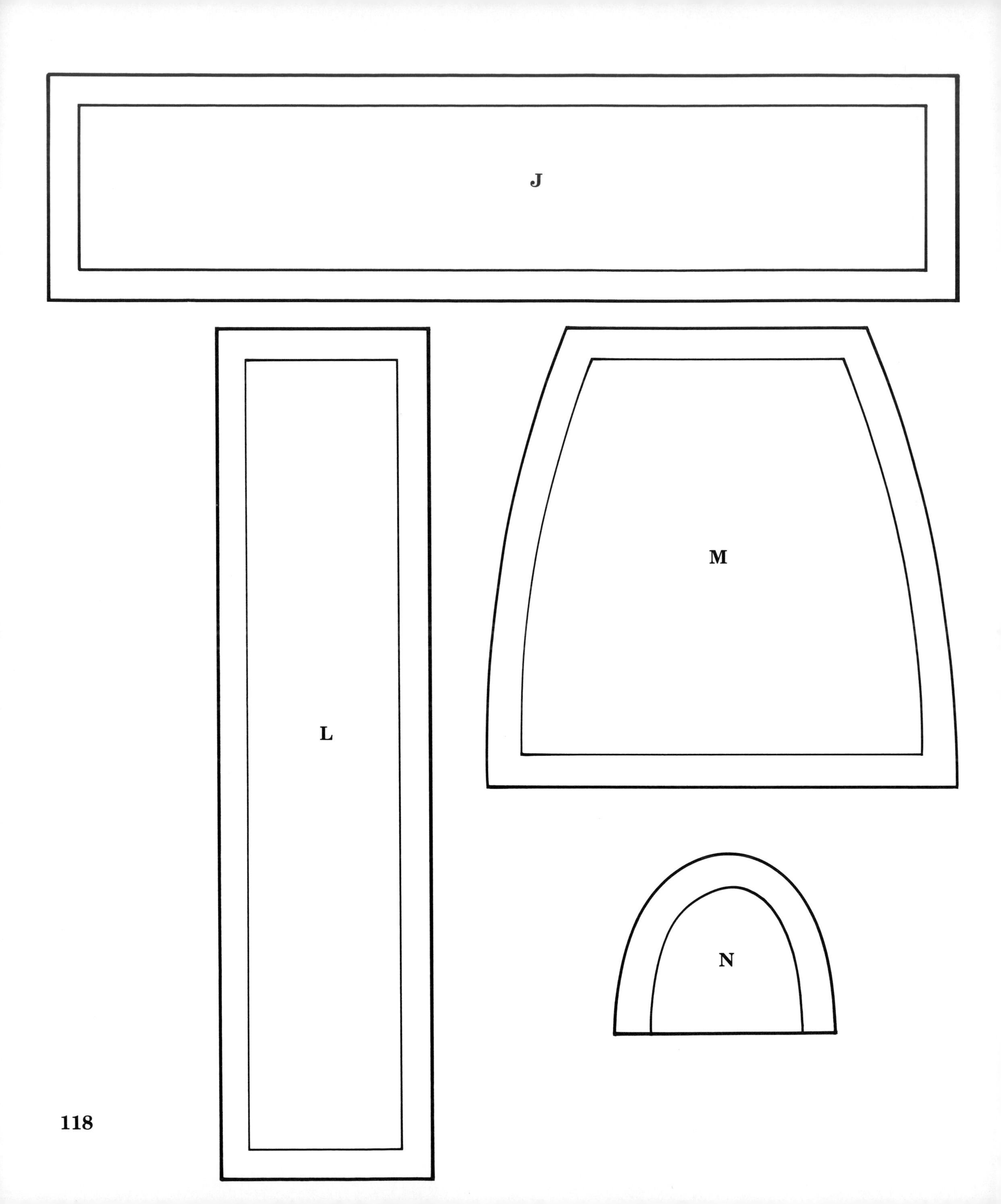
J
L
M
N

SANTA'S HELPER

Make a whole crew of little green friends to accompany Santa and Mrs. Santa on the tree or around the house. Here again, all you need are scraps of fabric—green, white, and pink.

Piecing Diagram

MATERIALS

Fabric

Pattern piece	Number of pieces
A (head)	4 green
B (head)	4 pink
C (body)	4 green
D (body)	4 green
E (sleeve)	2 green
F (apron)	2 white
G (cap trim)	1 white
H (mittens)	4 white

Other Materials

Polyester stuffing

Small amount of polyester quilt batting cut into ½ × 7-inch strip

Red button for nose

White yarn for pom-pom

⅛ yard of ½-inch gathered white cotton eyelet lace

Hook or nylon filament for hanging

SEWING INSTRUCTIONS

To make sewing curves easier and more accurate, set a short stitch length on the sewing machine. Use normal setting for straight seams.

1. With right sides facing, sew the four **A** pieces together in two sets of two (Diagram 1). Repeat for **B, C,** and **D**. Trim all seams to within ⅛ inch of stitch line.

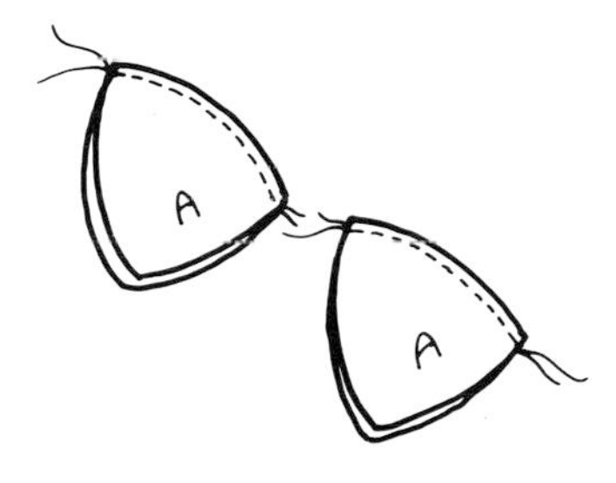

Diagram 1. Sew the **A, B, C,** and **D** pieces together in sets of two (see Diagram 1 for Santa).

2. With right sides facing, sew the two **A** units together, matching seams at intersections (Diagram 2). Repeat for the two **C** units. Trim seams.

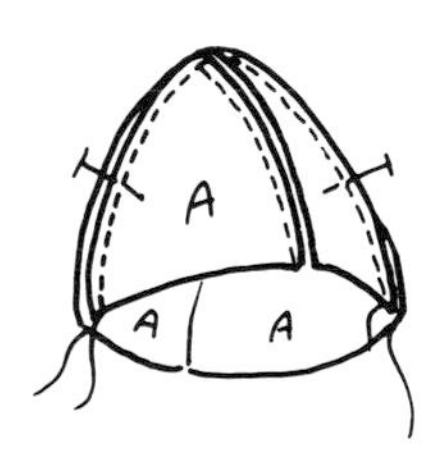

Diagram 2. Sew the two **A** units together.

3. Fold over the bottom edge of the sleeve (the long, straight edge of **E**) to the wrong side twice for a ¼-inch hem; top-stitch.

4. With right sides facing, fold sleeves in half along fold line and sew. Turn sleeves right side out and press.

5. Sew the sleeves in place between the notches on the jacket front ⅛ inch from the edge (Diagram 3).

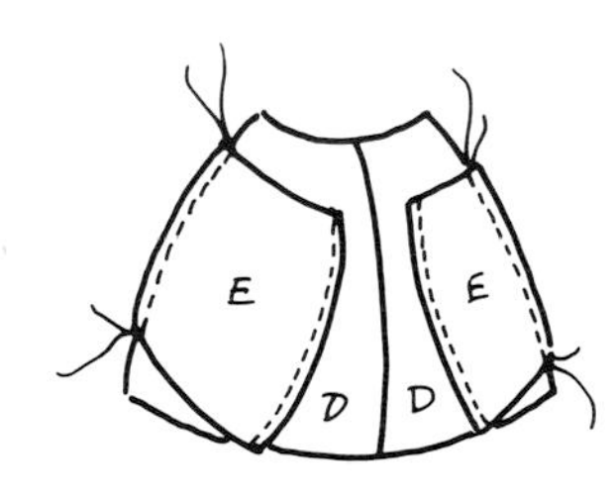

Diagram 3. Sew the sleeves in place between the notches on the jacket front.

6. To make the apron, sew the two **F** pieces together, right sides facing. Leave one long side open to turn right side out. Clip the corners to eliminate bulk and turn right side out. Gently push out the corners with the points of your scissors. Press.

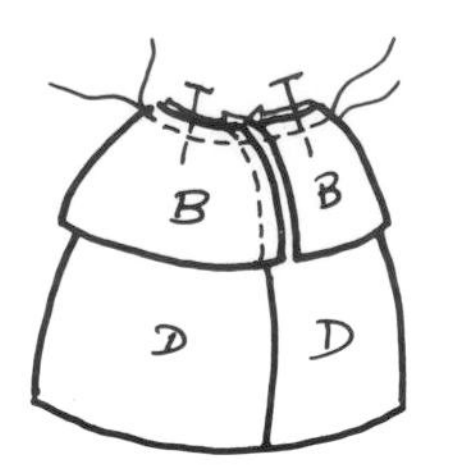

Diagram 4. Sew the **B** unit to the **D** unit.

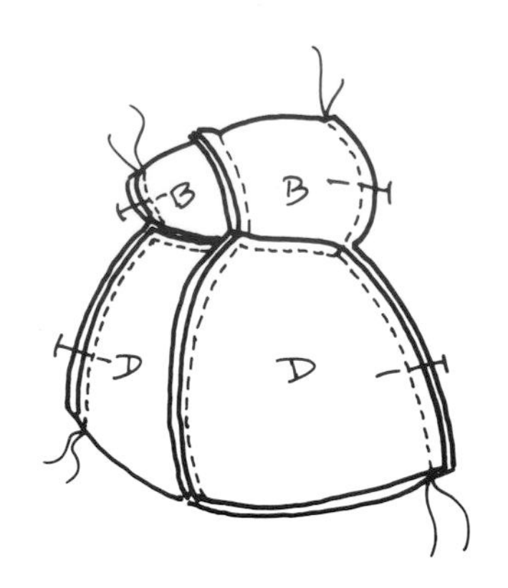

Diagram 5. Sew the **B-D** units together.

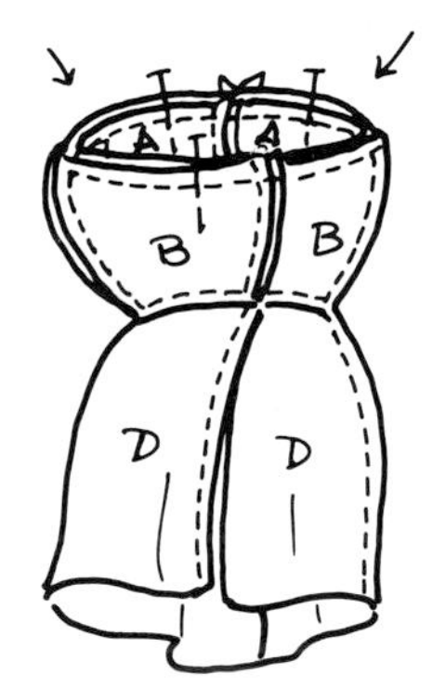

Diagram 6. Sew cap (**A**) to head (**B**)

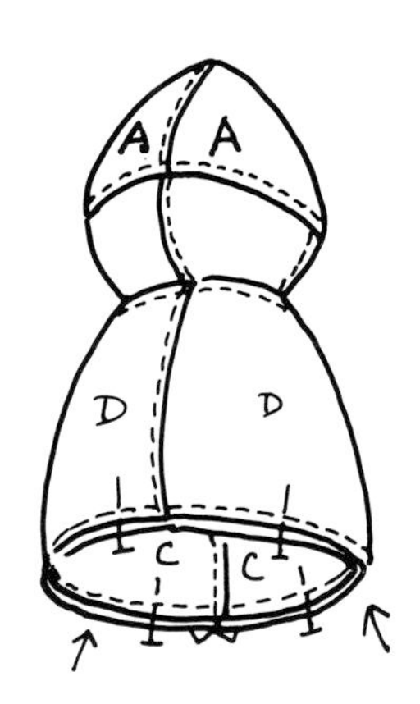

Diagram 7. Sew the **C** unit to the **D** unit around waistline.

7. Center the apron on the center-front of the bottom half of the body (**C** unit) and sew in place ⅛ inch from the edge.

8. With right sides facing, sew a **B** unit to a **D** unit around the concave curve of the neckline, matching seams at intersections (Diagram 4). Repeat for the other **B** and **D** units. Trim seams.

9. With right sides facing, pin and sew both **B-D** units together along one side, matching the notches (with sleeves) and the seams at intersections (Diagram 5). Repeat for other side. Trim seams.

10. With right sides facing, pin and sew the cap (**A**) to the bottom half of the head (**B**), matching seams at intersections (Diagram 6). Trim seams.

11. Repeat for the bottom half of the body by sewing the **D** unit to the **C** unit, leaving an opening in the seam at the center-back for turning (Diagram 7). Trim seams.

12. Turn right side out, stuff firmly with polyester stuffing and sew opening closed by hand.

13. Pin the lace in place around the bottom of the face to make a beard and tack in place by hand.

14. To prepare the trim for the cap, fold **G** in half lengthwise and insert a ½-inch strip of batting. With the strip in the middle, sew the sides of **G** together ¼ inch from the edge. Lightly press so that the seam lies open down the center.

15. With the ends at the center-back, wrap the cap trim around the head over the seam line between **A** and **B**. Fold one end over the other and sew in place by hand.

16. Sew a red button at the center-front intersection of the head for the nose.

17. To make pom-pom, wind yarn around three fingers about twenty-five times. Pull yarn off fingers and tie tightly in the middle with a strand of yarn. Clip the loops at both ends. Pull all the strands away from the knot and pinch tightly with your fingers. Trim the ends. Attach pom-pom to the top of the cap.

18. To make the mittens, sew two sets of **H** pieces together around the curved side, leaving the straight side open for turning. Trim the seams, turn right side out, and stuff lightly with polyester batting. Hand tack each mitten in place inside the sleeve.

19. To hang Santa's helper on the tree, add a thread loop of nylon filament at the top of the head for a hook.

SANTA'S HELPER

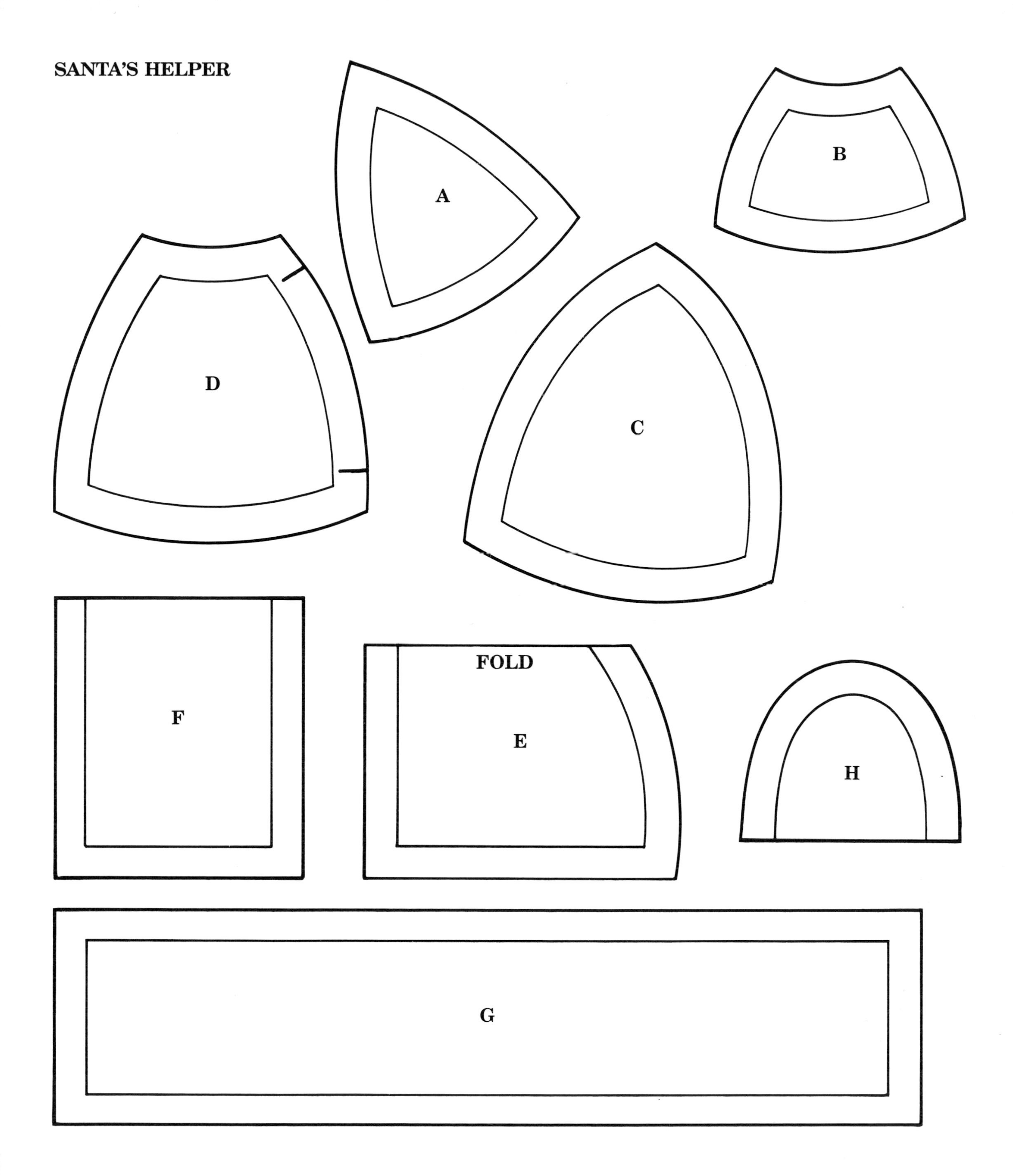

CHRISTMAS PINE TREE SKIRT

In *A Patchwork Christmas,* I came up with a number of designs that were variations on one basic motif: a triangular shaped tree. Since then, I discovered yet another way of using this motif that's perfect for a Christmas tree skirt. Here the design fits into a circle instead of a square. There's a hole in the center for the tree trunk, and the opening is tied with ribbons.

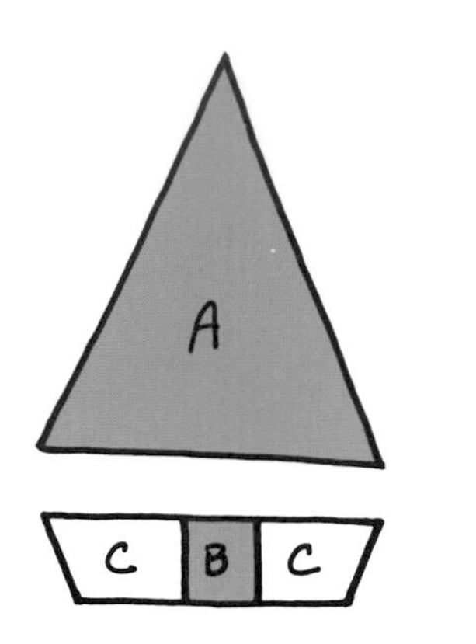

Diagram 1. Sew a **C** to opposite sides of each **B**.

MATERIALS

Fabric

You will need approximately ½ yard of red, ¼ yard of green, and 2½ yards of white fabric.

Pattern piece	Number of pieces
A	8 green
B	8 green
C	16 white
D	64 red, 64 white
E	8 green
F	8 white
G	8 red
H	8 white
I	8 white
J	64 red

One 5 × 24-inch, two 5 × 12-inch, and two 5 × 33½-inch white rectangles for borders (⅔ yard)

One 34-inch square of white fabric for the lining (1 yard)

One 34-inch square of red fabric for the back (1 yard)

Diagram 2. Sew two **E** pieces together to make a square.

Other Materials

One 34-inch square of batting

2 yards red or white 1-inch ribbon for ties

Ruler or tape at least 15 inches long with a hole at one end

SEWING INSTRUCTIONS

1. Sew one **C** to one side of each **B.** Sew another **C** to the opposite side of each **B.** Press seams open. Sew one **A** to the top of each **B-C** unit (Diagram 1). Press seams open.

2. Set aside sixteen white and sixteen red triangles (**D**) to use later. Sew a white triangle to each of the remaining red triangles along the diagonal side to make squares (Diagram 2). Press seams open. You should now have forty-eight red and white squares.

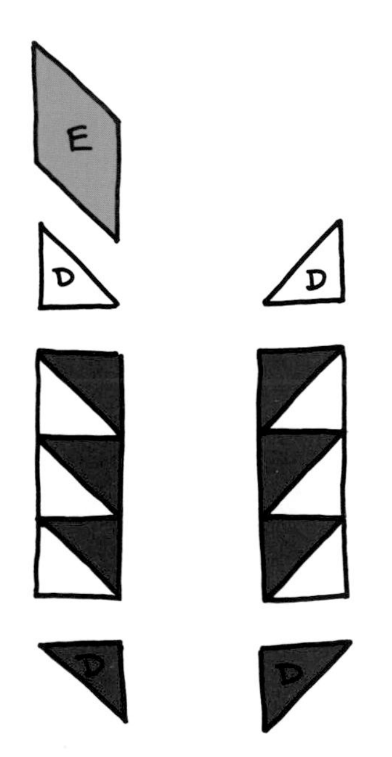

Diagram 3. Sew pieced squares together into rows.

3. Sew three of these squares together in a row with the red triangles pointing to the right. Repeat for a total of eight rows. Sew three squares together in a row, with the red triangles pointing to the left (Diagram 3). Repeat for a total of eight rows. Press seams open.

CHRISTMAS PINE TREE SKIRT

Piecing Diagrams

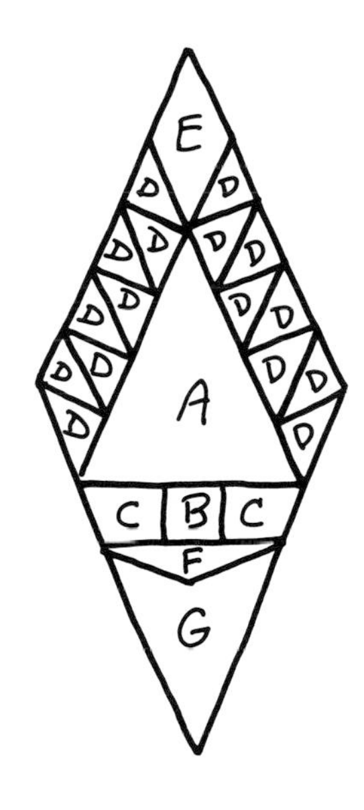

Diagram 4. Sew "branches" to trees.

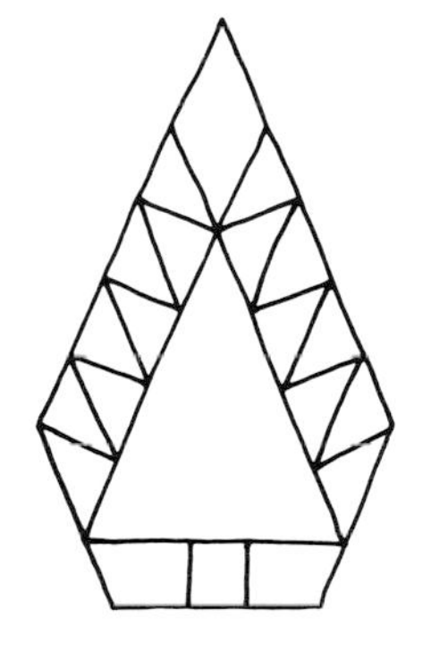

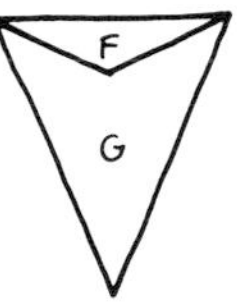

Diagram 5. Sew star unit (**F-G**) to tree unit.

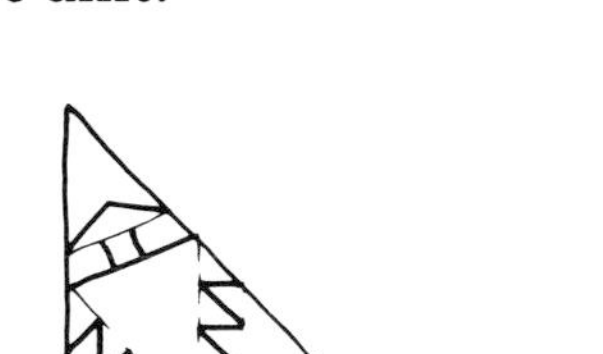

Diagram 6. Sew one **H** to the *right* side of four trees. Sew one **H** to the *left* side of four trees. Sew one **I** to the remaining side of all trees.

4. Sew a red triangle (**D**) to the bottom of each row so that it points in the same direction as the other red triangles. Sew a white triangle to the top of each row in the same way (Diagram 3). Press seams open. Sew a green **E** to the top of each row of triangles pointing to the left. Press seams open.

5. Sew a row of triangles pointing to the right side of each tree (Diagram 4). Press seams away from trees.

6. Sew a row of triangles with an **E** on top to the left side of each tree, matching the seams at the top of the tree (Diagram 4). Press seams away from trees.

7. With right sides facing and with the **F** on top, sew one **F** to each **G,** matching notches. To turn the corner at the center, leave the needle down and lift the presser foot. Clip the seam allowance on piece **G** up to the needle. Pivot and adjust the pieces so the notches match on the other sides of **F** and **G.** Lower the presser foot and continue sewing. Repeat for a total of eight **F-G** units. Press seams toward **G**.

8. Sew one **F-G** unit to the bottom of each tree unit (Diagram 5). Press seams open.

9. Sew one **H** to the right side of four trees. Sew one **H** to the left side of the other four trees. Press seams toward **H**.

10. Sew one **I** to the remaining side of all the trees (Diagram 6). Press seams toward **I**.

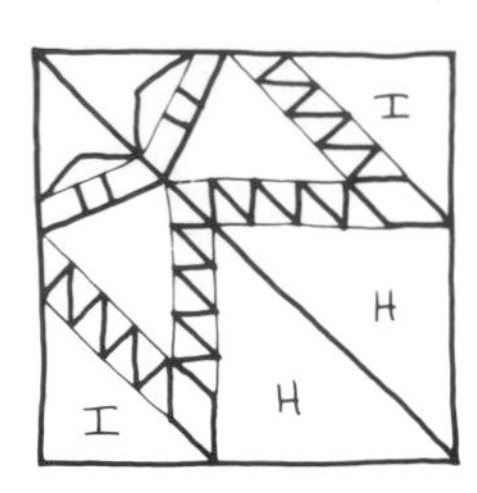

Diagram 7. Sew two trees together along sides with **H** pieces to make square.

11. Matching seams at intersections, sew two trees together along the sides to which the **H** pieces are sewn to make a square (Diagram 7). Repeat for a total of four squares. Press seams open.

12. Matching seams at intersections, sew two of these squares together to make one half of the tree skirt. Repeat for the other half. Press seams open.

13. Matching seams at intersections, sew these two halves together, leaving one side open (Piecing Diagram). Press seams open.

14. To each side of the tree skirt which has the opening, sew one 5 × 12-inch white rectangle (Diagram 8). Sew the 5 × 24-inch rectangle to the opposite side. Press seams open.

15. Sew one 5 × 33½-inch white rectangle to each of the remaining two sides. Press seams open.

16. Lay out the 34-inch white square for the lining. Place the square of batting on top. With the right side up, lay the tree skirt on top of the batting. Pin all three layers together.

17. Many rulers or tapes have a hole at one end. Use one at least fifteen inches long as a compass. Standing a pin straight up in the center of the tree skirt, place the hole of the ruler over the pin. Mark off a circle with a 15-inch radius by rotating the ruler around the pin. The circle should clear the treetops by about three or four inches. Mark off another, smaller circle with a 1½-inch radius (Diagram 9).

18. Baste all three layers. Hand quilt ¼ inch around the outside (and

Diagram 8. Sew border rectangles to tree skirt.

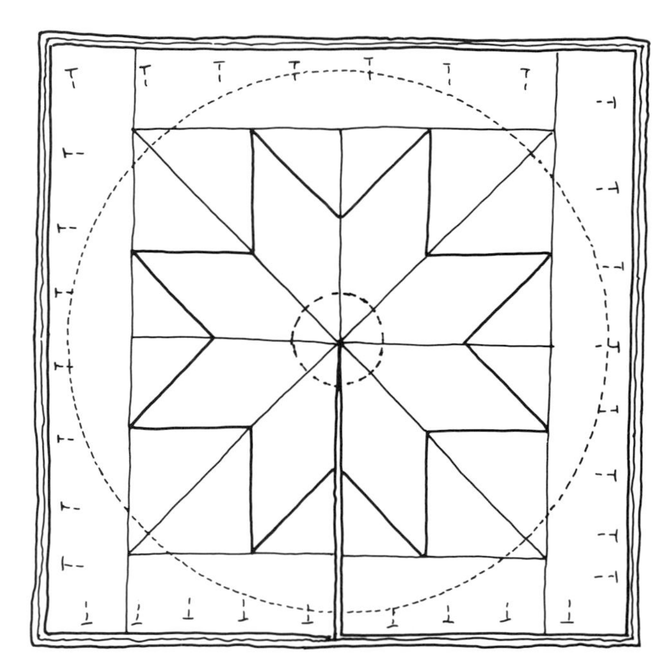

Diagram 9. Mark off one circle with a 15-inch radius and one with a 1½-inch radius.

inside, too, if you like) of all the trees. I added 5½-inch feathered wreaths between the trees. The remaining white areas were stippled (stitched with random, winding rows of quilting).

19. When all the hand quilting is finished, stay-stitch all three layers around the circumference of both circles marked off in Step 17. Trim all layers to within ¼ inch of the circles.

20. Fold one **J** diagonally in half. Fold diagonally in half again. With the point facing toward the center of the circle, place the long side of the triangle on the circumference. Pin it in place on the top edge, allowing it to curve slightly with the curve of the circle (Diagram 10). With all the folds on the same side, add the remaining **J** pieces, filling the circumference of the circle. Stitch in place.

21. With right sides facing, pin the tree skirt on top of the back (Diagram 11). Cut the ribbon into four equal parts. Pin two pieces between the top and back, pin one piece of ribbon at each of the four corners of the opening. Pin the remaining two pieces of ribbon in the middle of each side.

22. Stitch all layers together around the outside edge of the circle. Turn the corners at the opening and, leaving a six-inch opening on one side for turning, sew down each side of the opening and around the circle in the center. Trim the seam allowance around the entire edge and clip the corners.

23. Turn the piece right side out. Turn the edges of the six-inch opening to the inside and close the opening by hand. With the trunk in the center, wrap the tree skirt around your Christmas tree. Tie the sides of the opening together with the ribbons.

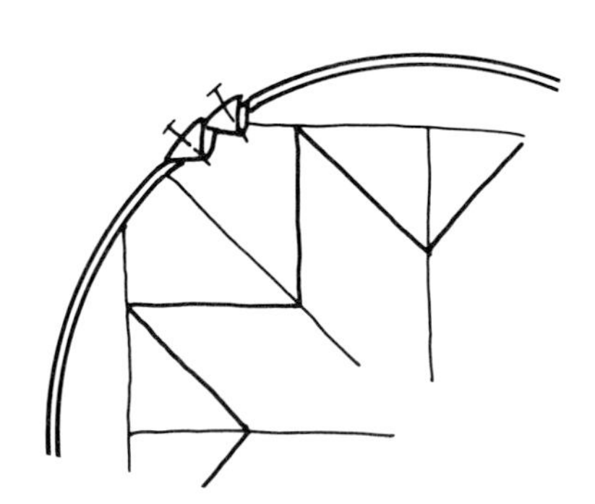

Diagram 10. Pin folded **J** to edge of circle.

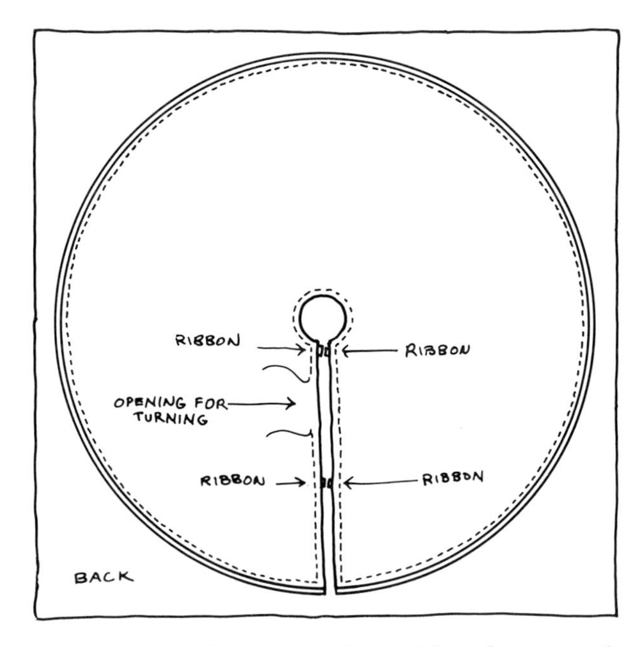

Diagram 11. Sew around outside edge, opening, and inside edge.

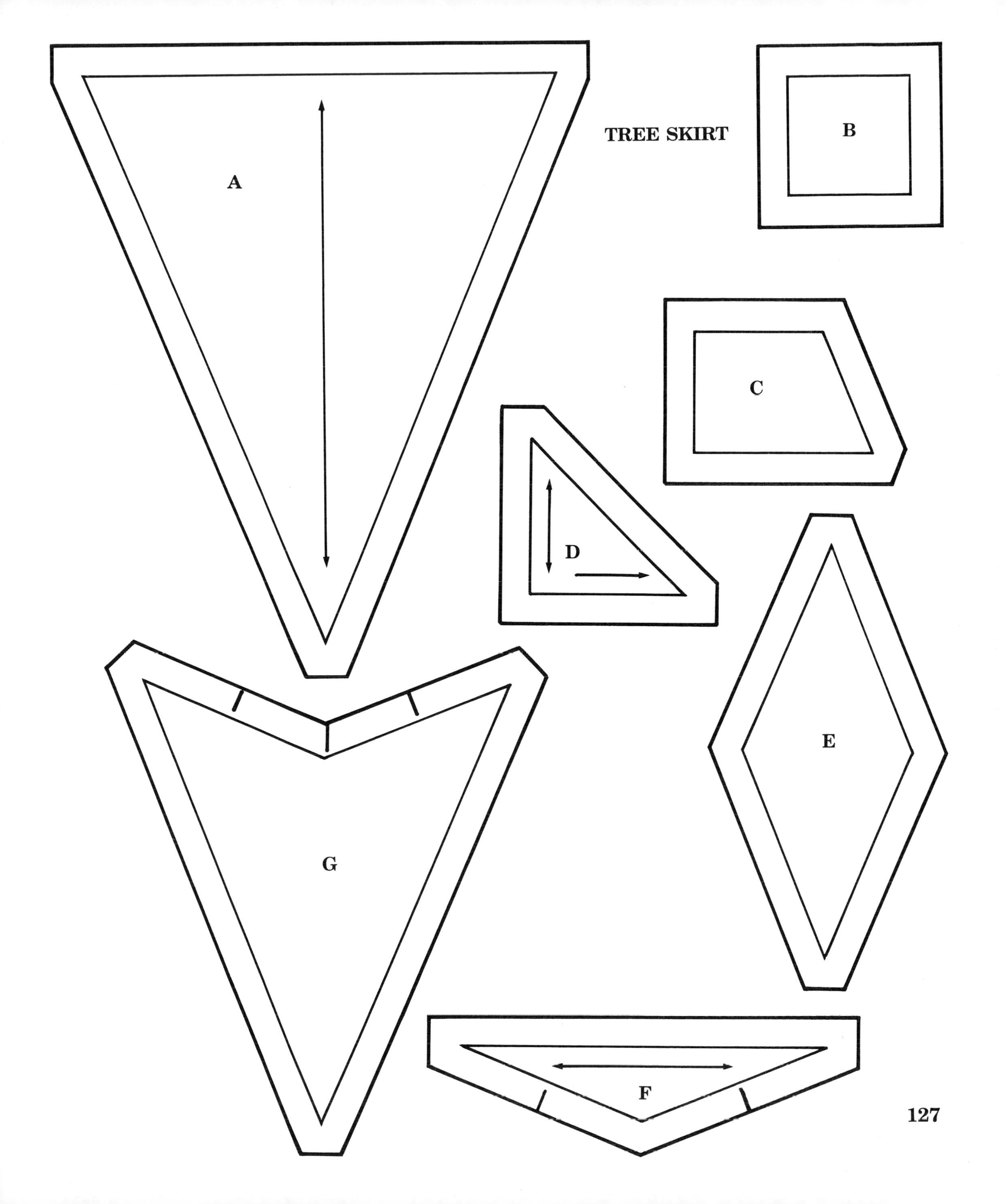
TREE SKIRT
A
B
C
D
E
F
G

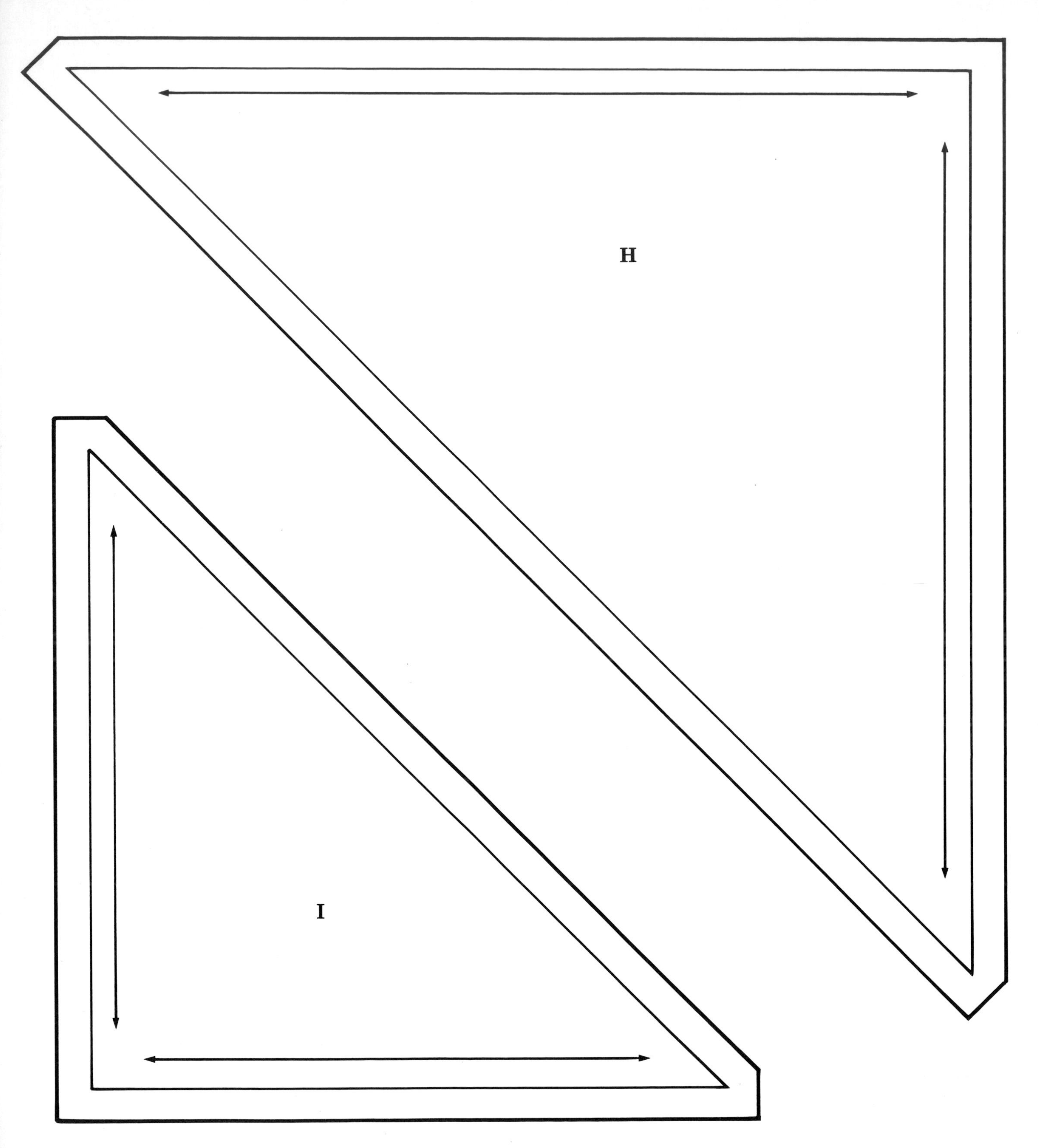
H
I

QUILTED BAGS

QUILTED QUILT BAG

If you're like me, I'll bet that in spite of all the quilts you've made, you don't have anything really nice to carry them in.

I remember having to lecture at Bloomingdale's in White Plains, New York. I had a lot of quilts to take with me and all I could find to carry them in was big, black, plastic garbage bags. Practical, but not the smartest kind of luggage for making an entrance as an authority on quilt lore.

After a few long looks from the ladies who met me at the door, I decided that it was about time to come up with something respectable, lest I risk being ushered to the loading dock. I could never find anything that seemed quite right, and it's only now, after many years, that I've gotten around to making my own quilt bag.

I had planned to make only a quilt bag, but after visiting one of my favorite fabric companies, where I saw a wonderful new group of fabrics with medallions and coordinating prints and borders, I wound up making a matching tote bag, shoulder bag, and sewing (or make-up) case. The versatility of such a fabric collection inspires all sorts of possibilities.

These particular fabrics may not, of course, be around for too long, and they may not even be available now. However, the following patterns and instructions can be used for any fabrics with or without coordinating details. Select colors and prints the way you would for a quilt, using those that work well together. Make borders from contrasting colors, and if you're really feeling ambitious, substitute a printed medallion with a pieced square or octagon.

If pre-quilted fabric is available in your area, you can save time by skipping the first few steps in the instructions that follow. Whatever you decide, a nice quilt bag will make you and your quilts feel properly dressed when you take them out for a walk.

The quilt bag that follows is essentially a folded rectangle with side panels. Its handles are a loop made out of a printed border, and its edges are finished with bias binding.

The finished size is 18 × 25 inches.

Piecing Diagram

MATERIALS

Fabric

1⅔ yards of fabric or pre-quilted fabric

2¼ yards of fabric for lining and bias binding (Omit if using pre-quilted fabric.)

Two 6 × 58-inch borders, if different from bag

4¼ yards of 2-inch bias binding (can be cut from leftover lining)

Other Materials

44 × 58-inch piece of batting (Omit if using pre-quilted fabric.)

3 yards cotton cord, or something else to pull the handles right side out

Note: All seams are sewn with ½-inch seam allowance unless otherwise indicated.

SEWING INSTRUCTIONS

1. Trim ½ yard off the 2¼-yard piece of lining. Use this piece to make 4¼ yards of 2-inch bias binding. For instructions in cutting and making bias binding, see page 19.

2. Draw a diagonal grid pattern on the right side of the lining. I used the width of my steel ruler, approximately 1¾ inches wide, as a guide.

3. Lay out the unmarked fabric with the right side down. Place the batting on top. Place the lining right side up on top of the batting. Pin the three layers together.

4. Using the longest stitch length on your sewing machine, sew all three layers together, following the grid pattern marked on the top layer (Diagram 1).

5. Cut the following pieces from the quilted fabric: one 25 × 50-inch rectangle, two 6 × 58-inch handles, and two 6 × 18-inch rectangles (Diagram 2).

6. With right sides facing, fold one handle in half lengthwise and sew

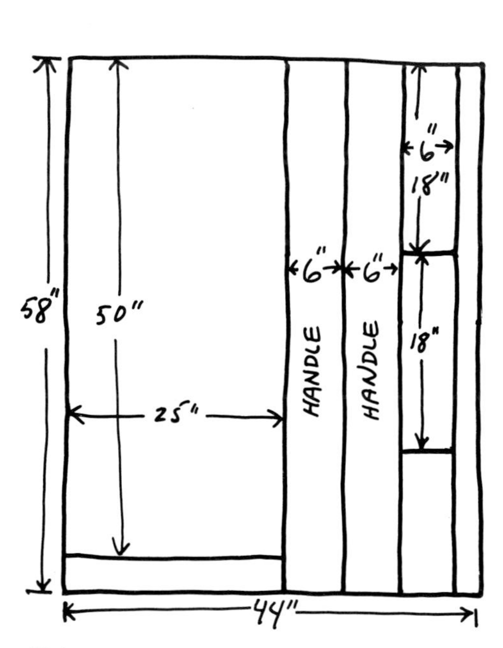

Diagram 1. Sew all three layers together in diagonal grid pattern.

Diagram 2. Cut bag, handles, and side pieces from quilted fabric.

the two sides together to make a tube. Repeat for the other handle. Lightly press the seams open.

7. A quick and easy method of turning the handles right side out is by using a large paper clip or a safety pin to insert the cotton cord into the tube so that one end of the tube is at the center of the cord. Tack one end of the tube to the mid-point of the cord by hand or machine (Diagram 3). Pull the tube toward the exposed half of the cord, turning it right side out as you go. When the tube is completely turned, remove the stitching and the cord. Lightly press so the seam lies in the center on one side of the handle. Repeat for the other handle.

8. Sew the ends of the two handles together to make a loop. Press the seams open.

9. Pin the loop in place on the quilted rectangle as shown in Diagram 4, with the seam on the underside, and the seams that join the two handles at the center bottom, 18 inches from one end and 8 inches from the sides.

10. Sewing ¼ inch from the edge, sew both sides of the loop to the bag, stopping and turning the corners 14 inches from the center bottom (Diagram 4).

11. Sew a 24-inch piece of 2-inch bias binding to the top edge of the bag (the end that's 18 inches from the center bottom). Sew a 6-inch piece of binding to one end of each of the side panels (6 × 18-inch rectangles).

12. Sew the side panels to the side top of the bag so the ends with the binding meet, and so the seam allowance is on the *right* side of the bag (Diagram 5).

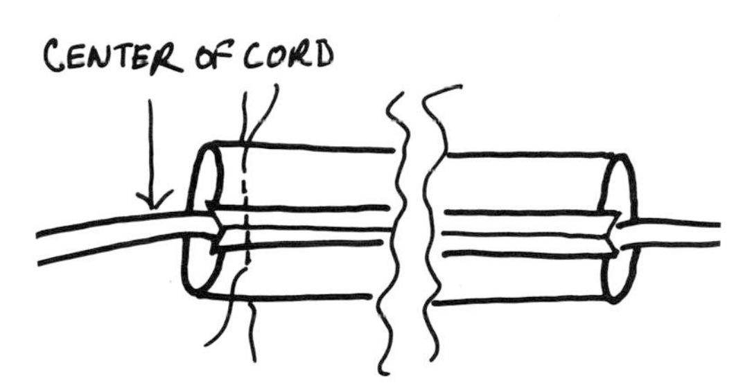

Diagram 3. Tack end of tube to mid-point of length of cord.

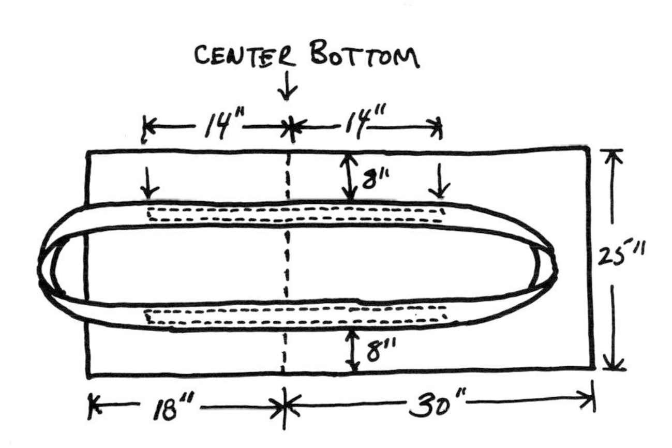

Diagram 4. Sew handles to quilted fabric.

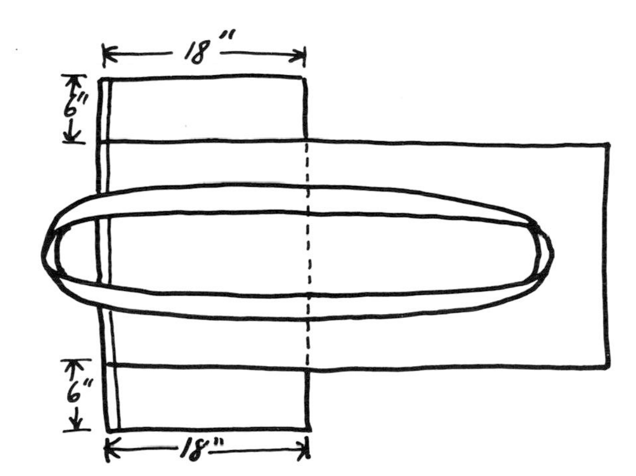

Diagram 5. Sew side panels to bag.

13. Continue sewing the bag around the side panels, turning the corners at the bottom (Diagram 6). To release the corners, clip the seam allowance ½ inch at the bottom corners on the panel (Diagram 7).

14. Allowing ½ inch of the binding to extend beyond the ends of the starting and finishing points, sew the remaining piece of bias binding to the exposed seam allowance (Diagram 8).

15. Starting at top right side of the bag, sew down the side front, turn the corner at the bottom of the right side panel, continue across the bottom and up the other side of the panel, around the flap, down the other side of the bag, turning the corners at the bottom of the left side panel, and up to the top of the bag front (Diagram 8).

16. Turn the ends of the binding under at the top of the seams at the right and left sides of the front of the bag. Fold the binding over to the other side of the seam allowance, turn the edge under ½ inch, and hand-sew the edge to the bag. For more instructions for handling bias binding, see page 19.

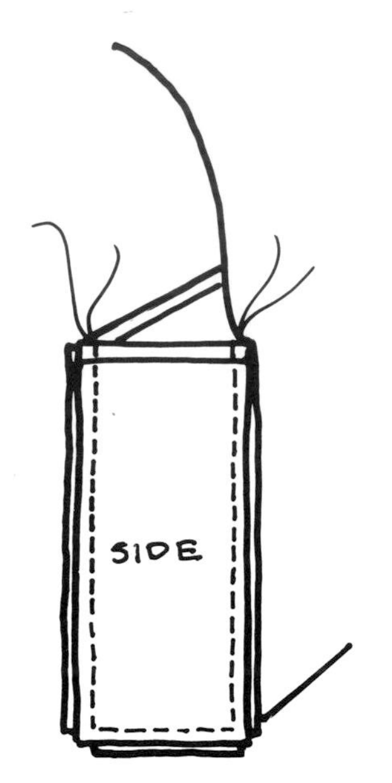

Diagram 6. Turn corner and sew across bottom of bag and up other side.

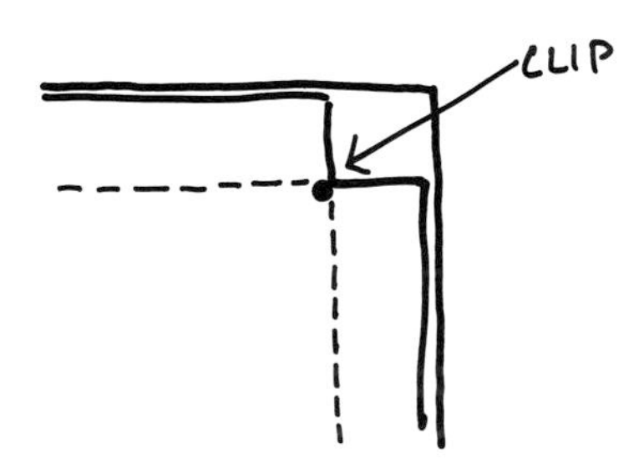

Diagram 7. Clip seam allowance to turn corner.

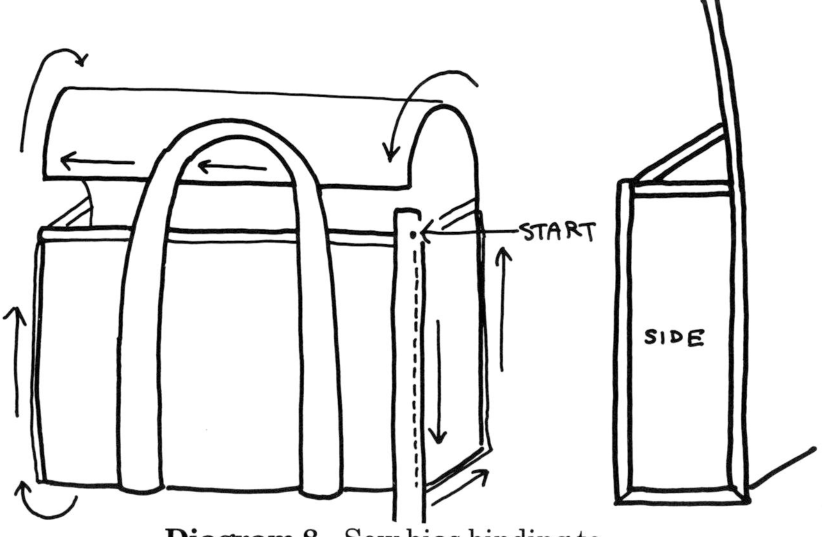

Diagram 8. Sew bias binding to unfinished seam allowance.

SEWING CASE OR MAKE-UP BAG

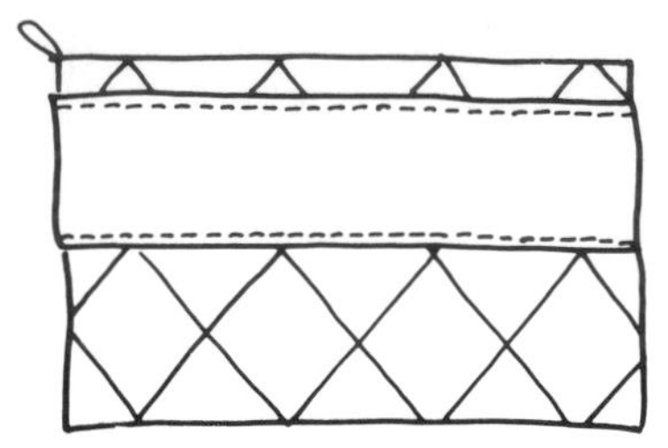

Piecing Diagram

To match your quilt bag, make your own accessories with coordinating prints and borders. I made a make-up case, which can also be used as a sewing case, with the same border trim I used for handles on the quilt bag. If a border fabric is unavailable, you can leave it plain, or substitute a contrasting fabric or a piece of lace.

If you're making a make-up case, a plastic inner lining can be added. I used a clear, lightweight plastic I found at a five-and-dime store. The finished size is 6 × 9 inches.

I made a second, smaller make-up bag with leftover quilted fabric and used one border strip running up the middle instead of along the sides (page 135). This bag is 5 × 7 inches—a little smaller than the other one. It's made in exactly the same way, but with a 7-inch zipper.

MATERIALS

Fabric

Two 10 × 13-inch fabric rectangles of the same or coordinating colors

Two 3½ × 10-inch borders: pre-printed, lace, or contrasting color

Other Materials

10 × 13-inch piece of batting

7-inch zipper

10 × 13-inch plastic rectangle

Note: If using pre-quilted fabric, skip the first three steps.

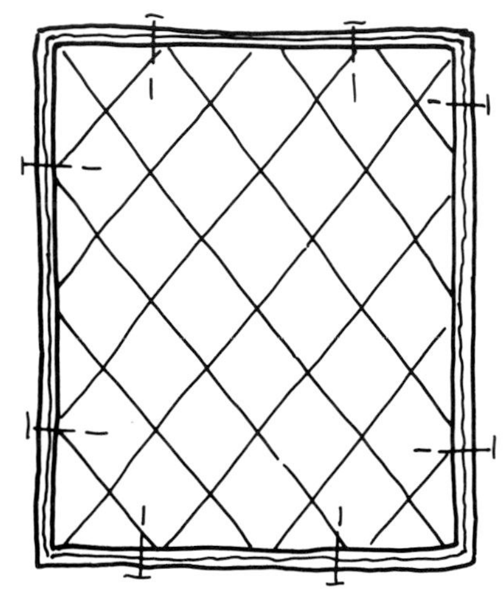

Diagram 1. Sew three layers together using grid pattern.

SEWING INSTRUCTIONS

1. Draw a diagonal grid pattern on the right side of the 10 × 13-inch fabric lining. I used as a guide the width of my steel rule, which is about 1¾ inches wide.

2. Lay out the unmarked fabric rectangle with the right side down. Place the batting on top. Place the lining right side up on top of the batting. Pin the three layers together (Diagram 1).

3. Using the longest stitch length on your sewing machine, sew all three layers together following the grid marked on the lining.

4. Fold the edges of the borders over ¼ inch on each side and press to make a 3-inch border. Pin borders across the top and bottom of the quilted piece, 1¼ inches from the edges. Top-stitch the borders in place (Diagram 2).

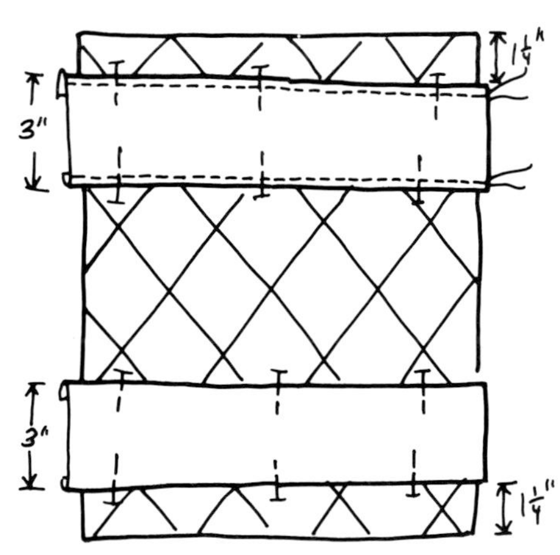

Diagram 2. Top-stitch the borders in place.

5. Place the plastic rectangle on top of the right side of the quilted piece. Pin it in place along the sides. Stitch the sides together ¼ inch from the edges (Diagram 3). Remove the pins and turn the plastic to the lining side of the bag. This will give the inside seams a finished edge.

6. Placing the zipper face down on one end of the bag as illustrated in Diagram 4, sew the zipper to the edge of the bag (Diagram 4). Fold the zipper over to the back of the bag. Top-stitch the bag to the zipper tape as shown in Diagram 5.

7. With the inside facing out, fold over the other end of the bag and sew it to the other side of the zipper (Diagram 6).

8. Turn the piece right side out and top-stitch the other side of the zipper as far as you can without sewing into the back underneath (Diagram 7). Remove the piece; slide the back up toward the top and out of the way. Re-insert the piece under the presser foot, and continue sewing to the end of the zipper.

9. Unzip the zipper, turn the bag inside out, and sew the two sides together (Diagram 8). Turn right side out, zip up your new bag, and admire your work!

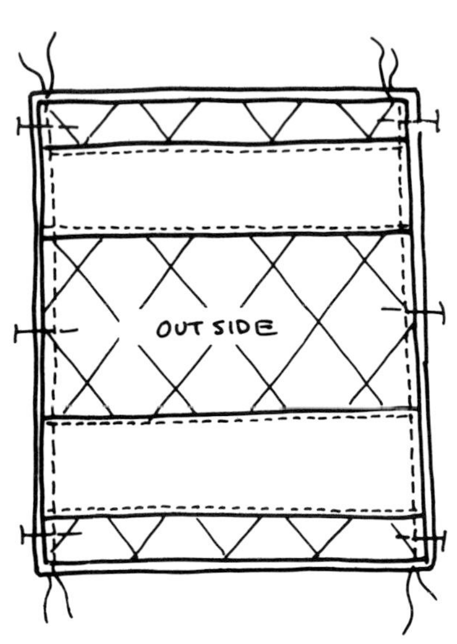

Diagram 3. Sew the plastic down both sides of the bag.

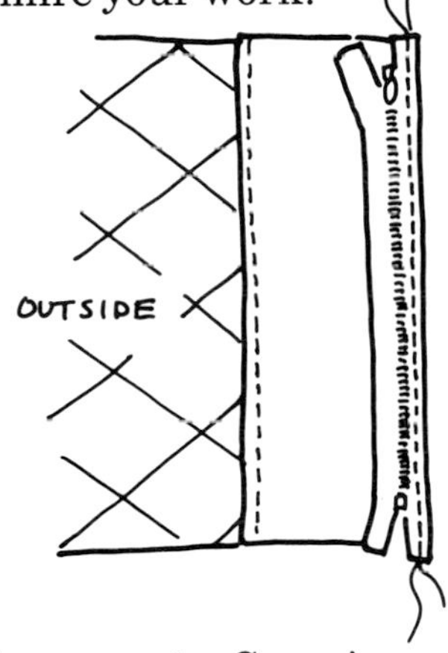

Diagram 4. Sew zipper face down to one end of the bag.

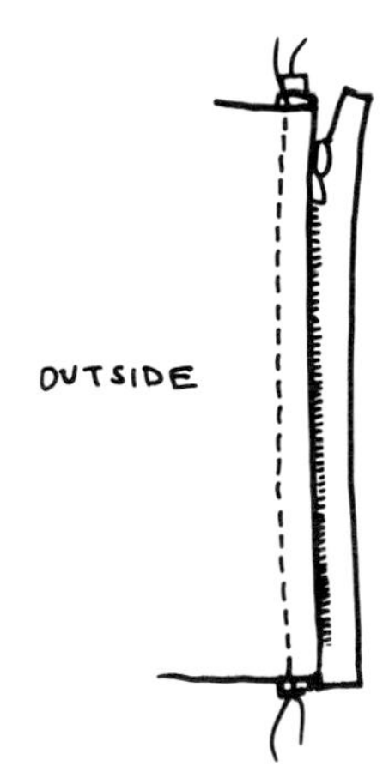

Diagram 5. Fold the zipper over to the back of the bag and top-stitch.

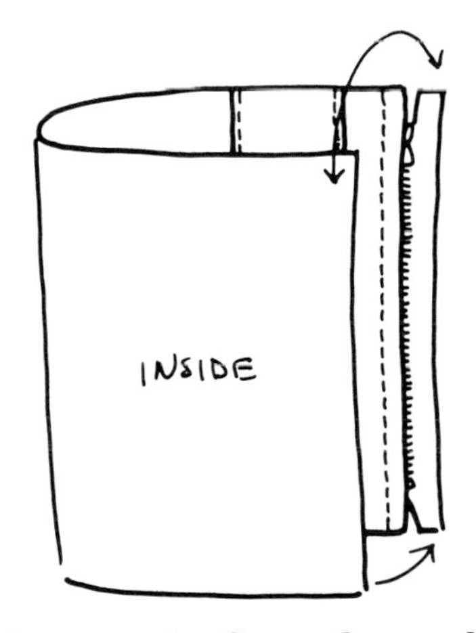

Diagram 6. Sew other end of bag to other side of zipper.

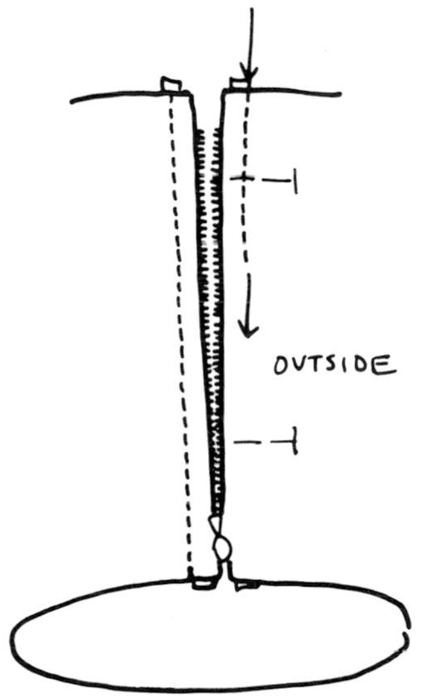

Diagram 7. Top-stitch the other side of the zipper.

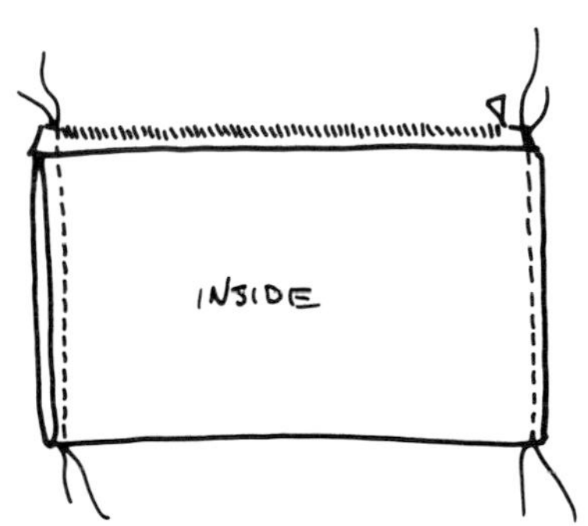

Diagram 8. Stitch the sides together.

EASY TOTE BAG

I used a fabric with pre-printed panels that happened to be just the right size for the tote bag. The panels were 14¾-inches square with octagonal medallions, separated by 3-inch coordinating borders. I cut one piece which included two medallions and a border in the middle, and lined the bag with a coordinating print.

You can use other pre-printed panels and adjust the size, if necessary. Or you can use any fabric you like, with or without medallions and borders, with these instructions.

MATERIALS

Fabric

Two 15¾ × 35½-inch fabric rectangles of same or coordinating colors (1 yard)

Four 2½ × 21-inch strips, two of one color, two of coordinating colors, for the handles (⅓ yard)

SEWING INSTRUCTIONS

1. With right sides facing, sew the two fabric rectangles together along the sides using ¼-inch seam allowance (Diagram 1). Press seams open and turn right side out. Press flat so the two layers behave as one piece.

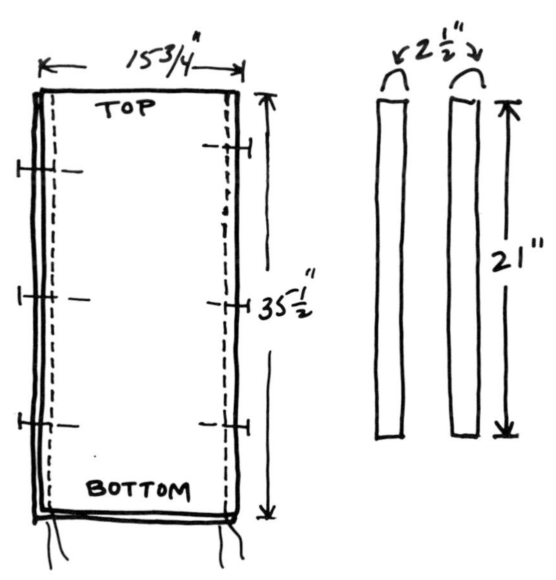

Diagram 1. With right sides facing, sew the two rectangles together along sides.

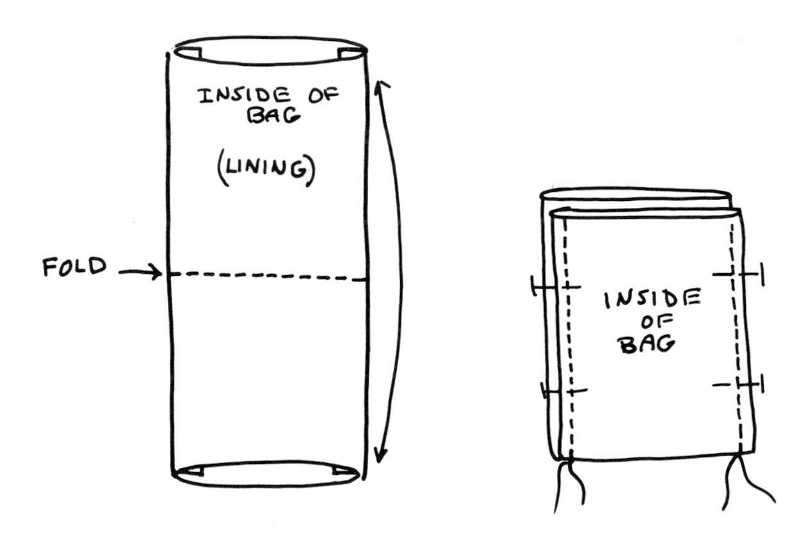

Diagram 2. Fold piece in half and sew sides together.

2. Leaving the top and bottom open, fold piece in half and sew together along the sides, using ¼-inch seam allowance (Diagram 2). This procedure will produce finished inside seams.

3. Fold the bottom corner so the end of the side seam is in the center of the fold (Diagram 3). Sew across the corner as shown so the seam line measures 3 inches in length. Repeat for the other corner.

4. With wrong sides facing, sew together two of the 2½×21-inch handle strips (one of one color, one of a coordinating color) along one side, ⅛ inch from the edge. Roll this edge over ¼ inch twice and sew a hem along the entire side. Repeat for the other side of the handle (Diagram 4), trimming the edge of the inside strip, if necessary, to match the outside strip. Repeat to make two handles.

5. Turn the bag right side out, fold the top edge over ¼ inch and topstitch ⅛ inch from the edge.

6. Sew both ends of one handle under the top of the bag on one side, with each end 4 inches from the outer edge of the bag (Diagram 5). Repeat for the other handle on the other side of the bag.

7. Fold the handles back over to the outside of the bag and sew them in place, making a square of stitching (Diagram 6).

8. Fold the top of the bag to the inside and sew it to the body of the bag all the way around, 1¼ inches from the top (Diagram 7).

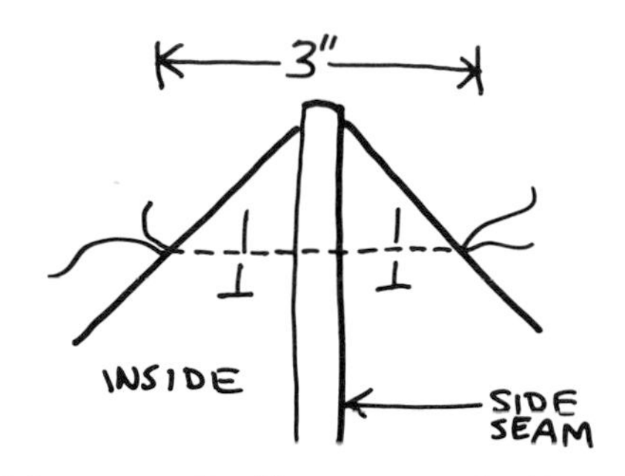

Diagram 3. Sew across bottom inside corners.

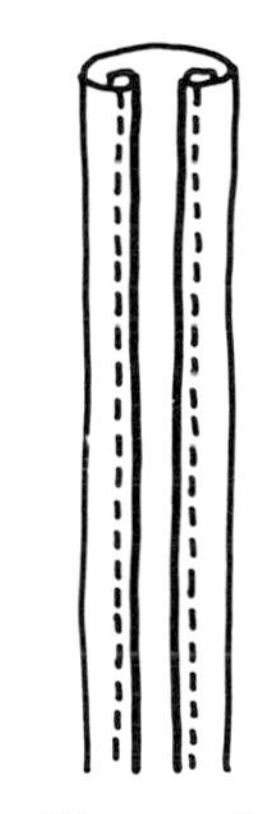

Diagram 4. Turn edges under ¼ inch two times on each side and sew.

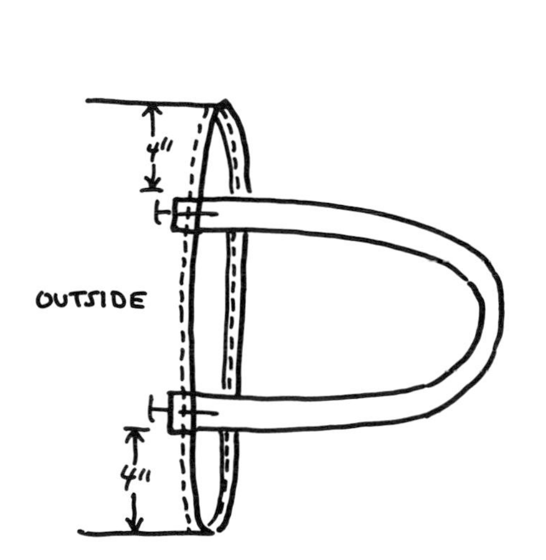

Diagram 5. Sew ends of handles under top edge of bag.

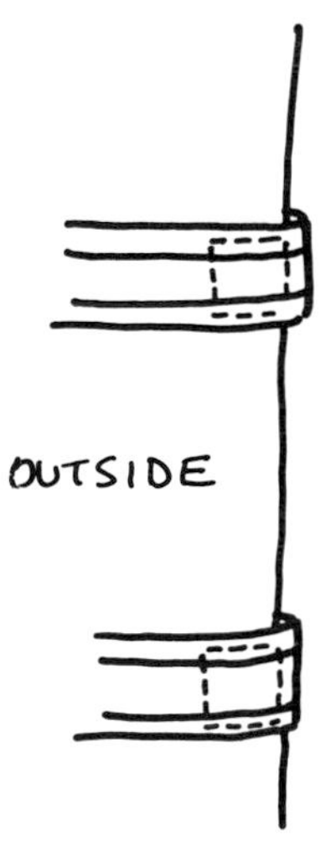

Diagram 6. Fold handles back over to outside of bag and sew ends in place, making a square of stitching.

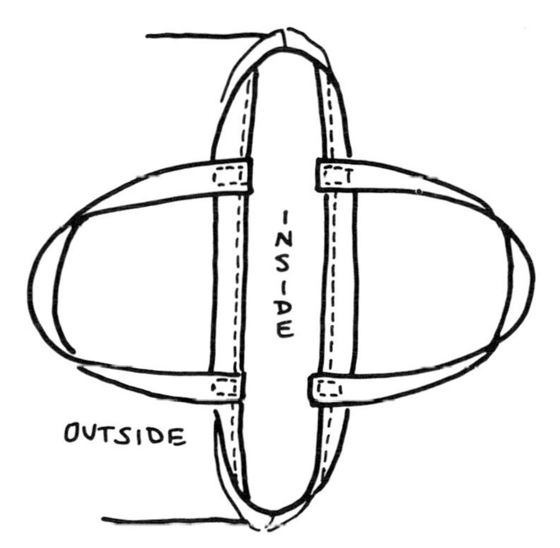

Diagram 7. Fold top under to the inside of the bag and sew hem 1¼ inches from top of bag.

SHOULDER BAG

This bag was decorated with a printed border. It can be left plain or decorated with lace or a border of a contrasting color. A wider border could be sewn up the middle instead of the sides.

Piecing Diagram

MATERIALS

Fabric

Pattern piece	Number of pieces
A	2

$\frac{2}{3}$- yard piece of fabric or pre-quilted fabric

Two $3\frac{1}{2} \times 30$-inch borders

1 yard of fabric for lining (Omit if using pre-quilted fabric.)

$1\frac{1}{2}$ yards of 2-inch bias binding

Other Materials

18×44-inch piece of batting (Omit if using pre-quilted fabric.)

12-inch zipper

Note: All seams are $\frac{1}{2}$ inch wide unless otherwise indicated. If using pre-quilted fabric, skip the first three steps.

SEWING INSTRUCTIONS

1. Trim off $\frac{1}{3}$ yard from the lining to use for bias binding. Draw a

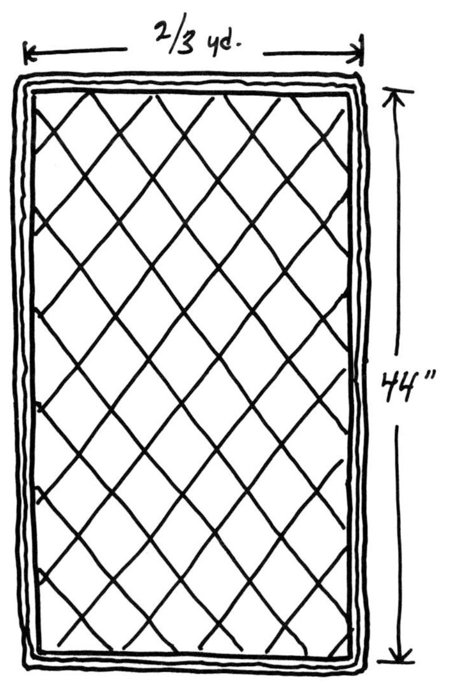

Diagram 1. Stitch all three layers together.

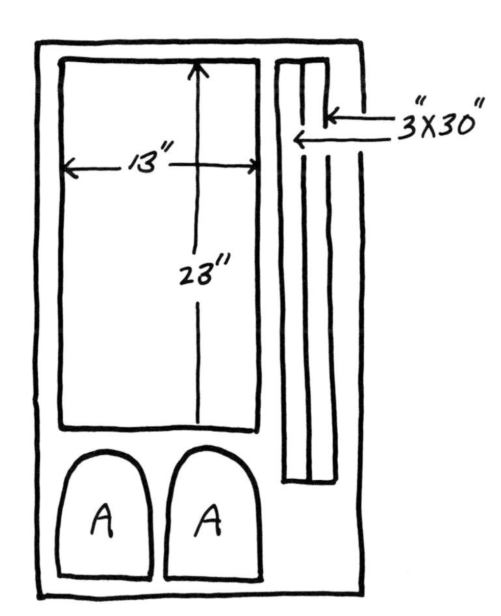

Diagram 2. From quilted piece, cut two ends (**A**), two straps, and one 13×23-inch rectangle.

diagonal grid pattern on the right side of the remaining 24 × 44-inch piece. I used as a guide the width of my 1¾-inch steel rule.

2. Lay out the unmarked fabric rectangle with the right side down. Place the batting on top. Place the lining right side up on top of the batting. Pin the three layers together (Diagram 1).

3. Using the longest stitch-length on your sewing machine, sew all three layers together, following the grid marked on the lining (Diagram 1).

4. From this quilted piece, cut one 13 × 23-inch rectangle, two 3 × 30-inch strips for shoulder straps, and two **A** pieces (Diagram 2).

5. Turn the sides of the borders under ½ inch and press. Pin them to the sides of the quilted piece 1 inch from the edge. Sew the borders to the quilted piece ⅛ inch from the edges (Diagram 3).

6. Fold over right side of the quilted shoulder straps ½ inch and sew (Diagram 4). Folding the left side over the right, turn the edge under and sew it to the strap (Diagram 5). Repeat for the other shoulder strap.

7. Sew the ends of one strap to one side of the bag 2½ inches from the top and just inside the borders (Diagram 6). Fold the strap up toward the top and top-stitch both ends in place with a square of stitching. Repeat for the other strap.

Diagram 3. Sew borders along sides, 1 inch from edge.

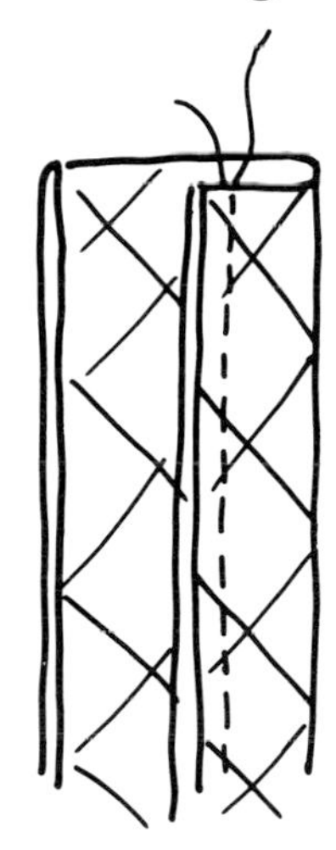

Diagram 4. Fold and sew one side of shoulder strap.

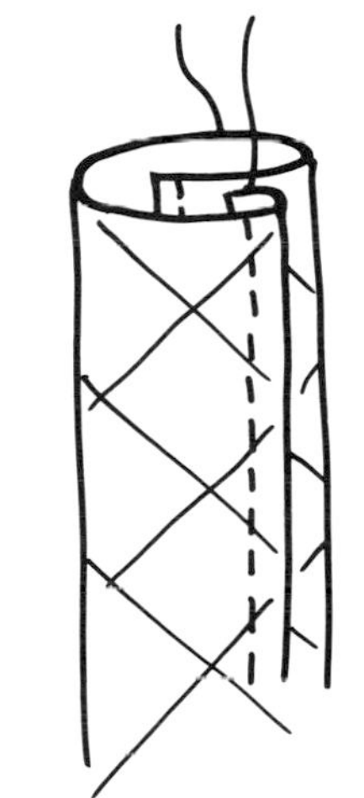

Diagram 5. Fold left side over right side, turn edge under and sew.

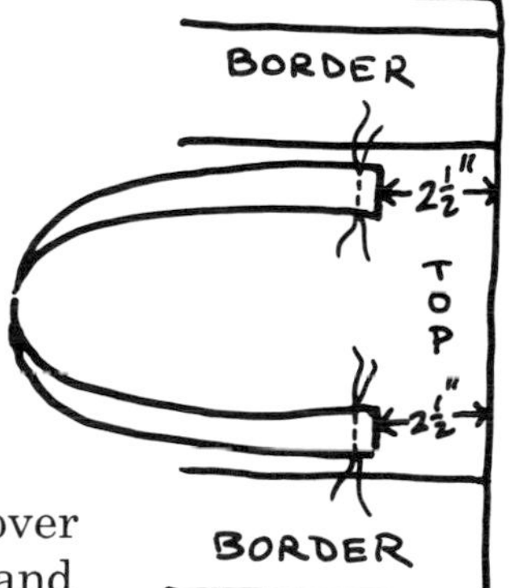

Diagram 6. Sew ends of straps 2½ inches from top of bag.

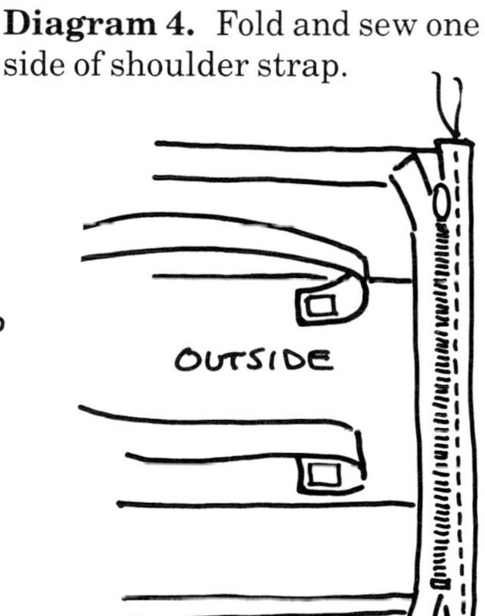

Diagram 7. Sew the zipper face down on top of bag.

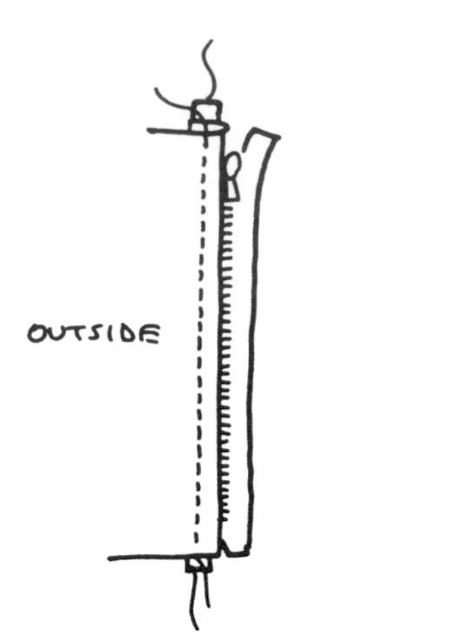

Diagram 8. Fold zipper over to back and top-stitch.

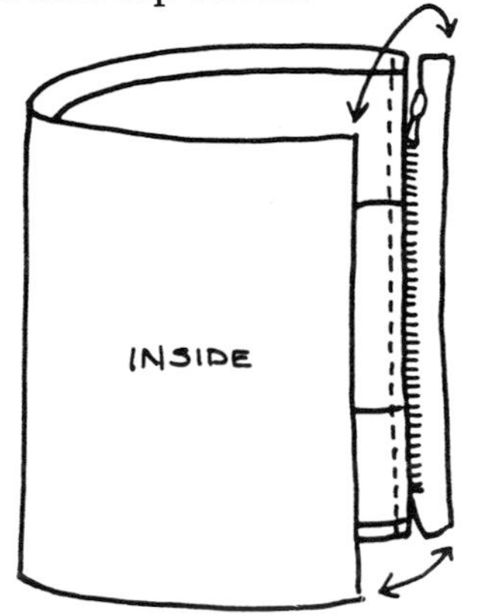

Diagram 9. Sew other end of bag to the side of zipper.

8. Sew the zipper face down on top of one end of the bag (Diagram 7).

9. Fold the zipper over to the back and top-stitch through the bag and the zipper tape (Diagram 8).

10. Sew the other end of the bag to the other side of the zipper (Diagram 9).

11. Turn the bag right side out, open the zipper, and from the open end, top-stitch through the bag and the zipper tape as far as you can go (Diagram 10). Remove the bag, slide the underside up and out of the way, re-insert the bag under the presser foot, and continue to top-stitch to the end of the zipper tape.

12. Turn the bag inside out, fold in half, and clip a notch at the center bottom of each side (opposite the zipper). Matching the notches, pin the bottom of **A** into the side opening of the bag. To turn the corners, clip the seam allowance on the bag where it meets the corners of **A** (Diagram 11). Pin the notch on the top of **A** to the center top of the bag (at the zipper) and ease the curve to fit. Clip the seam allowance on the bag around the top to help ease the curve (Diagram 12).

13. For a finished inside edge, sew one side of the bias binding made from the leftover piece of lining fabric to the seam on the inside where the bag and piece **A** are joined. (For instructions in making bias binding, see Binding the Quilt, page 19).

14. Instead of turning the corners inside the bag with the binding, it is easier to cut the binding ½ inch beyond each corner, turn the ends under, and finish the ends by hand. Then, fold the other side edge of the binding over the seam allowance, turn the edge under ½ inch and pin it to the seam line. Handsew the edge of the binding to the seam line.

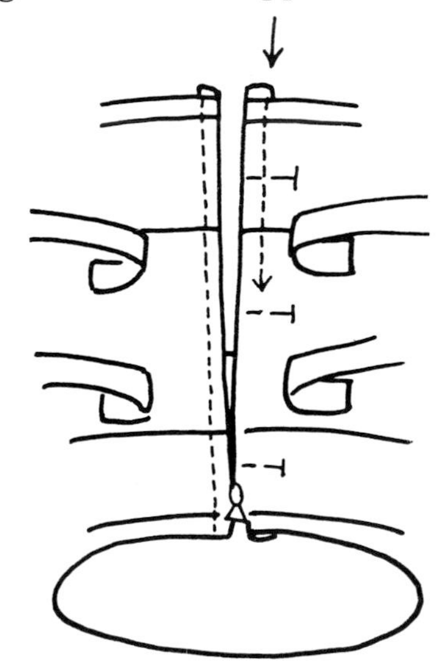

Diagram 10. Top-stitch left side of zipper.

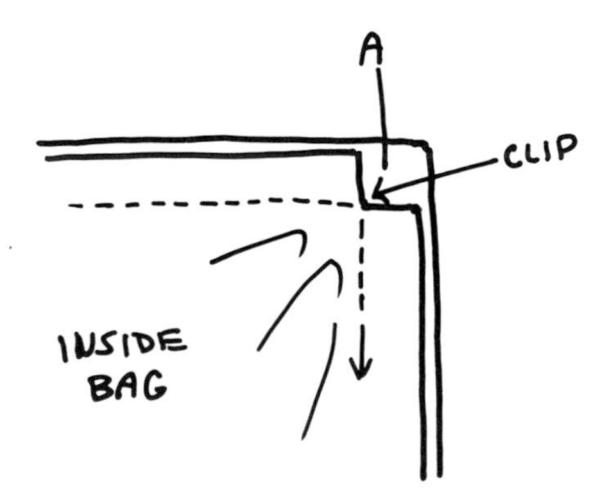

Diagram 11. To turn corners, clip seam allowance at corners of **A**.

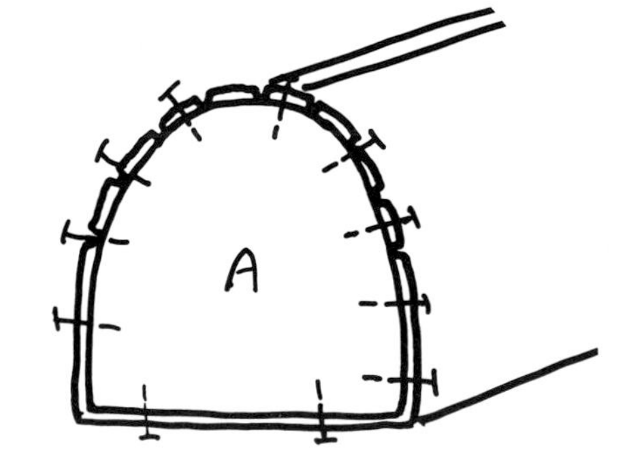

Diagram 12. Pin **A** into the side of the bag. Clip seam allowance to ease curve and sew.

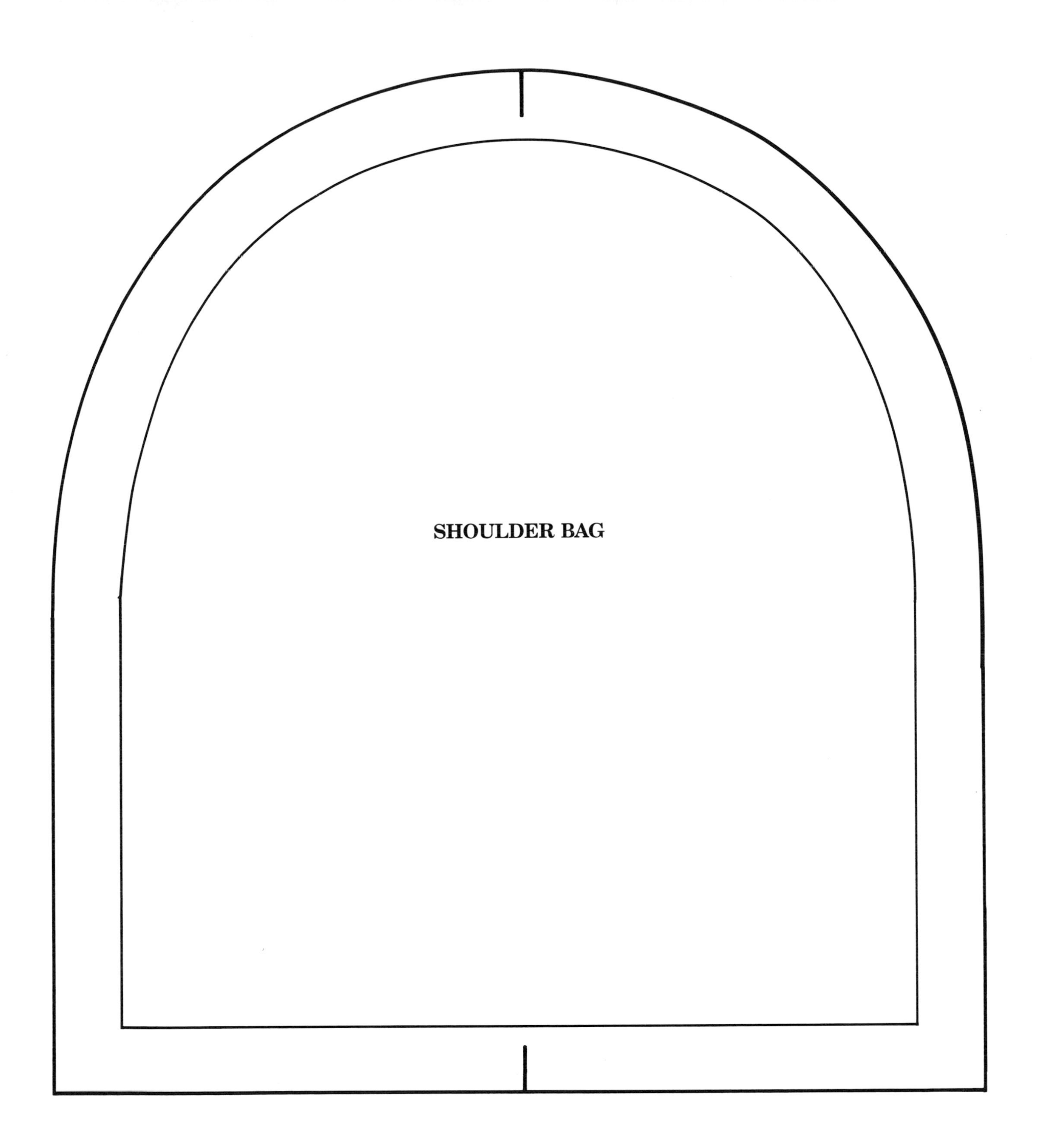
SHOULDER BAG

INDEX

All of us at Sedgewood® Press are dedicated to offering you, our customer, the best books we can create. We are particularly concerned that all of the instructions for making the projects are clear and accurate. We welcome your comments and would like to hear any suggestions you may have. Please address your correspondence to:
Customer Service Department, Sedgewood® Press,
Meredith Corporation, 750 Third Avenue, New York, NY 10017.

CLASSIC PATCHWORK & QUILTING: *Patchwork & Quilting 1990* is the third in a series of patchwork and quilting books. If you would like the first and second books in the series, COUNTRY PATCHWORK & QUILTING and ROMANTIC PATCHWORK & QUILTING, please write to the address above.